An Unfinished Canvas

An Unfinished Canvas

A True Story of Love, Family,
and Murder in Nashville

Michael Glasgow
Phyllis Gobbell

BERKLEY BOOKS, NEW YORK

THE BERKLEY PUBLISHING GROUP
Published by the Penguin Group
Penguin Group (USA) Inc.
375 Hudson Street, New York, New York 10014, USA
Penguin Group (Canada), 90 Eglinton Avenue East, Suite 700, Toronto, Ontario M4P 2Y3, Canada
(a division of Pearson Penguin Canada Inc.)
Penguin Books Ltd., 80 Strand, London WC2R 0RL, England
Penguin Group Ireland, 25 St. Stephen's Green, Dublin 2, Ireland (a division of Penguin Books Ltd.)
Penguin Group (Australia), 250 Camberwell Road, Camberwell, Victoria 3124, Australia
(a division of Pearson Australia Group Pty. Ltd.)
Penguin Books India Pvt. Ltd., 11 Community Centre, Panchsheel Park, New Delhi—110 017, India
Penguin Group (NZ), 67 Apollo Drive, Rosedale, North Shore 0745, Auckland, New Zealand
(a division of Pearson New Zealand Ltd.)
Penguin Books (South Africa) (Pty.) Ltd., 24 Sturdee Avenue, Rosebank, Johannesburg 2196,
South Africa

Penguin Books Ltd., Registered Offices: 80 Strand, London WC2R 0RL, England

The publisher does not have any control over and does not assume any responsibility for author or
third-party websites or their content.

AN UNFINISHED CANVAS

A Berkley Book / published by arrangement with River Valley Ventures LLC and Phyllis Gobbell

PRINTING HISTORY
Berkley mass-market edition / October 2007

ISBN: 978-0-425-21828-0

BERKLEY®
Berkley Books are published by The Berkley Publishing Group,
a division of Penguin Group (USA) Inc.,
375 Hudson Street, New York, New York 10014.
BERKLEY® is a registered trademark of Penguin Group (USA) Inc.
The "B" design is a trademark belonging to Penguin Group (USA) Inc.

PRINTED IN THE UNITED STATES OF AMERICA

10   9   8   7   6   5   4   3   2   1

Authors' Note and Acknowledgments

"For though usurpers sway the rule a while, yet heav'ns are just, and time suppresseth wrongs." —Shakespeare, 3 Henry VI, III.II.76

The March story captivated Nashville from the first reports that Janet March was missing. Like other Nashvillians who followed the unfolding events, year after year, we were touched by the tragedy and compelled by the drama. But after the investigation produced an arrest and the case proceeded toward a murder trial, we began to consider how all the pieces of this incredible puzzle might come together in a book.

We are indebted to our friend and fellow writer Doug Jones for convincing us that we should write the story. We also thank the members of the Nashville Writers Group for their support, and our special appreciation goes to Rita Bourke, our first reader, for her time and excellent advice.

Thanks to our skillful and tireless literary agent, Sharlene Martin, who helped us navigate the publishing world. We have had the privilege of working with two fine editors at Berkley. We thank Samantha Mandor for believing in this book and Shannon Jamieson Vazquez for her meticulous editing, patience, and diligence.

Our deep gratitude goes to detectives Pat Postiglione and Bill Pridemore for taking the time to answer our endless questions and share their years of experience in homicide investigations. Their insights were invaluable as we shaped the narrative, and we came to appreciate their tremendous dedication to the work of finding justice for victims and their families.

We are most grateful to our families, friends, and colleagues who are a continual source of encouragement.

Throughout the text we refer to details provided by print and media journalists, some of whom documented the investigation for years. We acknowledge their work in illuminating particular aspects of the story as we put together the ten-year sequence of events.

Due to the limitations placed on the interviewing of certain parties or individuals by judicial orders and the unavailability of certain witnesses, we have reconstructed certain scenes based on the official trial records and other public records, evidence, and documentation in conjunction with the completed interviews of witnesses that were available in an effort to provide a faithful re-creation of the likely actual events.

As we wrote this story, we came to feel that we knew Janet March. We will not forget her.

PROLOGUE

A flock of white pelicans sail in a perfectly straight line across the blue sky. Leather-faced fishermen in wooden boats cast their nets into the still, translucent waters of the lake. The chimes atop an ancient chapel peal with the music of a new morning in Ajijic, Mexico.

Perry March leaves his spacious home just before eight on the bright morning of August 3, 2005, walking to the café that he and his Mexican wife, Carmen, own. The perpetual sunshine angles its rays through the colorful windows of the shops and markets as he strolls along the cobblestone streets. At the Media Luna Bistro & Café, a buttery-yellow stucco building in the heart of the vibrant little town, Carmen is already putting out delectable baked treats for the day's customers. The smell of strong Mexican coffee mixes with the scent of fresh mangoes, papayas, pineapples, and guavas.

Another day in paradise.

Ajijic, a retirement haven for more than five thousand American and Canadian expatriates, is located on Lake Chapala, Mexico's largest natural lake. Surrounding the lake are villages and small towns that date back to twelfth century, pre-Hispanic settlements established by a migrating tribe of the Nahuatl Indians. The Ajijic convent was constructed in 1531, and after 350 years of an amalgamation of

Indian and Hispanic cultures, Ajijic began to experience an influx of citizens from many other countries. Tourists discovered the picturesque natural beauty of the Lake Chapala region and the ideal climate known as "eternal spring." In 1895 the first major hotel, the Arzapalo, opened to accommodate the growing stream of visitors. The Palacio Municipal—Town Hall—was constructed in 1913, and by 1930 the first railroad station was opened. Guadalajara's high society began to take the train to the Chapala lakeside for leisurely weekends and the Christmas holidays.

In 1999 the Chapala lakeside was a logical destination for Perry and his children, Sammy and Tzipi; his seventy-one-year-old father, Arthur March, had come to Ajijic in the mid-1990s. Perry knew he could count on his father to help him start over. In this land of "eternal spring," Perry believed he could finally escape all his problems.

The Lake Chapala region was everything Arthur had promised. Wealthy tourists of many nationalities flocked to the bed-and-breakfasts and excellent hotels. Guides conducted tours high into the Sierra Madres' El Tigre Mountains. Restaurants flourished, offering exquisite cuisine from varied cultures. The local yacht club held regattas on Lake Chapala. There were shops and open-air markets filled with busy shoppers and mariachi music. There were banks, and pharmacies, and dentists, and doctors.

Perry smelled opportunity. He joined forces with a Mexican entrepreneur and formed a diversified group of business enterprises. He married a beautiful Mexican woman with three children, and soon they added a baby girl to their blended family.

Life was good.

On this sun-splashed August morning, Perry March strolls past walled houses and colorful shops, decorated with fragrant bright flowers that drape to the ground from earthenware pots. He is in sight of the Media Luna Bistro & Café when four unmarked cars approach at a high speed and screech to a halt, pinning him in on the sidewalk.

"Hey, what the hell!" Perry demands as several men jump from the vehicles and grab him. He struggles. "Where are you taking me?"

One of the Mexican immigration officers tells him with a sneer, "Your visa has been revoked, Señor March. You are going to the United States."

Perry protests. "My wife is inside the café. Let me tell her. Let me at least call my father!" But already rough hands are hustling him toward one of the unmarked cars.

The cars speed away as an official convoy down the narrow cobblestone streets of Ajijic.

Perry March has just been arrested Mexican style.

Perry March is used to being the one in control, always sure he is the smartest person in the room. Today he is powerless.

He is formally deported based upon a federal criminal complaint charging him with fleeing the United States to avoid prosecution. The Mexican agents won't even let him make a call. By nine a.m. he is in FBI custody, in the air above Guadalajara—a short plane ride that changes everything. Once in Los Angeles, he learns he has been indicted and charged by the criminal court of Davidson County, Tennessee, with three felony charges: second-degree murder, abuse of a corpse, and tampering with evidence in the 1996 disappearance of his former wife, Janet March.

In the Los Angeles suburb of Van Nuys, night comes to the community police station. Inside his cell, Perry sits on a hard bed, on a scratchy, musty blanket. It is not lost on him that he's in the cell once occupied by O. J. Simpson. The incredible events of the day begin to sink in. His arrogance falls away like discarded clothing. It is incomprehensible to Perry that his world is collapsing so suddenly, all in one nightmare of a day, since that moment—just this morning—when he strolled along the street of Ajijic, the sun on his shoulders.

Perry March has been expelled from paradise. He wonders if he will ever again warm himself in the bright Mexican sun.

PART ONE

Chapter 1

A Perfect Life

It is only a fifteen-minute drive along West End Avenue for Perry March from downtown Nashville and the family law firm Levine, Mattson, Orr, and Geracioti, to his massive new home at 3 Blackberry Road, in the affluent Forest Hills neighborhood in this Southern city on the rise.

The air is crisp on this fall night in 1995. Maple and oak leaves of varying hues of red and gold litter the roadway like confetti from a heavenly parade as he turns from West End into the exclusive enclave of Belle Meade. He follows its divided boulevard lined with huge mansions—a display of tasteful old Nashville money and ostentatious new Nashville money, side by side. With windshield wipers knocking off the occasional stray leaf, Perry continues through Belle Meade, and crosses the boundary of his private city domain, Forest Hills. Nashville, like many Southern cities, contains numerous geographically defined interior entities—mini-cities with their own elections, and their own mayors or city managers; defined geographical boundaries that are firmly controlled by the residents within those boundaries. And all newcomers have to play by the local rules.

Nashville is a city once known as the Athens of the South, after the city fathers in 1876 elected to project a new image of art and culture by building an exact replica of the Greek temple the Parthenon, which was Nashville's contribution to the landscape of the South during the country's Centennial celebration. As the end of the twentieth century looms, Nashville is doing its best to forge its own unique urban mark upon the Southern landscape, to step from behind the broad shadow of the Southeast's premier city, Atlanta. Known for decades now as Music City USA, Nashville has determined forces at work constructing the multilayered dimensions of a more urban sophistication, a citywide goal to outrun the hayseed image burned into the collective national memory by television shows such as *Hee-Haw*. The blue bloods of Nashville have never fully embraced or understood the music industry, which is a combination of two primary groups. There are the artists and performers, with their tour buses and cowboy hats, and there are the record producers and music executives, with their designer jeans and Porsches. Although it employs thousands of people and generates billions of dollars annually, the music industry has always remained a subculture within Nashville, never the power behind the urban throne.

Many of the Nashville streets bear the names of Confederate generals whose blood stained the soil of its Middle Tennessee hills during what is still referred to as "the War," and historical markers appear on street corners throughout the city like postcards from the past. But broad changes in the makeup of the city's population and its leaders are readily evident. The most obvious is the city's mayor, Phil Bredesen, elected in 1991. Unlike his predecessors, Bredesen is not from an old Nashville family. In fact, he is not only from above the Mason-Dixon Line, but from New York, of all places, and with a wife, Andrea, who insists on maintaining her maiden name, Conte.

Bredesen, a Harvard-educated entrepreneur, is a poster child for the dramatic changes stampeding through this once quaint and provincial city, which for decades was controlled primarily by families who had made their fortunes in companies selling life insurance door-to-door, businesses like National Life and Accident Insurance. The audacity of a New Yorker asking the voters of a conservative Southern city in the heart of the Bible Belt to elect him as their leader comes from his connections with the new power brokers of Nashville. This crucial connection comes from his wealth, and his wealth comes from the new currency in Nashville: health care.

In the 1980s, Bredesen was one of an elite number of businessmen who amassed staggering sums of money in very short periods of time through health management organizations. It was the beginning of fundamental changes in America's health care system, the introduction to both patients and doctors throughout the nation of health management organizations (HMOs) and preferred provider organizations (PPOs). The radical shift in the nation's health-care system found Nashville and companies like Bredesen's HealthAmerica at the heart of it all.

Nashville has had its share of visionaries. One of the first was Joel Cheek, a coffee merchant in the 1920s who created a blend known as Maxwell House, named for a famous hotel in Nashville. In 1928, when General Foods came calling, Cheek sold his blended coffee that was "good to the last drop" for the staggering sum of $42 million.

The enormity of the business transaction, and the legal fees it generated, also catapulted the Cheek family's attorney (and his firm) to the top echelon of law firms in the South and set the pace for its steady growth throughout the next seven decades. It was this firm—Bass, Berry, and Sims, always on the lookout for the brightest legal minds—that hired Perry March straight out of Vanderbilt in 1988.

Then there was Jack C. Massey, who in 1964—after retiring from a highly successful surgical supply business that he took public on the New York Stock Exchange, handing out bedpans on Wall Street the day the stock became listed—purchased Kentucky Fried Chicken from the white-haired and white-suited Colonel Sanders for a cool $2 million. Then, along with his partner, former Kentucky governor John Y. Brown, Massey expanded it into the first international fast-food chain to challenge the dominance of McDonald's. Massey would become known as the father of the fast-food franchise in America.

And then there was Dr. Thomas Frist, founder of Hospital Corporation of America in 1968. Through HCA, which was controlled by the Frist family, Dr. Frist and his oldest son, Dr. Tommy Frist, Jr., began purchasing government owned and operated hospitals first in the South and then throughout the country. The Frists and HCA conceptualized a plan to secure a stream of cash that would literally never dry up—the United States Treasury. With an ever-aging population of baby boomers, the billions of dollars in annual Medicare reimbursements that used to keep the locally owned government-run hospitals afloat were now flowing into the coffers of the privately owned hospitals. HCA had brilliantly engineered one of the largest transfers of public monies into private hands in the history of the country, a transfer of wealth that would lead to Nashville's first billionaires.

This seismic shift of power and wealth from public to private hands came full circle in Nashville in 1995. The younger Frist brother, William Frist, was elected United States senator from Tennessee in the fall of 1994, the first step in what would become a powerful national political career, with his rise to the position of Senate majority leader and potential presidential candidate. Bill Frist had originally followed his father and older brother into the medical profession and was a Nashville cardiac surgeon. Even though it was rumored during his first campaign that he never even voted until the age of thirty-six, he was encouraged by the Republican power brokers in Washington, primarily former Tennessee senator Howard Baker, to enter politics. Frist was victorious, unseating political veteran and seemingly untouchable Tennessee Democrat senator Bill Sasser.

The merger of private and public power is complete. One brother, Tommy Frist, is head of the country's largest provider of health care services, and the other brother, Bill

Frist, is a leader of the public bureaucracy from which HCA receives its billions in medical reimbursements.

Nashville is truly no longer a provincial Southern city.

Perry March, like Phil Bredesen, was an outsider who came to Nashville and worked his way into the social and business fabric of this evolving Southern city. Perry's journey to Nashville began in Michigan, where he met his future wife, Janet Gail Levine, while they were attending the University of Michigan in Ann Arbor. Somehow, among the tens of thousands of university students crisscrossing the enormous campus that is U of M, these two attractive people with bright minds connected, and forged first a friendship and then a romance.

Perry was a person of small stature, only five seven and less than 150 pounds, with curly brown hair and large expressive eyes that stared out at the world with a look that could be construed as either eager anticipation or bewilderment. He was an outgoing and confident individual who knew he was brighter than most of his fellow students. Perry graduated in 1985 with a degree in Asian studies, becoming fluent in several Asian languages. He was an involved collegian, serving as a member of the University of Michigan Honor Student Council.

Janet Levine was the daughter of Lawrence and Carolyn Levine, established Nashvillians, prominent in both social and business circles, but especially influential and generous with their wealth within Nashville's Jewish community. Janet was an exceptionally beautiful young woman with thick dark hair, high cheekbones, and full, sensuous lips. At five four and weighing barely over a hundred pounds, she was a gifted and talented artist who gave off a glowing radiance and a compelling energy. Janet studied political science at U of M as well as art and illustration. She had deep, soulful brown eyes that the artist in her used to take in the world and interpret it. Beside her picture in her high school yearbook is the notation, "Pretty eyes." Some would say she had it all—beauty, brains, and talent.

As Shakespeare said: "For the eye sees not itself, but by reflection." The question remains to this day, and Janet will never give an answer: Did she paint what she saw, or the reverse of what she saw—not what life is, but what she wanted life to be?

Lawrence Levine, who most everyone refers to as Larry, is the senior partner in the law firm of Levine, Mattson, Orr, and Geracioti, an established firm with comfortable offices on Third Avenue in downtown Nashville, just blocks away from the courthouse, in the heart of the legal trenches. A thin and angular man, Larry combs his few remaining gray hairs across a balding scalp. With a constant look of seriousness, he peers from behind a pair of shaded oversize glasses, relics from the 1970s, his gaze intent and hard to read. He is known throughout the Nashville legal and business community for his tenacity in the representation of his clients. If Larry Levine is on a case, his opponent can rarely catch his breath before the next onslaught of legal pleadings is filed. When Larry Levine is suing, it is an all-out war.

Yet when it comes to family, there is an unconditional love, a generosity that Perry experienced firsthand when he followed Janet to Nashville and enrolled in the highly respected Vanderbilt University School of Law in 1985. Vanderbilt University, one of the schools referred to as an Ivy League of the South, has an excellent academic reputation; the institution has produced nationally recognized scholars, such as broadcast journalist David Brinkley, U.S. Supreme Court justice James Clark McReynolds, and the Pulitzer Prize–winning author of *All the King's Men*, Robert Penn Warren.

The tuition for Vanderbilt Law School was far beyond Perry's means, so Larry Levine stepped up and shouldered the entire cost.

Perry was up to the intellectual challenge of law school and its Socratic method of teaching, and performed well. He became associate editor of the prestigious *Law Review* and won nationally recognized academic medals through his performance in certain courses. He was a person with a fixed goal of transcending his middle-class background. During this time of growth and learning, Janet and Perry sealed their love in marriage in 1987.

The following year Perry graduated with honors and was immediately hired by the most prestigious and blue-blooded of all the law firms in the city, Bass, Berry, and Sims. In fact, he became only the second Jewish attorney hired by Nashville's most WASPy firm. The hiring committee was clearly impressed with Perry, his confidence, and his intellect.

Perry March, an outsider, a transplant, with his very first job, entered the Nashville legal community at the very top.

Perry turns the Jeep Cherokee into the driveway at 3 Blackberry Road, winding toward the house that his talented and artistic wife had meticulously designed. The windows, ablaze with light, appear from the woods, a welcoming sight on this dreary evening.

After Perry graduated from law school and was working as an associate with the city's top law firm, Janet was balancing motherhood with a blossoming art career. She had periodic showings, and her paintings began appearing in homes and businesses across the city. Some of her artwork appeared as illustrations in children's books. She even designed and patented an infant car seat. The architectural masterpiece that is the March home was the culmination of all her artistic talent, imagination, and energies. Janet was attentive to every detail, like the angle of the sun's rays. Her design allows for bright light in the house throughout the day. It is a beautifully designed creation worthy of the pages of *Architectural Digest*—with an exterior of natural stone, complemented and accented by an open interior, with the tasteful use of natural woods on floors, in staircases, and moldings, all nestled in a private valley paradise of several acres, completely out of view from the rest of the world.

It is a home whose occupants can live a life in which neighbors will not intrude—a private world, with their dependable housecleaner, Deneane Beard, and their devoted

Russian part-time nanny, Ella Goldshmid, where the actions of the March family are kept out of the reach or knowledge of others.

For the Levines, the absolute seclusion is a feature of their daughter's dream home that will come to haunt them forever.

For Perry, so much has changed in his life, a life that was touched by tragedy when he was only nine. In 1970, his mother, Zipora—thirty-two years old—was found dead at their home in the industrial town of East Chicago. Questions surrounding her death have remained unanswered: Was it an accidental overdose of barbiturates by an overstressed wife and mother of three who needed a temporary reprieve from the mounting pressures of life, or was it a willful and deliberate suicide in search of a permanent escape from her demons? Several of the March family friends had commented to Perry and others that Janet was the spitting image of his mother when she was young.

But now Perry has his own family—first with the birth of their son, Samson, in 1990, followed four years later by the birth of their daughter, Tzipora, named for Perry's mother.

He is also an integral part of the expanded Levine family, having left the lofty corridors of Bass, Berry, and Sims in 1991 to join his father-in-law's firm, Levine, Mattson, Orr, and Geracioti. Perry told friends and associates that he simply wanted to be part of the family firm. Now in his fourth year there, his client list is robust and the demands of his private law practice are growing. He likes to refer to himself as a "go-to guy" in the wealthy and business-savvy Nashville Jewish community.

Perry March is a rising star in a Southern city that is rising as well. He has a beautiful and talented wife who spends her days creating art within her own private studio at home, or visiting with her mother, or enjoying the conversation and laughter of her close friends, or playing with and caring for their two adorable children, to whom everyone agrees both Perry and Janet are truly devoted.

And they live these perfect lives in a private paradise, away from the intrusion and worries of the outside world.

Life is good, really good. Or so it would seem as Perry's Jeep Cherokee pulls up to the magnificent dream house on this fall evening in 1995.

No one knows that Janet and Perry March are keeping up an elaborate facade.

CHAPTER 2

Cracks in the Facade

Back from lunch on a summer day in 1996, Perry enters the offices of Levine, Mattson, Orr, and Geracioti and picks up his messages at the receptionist's desk—an inch-thick stack, all since ten this morning when he left for depositions. A fusion of sounds filters from the row of offices on each side of the carpeted pathway as he makes his way down the hall—muffled telephone conversations, a burst of laughter from one of the secretaries, a metal file drawer being shut. In his private office, Perry peels back one pink slip of paper after another. His desk is littered with documents, corners peeking out from other papers, all needing him, all demanding something of him, like young children competing for attention from a busy parent. No less than half a dozen of the phone calls need to be returned promptly.

He doesn't make it to his desk chair. His mind is somewhere else. The office walls are closing in on him, suffocating him. He's got to get out of here—go somewhere, anywhere. He drops the slips of paper on top of the two stacks from yesterday next to the telephone on his credenza, *grabs one of his several leather briefcases for proper effect, and makes a quick retreat down the hall.*

"Perry!" comes the unexpected greeting just as he reaches the heavy front door of the office suite.

He turns around. Larry Levine is standing in the hall, slipping into his gray suit jacket. "Have you had lunch?"

"Just got back from Satsuma's," says Perry.

"Is it crowded?"

"Just the usual, but good food, as always."

"Off to a meeting?" Mr. Levine asks.

"Yes. I just love clients who seem to always screw up," Perry jokes. He knows his father-in-law will equate screwups with tangled business affairs, and the more untangling required by him, the more fees for the firm. It is all fabrication, but Perry is rarely guileless. He prefers operating in a world of artful deception. Before Larry Levine can inquire further about the particular client, Perry dashes out the front door. The receptionist glances down at the appointment calendar. Under Perry's name the space is blank for the rest of the afternoon. She starts to say something about it to Mr. Levine, but her longtime employer gives a pleasant smile and says he's going out for a sandwich. "I won't be long," he says.

She swallows her comment. "Have a nice lunch, Mr. Levine," she says.

*A **typical summer day** in Nashville is characterized by ninety-degree temperatures, high humidity, and not a whisper of a breeze. Today the city gets a reprieve from the heat. It's a balmy, breezy day more like April than early August. Standing on the corner waiting for the light to change, Perry decides to get his car and drive somewhere, get out of downtown, go where he can breathe.*

The office buildings that line both sides of Third Avenue act like a mini–wind tunnel. As Perry walks briskly toward the parking garage, he comes upon a striking woman in a bright canary-yellow dress that accents her silky dark hair. She has ample breasts and a tiny waist. She is doing her best

*to keep the gusts from hiking her dress up in all directions,
like that famous Marilyn Monroe photograph. As she continues to lose the battle to the unseasonable winds, Perry
comes to a complete stop to enjoy the private show, pivoting
like a corkscrew to continue his appreciative gaze as the
young woman passes by.*

*Suddenly he knows exactly where he's going for the after-
noon.*

Janet has worked steadily *in her studio for over two hours.
She's ready for a break from the self-imposed pressure of her
creative endeavors. Stepping back from the painting, she ad-
mires her work for a minute and then heads to the kitchen
for something to drink.*

*Her newest client should be quite pleased. She should be
pleased, too, she tells herself. She's doing what she loves
best inside the inner sanctum of her private stone castle at 3
Blackberry Road. But there's a sadness inside her that she
can't fully suppress, a vague, sorrowful feeling that resides
in the pit of her stomach. It doesn't entirely go away, just
subsides, and then something else happens, and the sorrow
unexpectedly surfaces, temporarily consuming her. She's in
a maelstrom, and every day she is becoming more unsure
how to escape it.*

*Sammy bounces in the kitchen door, followed by Ella. A
ball of energy, the five-year-old has been playing outside on
this splendid day under the nanny's supervision.*

*"Be sure you wash hands," Ella calls to Sammy as he
heads to the bathroom.*

*"Sammy and I are going out for a while," Janet says. "I
need to buy him some school clothes."*

*"He is happy about school, yes?" Ella asks in her thick
Russian accent.*

*"I think so. Probably not as excited as I am." Janet is so
proud that Sammy has been accepted at her alma mater—
not that she ever doubted he would be.*

*She locates a large travel cup. She empties the contents
from a large bottle of chilled water, finds a slice of lemon,*

squeezes, and lets it splash into the clear, cool liquid. Ella has brought in the mail. Janet picks up the envelopes from the counter and takes a quick look—a couple of bills, something from the bank, one of those flyers with pictures of missing children. It breaks her heart to see those photos.

"I check on Tzipi. She takes long nap today, yes?" Ella says, stooping to pick up a wooden puzzle piece from the floor.

"We should be back by five thirty. Remember, we have dinner plans with friends tonight." Janet tosses the mail back on the counter. She takes a sip from her cup and fastens the lid. "When Tzipi wakes up, please take her outside. You know how she loves the sunshine."

"Yes, ma'am."

"Mommy, where are we going?" comes Sammy's singsongy voice. He runs to Ella and turns his palms up to her. She pats the damp hands with the hem of her blouse and nods approval.

"To the mall, sweetie. To shop for school clothes," Janet says.

Sammy's small shoulders sag as he whines, "Why do we have to shop?"

"Because you're going to start school in just a few weeks. Come on, let's go." Janet grabs her purse and keys and travel cup and hurries Sammy through the door.

She fastens his seat belt and closes the passenger door of her silver-gray Volvo. The wind plasters her dark hair against her face as she goes around the car. She pulls it into a ponytail at the nape of her neck, holding it until she gets into the driver's seat. What an unexpectedly pleasant day for early August, so exhilarating. She pictures Perry, cooped up in the office, hunched over a mound of paperwork, missing out on this splendid weather.

They call them "show bars." Some of them advertise as "gentlemen's clubs." There's a whole industry of strip joints located south of Broadway between downtown and the interstate, right here in the buckle of the Bible Belt, that

Perry has discovered since his client Paul Eichel introduced him to this exotic entertainment.

One of the girls—naked except for a tiny patch of cloth and obscenely high heels—writhes against a shiny pole, center stage. The others work offstage, weaving in and out among the small tables, shedding their frilly garments, bumping and grinding to the high-decibel, pounding music—a sensory overload. Perry checks his watch. It's dark inside, but as the strobe lights ricochet off the mirrors, he's able to make out the time: three thirty. He promised Janet he would be home by five thirty, so they can meet friends at the Tin Angel for dinner. Story of his life.

One of the girls is dancing so close to Perry now that he can smell her musky sweat. His gaze moves upward from the gyrating pelvis. The dreamy-eyed girl is wearing a pink lace bra, pink G-string, and black stiletto heels. These strippers are not necessarily what people imagine. Some of them are just regular girls, some trying to support their kids. He's met a couple of dancers who are taking college courses. They are girls who didn't have all the privileges Janet had. They're earning a buck; they just happen not to mind dropping their clothes in a room full of men.

Perry pulls a fifty-dollar bill from his money clip and tugs on the pink G-string with his left hand. He slowly slides the crisp bill down inside until he can feel her moistness for an instant before she backs away. He's not supposed to touch, but no one pays much attention in the afternoons when the crowd is sparse, mostly out-of-towners, guys in Nashville for conventions. It will be another couple of hours before the after-work crowd comes in and much later before things really start revving up.

In one deft movement, the dancer whisks off her pink bra and tosses it to Perry. She smiles and blows him a kiss. He knows this one. Her name is Tracy.

The traffic on Twenty-first Avenue *is busier than usual. Janet nudges her way past the expansive Vanderbilt campus, another link in a connected column of vehicular strangers, like* *part of a crawling caterpillar float in a Christmas parade. College students are everywhere as the summer semester draws to an end—on bicycles, mopeds, and walking, each dressed with almost uniform regularity, like ragged soldiers in a blue-jeaned and sweatshirted army, their most important belongings crammed inside their backpacks, which appear as mere extensions of their anatomy.*

Janet has taken a detour.

Nestled in the heart of what is now the ever-growing campus of Vanderbilt University, the University School of Nashville traces its academic roots all the way back to 1892, when this corner of academic Nashville real estate was a separate and competing center of learning across the street from a young but established Vanderbilt. In what would become known as the George Peabody College campus, this precollege institution was initially known as the Peabody Demonstration School.

After the racially charged 1960s, which included sit-ins, boycotts, and physical confrontations between the blacks and whites of Nashville, the University School, now called USN, became known as a K–12 campus that embraced ethnic and cultural diversity, and a school that strived to maintain its guiding educational mission of nurturing and fostering the artistic and intellectual potential of its students while inspiring their creative expression.

Janet's need and desire for creative expression, as well as her talent at expressing herself, began to surface while attending USN. Graduating in 1981 as vice president of her class, she loved her years at this unique urban institution, which had for decades produced talented alumni who would go on to receive international awards and hold positions of importance in the world of science, music, art, and journalism.

As she is finally permitted to escape the slowly tightening grips of the Nashville afternoon traffic, Janet turns onto the USN campus. She glances over at Sammy and says with pride, "This is your school, Samson."

"I know," he says. "USN."

"And did you know your mommy went to USN?"

"Yes."

"Won't it be fun to be in kindergarten here?"

"Uh-huh." He is a hard one to impress, this son whom she loves so much. Everyone tells her that he's the spitting image of his father. Sometimes the comments bother her. He's her little boy, her Sammy.

"Do we have to buy clothes?" he asks.

"Yes, we do. That's where we're heading right now."

She imagines the "hookup line," filled with cars at dismissal time during the school year. She looks forward to finding her place in line in the afternoon. The hookup line is a social gathering, mothers in tennis or workout attire, visiting, laughing, gossiping, planning playdates and luncheons while they wait for their youngsters to emerge from the historic columned buildings and race to their luxury chariots. It will give her a routine, a daily ritual, some time alone with her son. A reason to remember her priorities, to make things work out.

"Can we get some ice cream?" Sammy asks.

Janet is not a big believer in sweet snacks, but today she knows she's about to give in. It's a beautiful day and she has this beautiful child. *"Let's get some ice cream, then some new clothes for school."*

She maneuvers back into traffic. She cannot believe it has been fifteen years since she graduated. Where has her life gone? More important, where is it going? Janet wishes she knew.

Reentering the spring sunshine after two hours at the strip club, Perry has to adjust to the light. The cacophony of city sounds seems foreign. He turns his cell phone back on. Within seconds he is reconnected with the endless demands of the real world. There are eight new messages. One is from Janet, and one is from Dr. Thomas Campbell's office. Another is from Paul Eichel, and five others he does not immediately recognize. The one from Dr. Campbell pisses him off, even though it's just a routine call, confirming an appointment. *Marriage counseling is such a crock. He and Janet both know it's not working.* After months and months of appointments, Perry is ready to jettison the whole counselor routine.

He decides to stop by and see Eichel instead of returning his call. He can tell from the number and the time of the call that his client just called from one of his clubs. Paul Eichel is unlike any client Perry has ever had. They met when Perry represented someone who was purchasing an ownership percentage in a manufacturing plant that Eichel owned. After the deal closed, Eichel, impressed with Perry's confidence and tenacity, called him up one day and asked if he would like to represent all of his diverse business interests.

Although there was no way Paul Eichel could have known it at their initial meeting, he will be forever linked to Perry March—and the link to Eichel will come back to haunt Perry as well.

For most of the 1990s Paul Eichel has been the king of adult entertainment in Nashville. At one time he operated five popular nightspots at the same time: Club Platinum, Oasis, Malibu Beach, Big Daddy's, and the huge twenty-five-hundred-seat complex on Second Avenue downtown, the Music City Mix Factory.

Representing Eichel has opened up Perry March to this fascinating world, so far removed from the world that stifles him, the Levines' social circle, the Jewish community, life with Janet in her dream house. Eichel is someone who operates in the underbelly of Nashville, offering brief moments of entertainment and escapism to a certain crowd within Nashville and to the thousands in Music City on business, who want a taste of some late-night pleasure while far from home. As Perry quickly learns, all these nightlife enterprises generate a lot of revenue, and a good portion of it is cash. It is a setting where people with different priorities enter in through the shadows, find their own personal pleasure, and then leave again before the sun's rays can penetrate the darkness.

Arriving at the club, Perry exits his Jeep Cherokee. He can't help but think back to his days at Bass, Berry, and Sims. He would never have had a client like Eichel while practicing in the lofty towers of Bass, Berry, as it is referred to in local legal circles. Still, Perry regrets the way he had to leave the firm in disgrace. All the images from the hell of 1991 begin to flow back into his mind. He sees the letters he carefully typed and secretly delivered, as clearly if he had just authored them yesterday. He sees the appealing figure and the pale skin of the beautiful paralegal who drove him to open his heart and his soul with such total sexual honesty.

He still can't believe she betrayed him. How carefully he had chosen his words. Didn't she understand they were truly from his heart? He had meant no harm when he said he wanted to devour her, taste her. He simply could not contain the passion that had built up inside him. He was so sure she wanted him, too. But he escaped from the clutches of his betrayer and those at Bass, Berry who conspired with her. It has been five years since he'd been forced to resign, but he outsmarted his enemies. His legal mind protected him, gave him a future. No one knows, and no one will ever know, he reassures himself.

When police detectives later read the most private of words meant only for the young paralegal in each of Perry's three masterpieces of love and lust, they quickly realize that in dealing with Perry March, they are dealing with a beguiling character, a person living in two worlds, regularly passing through a private portcullis. With one foot in the public world of duty and responsibility, Perry is a husband, a father, a competent and bright attorney, and a resident of fashionable Forest Hills, who shops and dines and laughs with the beautiful people. But he has his other foot in that other world, the one that tempts him, beckons to him—the heady world of sexual freedom and experimentation, of immersing himself in all the pleasures that life has to offer, of an imagination not limited by the rules of established society.

•   •   •

As Perry pulls into the driveway, he sees Janet outside with Sammy and Tzipi. They are doing their best to fly a small kite on this August day with its rare breezes. The kite continues to jerk in concentric circles, thwarted from lifting into full flight by a homemade tail of insufficient length. The children see their daddy's car and drop the kite to run to him, but Janet intervenes, blocking their path across the expansive backyard. She directs them toward the back door, where Ella, the nanny, magically appears on cue.

Perry maneuvers into his normal parking spot in the driveway, waving to his youngsters as they scurry toward the house. Janet bounds across the yard toward the drive with a white envelope in hand, her long strides belying her tiny frame.

His car door is only partially open when the verbal barrage begins. "How could you let this happen?" Janet demands.

"Let what happen?" Perry asks, remaining calm, though he feels a flare of rage at the attack, another of his wife's harangues. She can't even wait until he's out of the car.

"This is so embarrassing!" Janet shouts, slapping the envelope onto his chest as he tries to shut the car door. "And at USN, of all places!"

"Janet, please calm down, and stop shouting." Perry speaks slowly and deliberately, his lawyer's voice. "The children will hear you. I don't have a clue what you are talking about."

"Just look, look at this." Again, Janet slaps the envelope across his chest.

Perry grabs the envelope from her hand and takes two deliberate steps away from the car. It's a notice from the bank saying a check has bounced—and not just any check. The check for Sammy's tuition at USN.

"That stupid damn bank!" Perry hisses, now in full defense posture.

"And why is this the bank's fault?"

"Because they've made a mistake."

The fire in Janet's voice begins to diminish. "You mean the money was in the account?"

"Janet, do you think I would allow a bad check to come from our home to Sammy's school?" His voice strains for acceptance.

"It sure looks that way," she says.

"Let me deal with this in the morning." Perry loosens his tie and starts toward the house. "It's either the fault of the bank, or the office bookkeeper forgot to direct-deposit my regular draw check. Either way I'll straighten it out first thing in the morning. Don't worry another minute about it," Perry says, shifting to a dismissive tone.

Janet, frozen in the driveway, closes her eyes and takes a long deep breath. For Perry, everything is always someone else's fault.

Almost to the house, Perry stops, turns toward her. "I'm going to take a shower. What time are we supposed to be at dinner?"

"Seven."

"The Tin Angel, right?"

"Yes."

"Good. I love to see your beautiful painting there every time we go." Perry does his best to smile. "It is one of your best works."

The hot jets of water *soothe Perry's arched shoulders. He wishes he could lock the bathroom and remain in the steamy shower until he can come up with a plan for his life. Things have gotten out of hand. He has allowed himself to become trapped by the Levines on all sides. His in-laws helped pay for the dream home Janet just had to have. They hold the mortgage on the home where he sleeps. Hell, his name is not even on the deed. He works for the family firm, but his name is not even part of the firm's name. He may be "in" the family, but he has never felt "of" the family. He needs to be his own boss, to have his own firm. He needs his own place, too.*

Perry rubs his scalp furiously, making a lather, ridding his hair of the smell of smoke and stale perfume, the smells of the strip club. He thinks of Paul Eichel and all that revenue that flows from all those businesses. He thinks about all that cash—and about the stripper Tracy. There has to be more to life than this.

Something has to give.

CHAPTER 3

"Don't Worry—She'll Be Back"

Janet March has a circle of friends who have been a vital part of one another's lives for a long time. She has known some of the girls since childhood. Janet and Perry regularly socialize with her friends and their husbands. Their children play together, swim together at the Jewish Community Center, attend one another's birthday parties. Although it is weeks away, Janet has already sent out invitations to Sammy's sixth birthday party at Dragon Park in Hillsboro Village. His birthday is August 27, but she has planned the party for August 25, a Sunday afternoon. Her friends and their children will be there. Janet, of course, plans to be the perfect mommy-hostess at her little boy's party.

Janet goes to lunch with her friends, and they confide in one another. A couple of her closest friends know that all is not well between her and Perry. They have watched Perry dominate and demean her; they have witnessed his arrogance and have seen her beautiful animated smile fade when he embarrasses her. Others suspect trouble, but none of them knows exactly what is going on inside Janet's dream house at 3 Blackberry Road as a languid, sweltering August slides into its third week.

Perry has spent the last several nights away from home— three nights in the Budgetel and two in the Hampton Inn. On Tuesday, August 13, as Lori Fishel passes through Janet's kitchen, she happens to see a note from Perry. It says something about leaving—"if I leave I will only take my guitar"—but she can't fully make out the writing. Janet sees Lori looking at the note and whisks it away without comment. Lori pretends she hasn't paid any attention to it. She doesn't want to embarrass Janet; it's not her business.

That evening, Janet goes with her friends to the Bound'ry, a trendy restaurant in the Vanderbilt area. She frequently goes to the Bound'ry for girls' night out. The girls are all young mothers with husbands in demanding, time-intensive professions. This is a chance to dress up, have a few drinks, complain a little, gossip a little. Janet is not in a party mood tonight. Diane Saks, another friend in her exclusive circle, is aware that Janet isn't herself. Usually she's talking about her kids and her painting, which has really taken off in the last couple of years. Diane knows about some of the tension between Janet and Perry. Janet also has been looking into the 1970 death of Perry's mother when he was only nine years old; she has told Diane that she feels certain Perry lied about the circumstances. Janet has told another close and trusted friend, Laura Zinker, that she believes Perry's father, Arthur, was somehow responsible for his wife's death. She even told Laura she is afraid of Arthur. Tonight, Janet tells Diane, "I can't believe this is my life." Even their waitress at the Bound'ry, a young woman who frequently serves Janet, notices that she is quieter than usual. The waitress, Ashley, asks if everything's all right. Janet shrugs and manages a smile. "Home problems," she says.

Tonight, for the first time in several nights, Perry does not go to a hotel. He's waiting for Janet when she comes in. They sit up late talking, their voices edged with frustration. They are tired, both tired of the friction that never eases, both tired of the inevitable arguments. Janet dictates a list of things Perry should do; he promises he will do better. Janet goes to bed, alone. Perry heads to Sammy's room for the night.

On Wednesday, Ella Goldshmid comes to take care of the children. She works for Janet twice a week. The Russian nanny is not completely fluent in English, so she and Janet don't do a lot of talking and Janet never talks about personal matters, but Ella senses that her employer is depressed. Janet spends most of the day in her studio, painting. Ella will later tell police that Janet was a devoted mother who liked to keep her children to a routine.

Like Perry, Janet is living a double life—the one she projects to others, and the one that is progressively disintegrating. A shuttlecock existence. Even though she has been going for marriage counseling for months, she tells Ella not to worry about job security, because she and Perry plan to have five kids.

When Perry comes home from the office, Janet is dressed to go out again. Her best friend, Laurie Rummel, is hosting their regular book-club meeting, but before the book club, Janet drives over to Sperry's restaurant, in Belle Meade.

The wealthiest pocket of Nashville is Belle Meade, a city of only 3.1 square miles where the residents are 98 percent white and the median household income is well over $100,000. It is not uncommon to find homes listed for over a million dollars. Sperry's, a dark wood, faux–English steakhouse, is a Nashville tradition and has not changed much since it was established in 1974. Located on Harding Road, the restaurant is a favorite of Nashville's old families, a mix of politicians, movers and shakers in business, and big names in the music industry. But Janet does not go to Sperry's to see and be seen. In the dimly lit surroundings, at one of the tables built from World War II Liberty-ship hatch covers and shined to a mirror finish, Janet sits alone, orders dinner, and reads a book. When she finishes picking at her food, she asks her waiter for a "to go" box. She takes the box to Laurie Rummel's and puts it in Laurie's refrigerator during the book-club meeting. After the meeting, there is a lot of chatter, a lot of laughter—but Janet is distracted. She excuses herself and leaves without her box from Sperry's.

Perry sleeps in Sammy's room again.

The last day Janet March is seen or heard from—Thursday, August 15—begins as another ordinary day at 3 Blackberry Road. Perry leaves for work early. A warm breeze stirs, pleasant enough now, but already in the air is the promise of a hot, humid day, typical of August in Tennessee. Sammy and Tzipi wake up happy, full of energy, ready to play. Janet gets them dressed and fed and plans her day.

She remembers the box of food from Sperry's that she left at Laurie Rummel's house the night before and drops by to pick it up. Laurie asks her to come inside for a while, but Janet says no, she has to go. Laurie will later describe her demeanor to police, saying she was "distraught." Her close friend wonders why she has to hurry. Possibly, Janet goes on other errands, but no one will report seeing her again until noon.

Belle Meade is mostly residential, except for Harding Road, which defines the tiny city's western perimeter. The Belle Meade post office, Sunflower Grocery, Bread & Company (an upscale bakery and café), and the gourmet deli Corner Market, are all located along Harding Road, just minutes from Sperry's restaurant. Forest Hills, itself a tiny enclave of more of the city's wealthy, where Janet and Perry live, borders on Belle Meade.

Janet and the children arrive at Bread & Company around noon. It's a short drive from Blackberry Road, along Tyne Boulevard, with its sprawling homes on spacious lots. The lawns are lush and green, despite the scorching August heat. Janet parks her new 1996 Volvo 850 in the Bread & Company parking lot between a Lexus and a Mercedes convertible, across from a Suburban and a BMW.

Inside the popular café, the air is thick with the smells of sugar and yeast and the sounds of laughing voices. The crowd is overwhelmingly female, with several knots of tanned women in tennis skirts fresh off the courts of their respective clubs: Belle Meade, Richland, and Hillwood Country Clubs; and Westside, Seven Hills, and Whitworth Tennis Clubs.

Janet is waiting to order when Jo Anne Copeland calls her name. Jo Anne makes her way over to Janet and the children, and they talk for a few minutes, mostly about the end of summer that always seems to come too soon. "Are you excited about starting to school?" Jo Anne asks Sammy.

It is the last time Jo Anne will ever see Janet.

Later, she will tell police that Janet said nothing about a trip, nothing at all to indicate that she wouldn't be taking Sammy to his first day of kindergarten, August 26.

None of Janet's friends knew that she had an appointment with a divorce lawyer scheduled for the very next day. Even Laurie Rummel, Janet's closest friend, didn't know. Janet's parents didn't know their daughter's marriage had reached this stage until Janet asked her father to suggest some divorce attorneys. She is a private person, not usually given to run crying to her mother after an argument with Perry. Perry is more likely than Janet to call Carolyn after one of their arguments, to tell his side first. Perry always seems to have an agenda when he interacts with others, and his conversations with his mother-in-law prove no different. But in recent weeks both Janet and Perry have come to Carolyn with their marital problems. Carolyn advised a "cooling off" period. If Perry would move out for a while, she said, she would pay for the apartment.

Janet knows she must consider something beyond a cooling-off period—but some weeks ago, she mentioned divorce to Perry and she has not been able to get his words out of her mind.

"I'll kill you," he'd said.

Janet has chosen Lucinda Smith, the sister of her best friend in the fifth grade, as her counsel for this excruciatingly personal legal matter. Telling an old friend will somehow soften the reality of her failure to make the marriage work. Her parents have been married for thirty-six years, and she just assumed her life would follow the same course of stability and growth. Her dream house, with all its months of planning and design and with all its beauty and precise craftsmanship, could not impose a symmetry on their swirling disharmony.

"Will you go with me?" Janet asks her mother in one of their last telephone conversations.

The thought of Janet and Perry divorcing is agonizing to Carolyn, but of course she will not refuse her daughter. She says yes, she'll go.

At about three forty-five in the afternoon, workmen arrive from Classic Interiors. John McAllister and John Richie are installing new butcher-block countertops in the kitchen at the March home, replacing ones that Janet had not been pleased with originally. She is meticulous and can be demanding. Janet has scheduled the workmen for late afternoon so their noise won't interrupt Tzipi's nap. The men talk with Janet about the project. At about four thirty, Perry comes home, but he defers to Janet's role as the home's designer and at first doesn't deal with the workmen. They tell Janet they'll need to come back to finish. She asks if they can fix a leaky kitchen faucet before they leave. Perry locates a plumbing tool for the job and gives it to the workmen.

"Call me on Friday," she says. "We'll set up another appointment."

They will remember what she is wearing: blue jeans, a blouse, and sandals. They will be asked to remember, because no one except Perry and the children will ever see Janet March again after John McAllister and John Richie leave the house at about five o'clock Thursday afternoon, August 15.

The only other person to speak with Janet on this day is Marissa Moody. They talk on the phone late in the afternoon and set up a playdate for Sammy and Marissa's son, Grant, for the next morning.

"Why don't you bring Grant over about nine thirty or ten?" Janet says.

"Great," says Marissa. "I have some things to do. I'll pick him up at about two if that's okay."

"Perfect. Sammy will be so excited," says Janet. "I'll see you then."

Perry and Janet and the children have dinner, Janet does some work in her studio, and Perry puts the children to bed. This time the arguing begins at the kitchen table. According to Perry's version of the night's events, their argument ends when Janet gets into her Volvo, slams the door, and drives away.

The story that Perry March will give police is this: At about eight, Janet packs some bags and says she's going on a vacation. "A vacation, like the vacation you've been having," she says, referring to his nights in the Budgetel and Hampton Inn. She takes his credit card, a bag of marijuana, and several thousand dollars in cash and says she'll be back for Sammy's birthday.

She leaves a to-do list for Perry, items like "change burned out light bulbs" and "clean up your closet," chores Perry has neglected doing. The document is saved on the computer at eight fifteen. Janet makes Perry sign the list.

Perry follows her outside, into the balmy night, thick with the summer sounds of frogs and crickets. He demands to know where she's going.

"None of your business. See how it is with the kids," she says.

A neighbor, Helen Ward, who lives at 1 Blackberry Road, will report hearing a "loud male voice" coming from their driveway. She will tell police that Janet and Perry were in the habit of arguing in the driveway, apparently to keep from waking the children.

Janet says, "See ya!" and drives away, and it's the last time Perry sees his wife.

That's Perry's story.

•   •   •

Laurie Rummel gets a call at about nine that evening. "Well, she's gone," Perry says. Laurie is Janet's best friend, but she has been a friend to Perry, too. He has asked her to do the interior decorating of a new office he is planning. Perry has decided to leave the family firm and practice law alone. He has complained to Laurie in the past that Janet is spoiled and used to getting everything she wants, that she's always making lists of things for him to do. Of course she's heard some of Janet's side, too—but never in her wildest dreams did she picture Janet just driving away, as Perry is describing. She hangs up, a sick feeling deep in her heart, wondering what has really happened.

At 9:11 Perry calls his brother, Ron, and at 9:14 he calls his sister, Kathy. Ron, an attorney, and Kathy, a dentist, both live in the Chicago area. He reaches Kathy at the home of her boyfriend, Lee Breitowich. He delivers the same message to both of his siblings: "Janet has left."

At midnight, he dials the Levines' number. There is a phone on each side of their bed. Carolyn and Larry both pick up at the same time. Larry's voice is thick with sleep but quickly turns anxious when Perry says, "Janet has left."

"Left? What do you mean? Where has she gone?"

"I don't know where."

"Perry, tell me exactly what happened," says Carolyn.

"We had an argument, and she packed some bags and just drove away," Perry says, not with the self-assured arrogance that normally resonates in his voice, but with the whine of a disappointed child.

Larry is quiet. He closes his eyes and listens, rubbing the skin between his eyes, as Carolyn continues the conversation. She asks about the children. Perry says they're sleeping. He recites the events of the night once again. He sounds bewildered, the way he often sounds after he and Janet argue and he rushes to call Carolyn. In some ways, she has been a surrogate mother to him. Her heart always went out to him because he missed having a mother as he was growing up.

Finally, Carolyn says, "Perry, don't worry. I'm sure if you

had an argument, she's upset. She's probably driving around to cool off. She'll be back. Call me when she comes home."

In a written statement Perry will make to the police, two weeks after Janet's disappearance, he says, "Janet had left like this before, so we all settled down to wait."

Carolyn Levine will tell police that Janet had *never* left home like that.

The dark night fades into dawn. Light streaks the sky as Nashville wakes up. It's another hot August day, an ordinary day for most of the city's residents, but life at 3 Blackberry Road has changed forever.

Janet does not come home.

CHAPTER 4

She Simply Vanished

For Deneane Beard, the day starts early. It is almost a twenty-mile drive from her home in Fairview, in the contiguous county of Williamson, to the home of Janet and Perry March in Forest Hills. Although Williamson County is gaining a national reputation as a growing residential area whose inhabitants enjoy one of the highest per capita incomes in the country, Fairview has been virtually overlooked by the influx of wealthy new residents. Located on the opposite end of the county from the affluent cities of Brentwood and Franklin, Fairview remains essentially a rural community.

Deneane has cleaned the March home since the family moved to 3 Blackberry Road in 1995. She and Janet are about the same age, but their relationship is distinctly that of employer and employee. They are clearly from two different worlds. Still, Janet has always been nice to Deneane. The money is good—seventy-five dollars for two to three hours' work—and Janet allows her to set up her work schedule around her class commitments at Belmont College. Just a few more semesters, and she will have the college degree she has worked so hard to earn while going to school part-time and cleaning rich people's houses.

August 16 begins earlier than normal for Deneane. Just after six thirty that morning, her phone rings. It's Perry March asking what time she will be coming to work.

"I should be there by eight thirty," she tells him, puzzled by the call. She has maintained the same alternating schedule for months, arriving at eight thirty on one day and then the next week at about eleven thirty.

As promised, Deneane arrives at Blackberry Road by eight thirty. Perry meets her at the door. "Come in. I'm getting the children dressed," he says.

"Where's Janet?" she asks.

"She's in California for a few days," Perry tells her.

Deneane will later inform the police that the last time she saw Janet was on August 9, 1996, during her regularly scheduled cleaning time. That week her hours were eleven thirty to two thirty. She will add in her formal statement that Janet discussed Sammy's sixth birthday party scheduled for August 25, and that the party invitations were already on Janet's desk. Janet did not mention a trip to California.

On this summer morning, Deneane's cleaning routine goes more quickly than usual. While she normally fills five or six bags with trash, today there are only two, and when she heads toward the kids' playroom, Perry informs her that it is not necessary to clean that room today. After completing her duties, she tells Perry that she is ready to leave.

"How do you spell your name?" Perry asks as he begins to write her check. "And how much does Janet pay you?"

She tells him. People are always misspelling her name, and she supposes Janet doesn't bother her husband with domestic details such as how much she pays for housecleaning, but Deneane can't help feeling offended that he knows so little about her and what she does at the March house. Perry writes the check, and before she goes, Deneane mentions that she left a note for Janet, a list of cleaning supplies that she needs for next time.

As she drives away from the March home, Deneane tries

to shift her mind to her upcoming classes at school. Yet she cannot help having an odd feeling about the entire morning, starting with the early call to her home. It would be more like Janet to have left the check already written, perhaps with a note to Deneane about particular items that needed attention. Or at least she would have left instructions about what time Deneane was to arrive and how much she should be paid. Janet is just that methodical. Maybe she didn't have time to make preparations, Deneane thinks.

Something must have come up suddenly.

As Marissa Moody and her young son, Grant, make their way to Blackberry Road on this same August morning, the sun is already high in the gauzy-white sky. Marissa's route takes her down Belle Meade Boulevard, with its landscaped median, an endless bouquet of vibrant red and white crepe myrtles that seem undaunted by the blistering sun. Marissa catches a glimpse of the golfers in their brightly colored shirts walking the manicured fairways of Belle Meade Country Club. They seem to be in another world. Behind each group of golfers in their pastel parade of carefree oblivion are caddies, the majority black, each wearing a starched white uniform with BMCC emblazoned on his back and carrying a load of weighty clubs that make a rhythmic clanking noise with each bouncy stride. It is as if time has stood still in this corner of the city.

Grant, excited about playing with Sammy, keeps asking his mom how much longer, though it's only a short drive to the March home. Marissa is glad her son is making so many friends. It's too bad adults can't make friends as easily as young children do. Everything gets so complicated for adults. The simple honesty of early childhood becomes clouded by the competing images of a complex adulthood. Marissa has learned that the game everyone plays, especially in this part of Nashville, is success, not friendship, and the images of wealth are how the score is kept.

"Here we are," she says to her impatient son as they arrive at 3 Blackberry Road, another jewel in the ever-expanding crown worn by the wealthy in Nashville. Each time she visits this private enclave of Forest Hills, she is taken aback by the complete seclusion that the March home enjoys. If it were not for the narrow meandering drive that disappears over the wooded hillside at the end of the cul-de-sac, no one would guess that among the oaks, maples, dog-woods, redbuds, and cherry blossoms, a home has been magically placed away from the daily noise of the world, as if dropped from the sky in its completed and majestic state.

Pulling her car up close to the house, Marissa sees Tzipi playing in the side yard along with the Marches' Russian nanny, Ella Goldshmid. Marissa waves as she and Grant make their way to the back of the house. She announces their arrival with a few gentle knocks on the kitchen door. After an unusually long time, the door opens. It is not Janet who greets her invited guests. It's Sammy.

"Hi," he says. Then he pivots and runs over to a large, dark-colored rug that is rolled up, lying on the floor just off the kitchen, in front of the doorway to Janet's studio.

Marissa and Grant take a couple of steps inside. "Is your mom here, Sammy?" Marissa asks, squeezing the hand of her excited son.

"She's not here," Sammy says.

"Will she be back soon?"

"I don't know."

Marissa frowns. Surely Janet didn't forget the playdate for this morning. They set it up only last night on the phone. "Is your dad at home?" she asks.

"He's in his study," Sammy says. "He's doing some kind of work."

As he talks to them, Sammy bounces up and down on the rolled-up rug as if it is an indoor trampoline. Marissa stays just inside the door, still holding Grant's hand. She has been to the March home before, but she and Janet are not close friends, not close enough for her to begin parading through the house calling out for Sammy's dad.

"Why don't you tell your dad that we're here, since your mom invited Grant to spend the day playing with you."

Marissa speaks gently, but she's aware of an edge to her voice. She doesn't think it's too much to ask that Perry at least come out and speak to her in Janet's place, parent to parent.

Sammy jumps off his perch atop the rug and races toward the back of the house. Grant, leaning in closer to her, seems to sense that the situation is awkward. Marissa is feeling more than discomfort; she feels snubbed that Janet is not here to greet them.

After a few minutes, Perry appears long enough to say that Grant can stay and play. "I was planning to take Sammy to the office, but it's all right. Ella's here," he says.

Not a warm welcome, by any stretch. Marissa says, "You're sure it's okay?"

"Sure," Perry says.

Grant pulls loose from his mother's grip and heads across the kitchen to meet his friend. At least Grant won't be disappointed, Marissa thinks. "I'll be back at about two," she says.

She lets herself out, amid the boys' giggles and tennis shoes slapping the floor. The two energetic young boys sprint off together across the hardwood floors, disappearing into the vastness of the house.

As she heads to her car, Marissa has the unsettled feeling of a parent who has left her child in a place where supervision and structure are questionable. She stops for a moment to watch Ella play with Tzipi and is comforted by the presence of the attentive nanny. She is still perplexed by Janet's absence, but by the time she reaches her car, she has convinced herself that she's making too much of the whole thing.

What could possibly happen in such a beautiful and magical setting?

Later in the morning, the phone rings. Perry has been making calls—to his office, to a few clients, and to Laurie Rummel, confirming their luncheon meeting later that day, to discuss decorating the new office space he has decided to lease. It is a huge decision to go out on his own, to leave the family firm, but he knows it is time. Time to be his own boss.

Perry knows that lunch with Laurie will center on Janet at first. Laurie is Janet's best friend; that's why he called her last evening to tell her Janet left. Talking with her this morning, he sensed that Laurie would rather not keep their appointment today under the circumstances. "Are you sure, Perry? We can reschedule."

"It's okay. I'm fine, Laurie," he says, determined to go on with his plans.

To a casual observer, August 16 appears to be a typical day at the March home. Sammy is romping through the house with his friend; Tzipi is playing under the watchful eye of her nanny, Ella; and Perry is attending to his business affairs, getting ready to have lunch with a family friend.

After the second ring, Perry wants to flip on the answering machine, but he knows it will leave the wrong impression in case the Levines call again. He answers. As he expects, it's Carolyn Levine. The concern in her voice is obvious, even more apparent than in her call earlier that morning, but still not at a panic level.

"Have you heard from Janet?"

"Not yet," Perry says.

"Did you check with any of the hotels?" his mother-in-law asks.

"Yes, of course," he says. "I just knew she was going to be at the Hampton Inn. She knew I had a reservation there, and I thought she would use it."

"What did they say when you called?" she asks.

"That no one checked in under the name of March."

A deep sigh comes across the wires.

"She'll call, I know she will," Perry offers, doing his best to project a tone of encouragement.

"I'm coming over there, Perry," Carolyn says. "I want to be with the children."

"Ella's here, and the children are fine," he says.

They've never been without their mother, not like this.

Carolyn blinks hard, rubs the chill bumps on her arms. "I just want to be with Sammy and Tzipi," she says.

Marissa Moody returns to 3 Blackberry Road a few minutes before two, the time she and Janet agreed upon the night before. Before she even knocks, Sammy and Grant rush to open the kitchen door.

"Is your mom back?" Marissa asks. "I want to thank her for letting Grant spend the day."

"She's not here."

"Did I miss her?"

"I don't know," Sammy says.

"Is your dad here? I can thank him," Marissa says.

"He had to go meet somebody."

Now feeling doubly snubbed, Marissa thanks Sammy and says, "Come on, Grant, it's time to go."

"My grandmother is upstairs with Tzipi."

"Oh—tell her thank you for me," Marissa says.

Then it hits her. The rug, the large dark-colored rug that was rolled up just beyond the kitchen—the one Sammy was bouncing up and down on—is gone. She starts to ask Sammy what happened to it but doesn't want to seem nosy.

Larry calls several times from the office to ask Carolyn if there has been any news of Janet. Neither can believe that Janet has really left for a vacation. She may have told Perry that's what she's doing, just to make him worry—but she wouldn't leave her children like this, her parents agree.

More likely she's at a hotel—but surely not for more than one night. Even *that* is hard to believe about Janet. Wherever she is, if she doesn't return soon, she will certainly call home. Janet will know how anxious her parents are. She'll want her children to know that she's all right.

Evening comes to Nashville, and Carolyn is still waiting. She thinks about Perry's call at midnight. She'd told him not to worry. She was so sure Janet would be back in a little while. Now Carolyn is worried.

Larry insists they should go to the police. "Tomorrow, it .

will be more than twenty-four hours. I don't care what Perry says. We need to report her missing."

"Surely we'll hear from her by tomorrow. Janet will know we're worried sick!"

"If we don't hear something by morning—"

"But if we contact the police, and it turns out that she really did just drive away—"

"Janet would call us. You know she would, Carolyn."

It's a conversation they will have over and over during the next two weeks.

The Levines spend the first of many long, restless nights waiting for the phone to ring, trying to imagine where Janet could possibly be. Both want with all their hearts to believe they will hear something from their daughter tomorrow, but for tonight, it seems she has simply vanished.

CHAPTER 5

The Critical First Two Weeks

On the second day of waiting, the Levines decide they must do something. Having left the earlier inquiries to Perry, they now begin to make some discreet calls of their own to some of Janet's friends, both in Nashville and out of town. They check with their son, Mark, in California to see if he has heard from his sister.

No one has heard from Janet.

Larry Levine himself begins to call hotels and motels around Nashville looking for any evidence that his daughter is somehow still in the area.

Nothing.

Later in the day, Larry goes to the airport with Perry, who has dropped the children off with Carolyn. They meticulously search through each of the parking lots and parking garages, scanning the hundreds of cars for Janet's Volvo 850.

Again they come up empty.

Perry has another important stop to make on this Saturday while the children are with their grandmother. Carolyn has offered to do what she can to help out with the children, and Perry takes her up on it. He asked Ella yesterday if she could start working every day for a while, but she informed him it would be at least September before she could take on such a schedule.

He drives to 900 Nineteenth Avenue South, the University Square Apartments. Weeks ago, Perry saw the handwriting on the wall and began to search for an apartment. Dr. Campbell even suggested that Perry and Janet separate for a while, sensing they needed a cooling-off period. Carolyn, always generous, had offered to pay for a place for Perry if it would allow for the couple to calm down. She was worried about Sammy and Tzipi. For the children's sake, she told Janet and Perry, they simply had to maintain some level of reasonable communication.

But Perry knew that he and Janet were not going to stay together. Marriage counseling was not helping—and he was sick of local motel rooms. He had to get on with his life.

His plans for a fresh start include a new office, the office Laurie Rummel is helping him decorate, and a new place to come home to. He checked with his client Paul Eichel about a downtown apartment that Paul maintains, but it was not available. He called local developer and new client Gary Zeitlin in early August to check on any available units, but nothing panned out. Unit 1004 at University Square will have to do. He signs the lease.

It is late afternoon by the time he arrives to pick up the children. Carolyn has heard him drive up. She meets him at the door and lets him in. Sammy and Tzipi come running.

"Time to go home, kids," he says.

Carolyn hands him a tote bag with some of Tzipi's things. "You should get some rest, Perry," she says. "You look exhausted."

Carolyn gives each of the children a kiss and a hug. Her embrace lingers. She does not want to let go.

•   •   •

That evening Laurie Rummel and her husband, David, stop by. The Rummel and March couples often go out together on Saturday nights.

"Any word from Janet?" Laurie asks, keeping her voice low. Perry has said the children are asleep, but Laurie isn't taking any chances that they might overhear. Her heart aches for Janet's children, who must be missing their mother terribly.

"Nope, nothing," says Perry.

"Are you all right? Are the kids okay?"

"We're fine. I want you to look at the note Janet left me." Perry steps away and comes back with a sheet of paper. "Her to-do list," he adds, in a lawyerly voice.

Perry hands the typewritten list to Laurie. Janet's closest friend examines it; David leans in to look as well. They study the list—each of the twenty-three items—for a couple of minutes. Centered in the title line is "Perry's Turn For Janet's 12 Day Vacation." The first item is "Feed the Children nutritious food—3 meals per day." The second is "Coordinate Deneane and Ella." Some of the imperatives deal with calls to make: "Call Steve Ward about driveway." Most are along the line of "Do Children's laundry," "Read to Tzipi," and "Do educational activities with Sam." Number sixteen is "Spend quantity and quality time with your Children—not your guitar or computer or clients." Perry's signature appears at the end of the page, after the line: "I agree to do all of the above before Janet's Vacation (in response to Perry's cowardly, rash, and confused vacation) is over."

Laurie looks up, furrowing her brow. "Perry, why didn't Janet sign it?" she asks.

Perry shrugs. "I don't know." An awkward silence follows.

Laurie grabs her husband's hand. "We need to be going. Perry, please let us know the minute you hear from Janet."

"Hang in there," David says. "She'll be home soon."

     •   •   •

Several days later, on Wednesday, August 21, Perry makes a stop at Universal Tires on Demonbreum Street in downtown Nashville. He goes to the sales counter and informs the sales associate that he needs four new tires for his Jeep Cherokee.

Weeks later, when police come to the tire store to interview the employee, Dave Roh, they learn that Mr. Roh is no longer with the company. However, another employee, Bobby Armstrong, will tell police that he remembers the occasion on August 21 and gives his account: Roh is busy, and Armstrong actually deals with Perry March, although Roh is credited with the sale. Armstrong points out that the tires on the Jeep Cherokee have at least twenty thousand miles of wear—50 percent—left on them, but Perry insists on new tires. "Do you want to keep the old ones?" Armstrong asks. Perry says no.

When Perry is interviewed in the press months later about the purchase of new tires just six days after Janet's disappearance, he will be quick to point out that "it was on the to-do list Janet had left me. Besides, I preferred Michelins." The police will note that the to-do list includes nothing about getting tires changed.

The next day, August 22, Perry is back at the law firm at Levine, Mattson, Orr, and Geracioti. Sometime during the day, he walks into the office of his law partner Michael Geracioti to ask for a referral.

"One of my clients, Paul Eichel, has gotten himself into some real trouble," Perry explains. "Can you recommend a good criminal defense lawyer?"

Geracioti, who is a friend of District Attorney Torry Johnson, says, "Let me call Torry and see who he recommends. He's a busy guy, so it may be a couple of days before I can get back to you."

"Great. That's fine, Mike. Thanks for your help," Perry says as he leaves the office and heads back down the hallway. It occurs to him that lying to his partner where a client is concerned is tricky business, but he needs a private investigator, and he knows that criminal defense lawyers use them frequently.

On August 23, Deneane Beard's day starts just like the previous Friday began. The phone rings. Before answering, she looks at her watch. It's not even seven.

The caller is Perry March. "I was wondering what time you would be here today," he says.

Deneane explains, "This is the Friday that I'm supposed to arrive at eleven thirty." She pauses, and then she just has to ask, "Has Janet forgotten my schedule?"

"Janet had to leave early this morning for some project she's working on downtown. She forgot to tell me what time you'd be here," Perry says.

"I'll be there at eleven thirty," Deneane says, thinking, once again, this is very odd.

The next morning, Saturday, phone calls start one right after another. Perry is expecting to hear from his father, Arthur, who is on his way from Mexico. He is driving his Ford Escort station wagon all the way from Ajijic, Mexico, to Nashville, and it is a long trip. When Perry called the previous week and said he needed some help with the kids, Arthur found it odd, since the Levines were right there in Nashville, always right in the middle of things, and Janet had hired that foreign nanny. When Perry also said he and Janet had been arguing and she had left for a few days, it didn't surprise Arthur. He didn't really get along with his daughter-in-law. They more or less tolerated each other.

But it's not Arthur calling. It's the first of several calls from Janet's friends. Their children have all received the invitations for Sammy's birthday party, the invitations that Deneane saw on Janet's desk when cleaning the house on August 9. Janet's friends all have the same question: "Is everything still on for Sammy's birthday party tomorrow?"

Perry knew there was a party but he is hazy on the details. He confirms that everything is still on go, and immediately hangs up and calls his mother-in-law. Janet had planned a Sunday-afternoon party on August 25 for the children and parents. Sunday is a perfect day for their circle of Jewish friends, and Dragon Park is a perfect location for the party. Dragon Park, officially the Fannie Mae Dees Park, named for a local civic leader, is located on Blakemore Avenue near the heart of Hillsboro Village, an area that Janet regularly frequented. The Village, as the name implies, is a small hamlet within the city, an eclectic mix of retail shops, offices, churches, private homes, apartments, and condominiums. It is one part of the old Nashville that has not been completely altered by bulldozers and developers. New buildings are interwoven with the older buildings, homes, and shops. Within walking distance of the Vanderbilt campus, Hillsboro Village attracts a youthful, effervescent crowd in designer clothes to its trendy restaurants, bars, and coffee shops. Janet and her girlfriends often found themselves at one of these fun culinary destinations for their girls' nights out.

The whimsical park, one area that the entire Nashville community seems to enjoy, is referred to as Dragon Park because of the two-hundred-foot-long sea serpent that is the focal point. It is a park truly designed for children. In 1972, the City of Nashville commissioned renowned artist Pedro Silva to create one of his signature sculptures. Silva, who was born in Chile, gave up his career in the Chilean diplomatic service to pursue his love for art full time, and developed a program in the sixties to get talented youths involved in creating massive art sculptures brought to life through their direct hands-on involvement.

Silva's massive sea serpent was just such a community project. It consists of thousands of pieces of cut or chipped tiles with pictures of faces, birds, flowers, and animals, painted by hundreds of local artisans. This is the setting Janet March had chosen for her son's birthday party—a place where her beautiful six-year-old and all his friends could play, climb, run, laugh, and dream.

Perry and the Levines know they will be bombarded with questions about Janet. They agree on their storyline ahead of time. What results is a penumbra.

"Carolyn, where on earth is Janet?" an early guest inquires.

"She's in California visiting Mark," Carolyn answers.

"I can't believe she's missing Sammy's birthday party!"

"Janet developed some type of inner-ear infection, so she couldn't fly."

"Oh, I'm so sorry. I know Sammy is crushed."

"He's disappointed, but she'll be home in a few days," Carolyn replies. She withdraws, thanking the guest for bringing her little boy. "I hope he has a good time."

"He's having a wonderful time!" the guest gushes. "Janet's parties are the best."

The party proceeds just as Janet planned. From all appearances, Sammy has a delightful sixth birthday, taking full advantage of Dragon Park, running and playing with all his friends, under the watchful eyes of his father and his grandparents, but amid the whispers of family friends.

If only his mom were there, it would be perfect.

On Monday, August 26, Mike Geracioti sticks his head in Perry's office.

"I have some names for you," he says.

"Excuse me?" Perry replies with a fixed gaze, his mind far away.

"The criminal attorneys you wanted for your client."

"Oh—right."

"I finally heard back from Torry Johnson's office. He gave me several names. I don't think your client could go wrong with any of them." Geracioti gives the names on the A-list: Lionel Barrett, Ed Yarbrough, Jim Weatherly, and David Raybin. "Let me know what you decide and how it turns out," Geracioti says as he exits the office.

"Sure. Thanks, Mike," Perry says, jotting the names on a notepad.

Approximately six weeks later Michael Geracioti will provide police with a typed statement outlining the substance of these conversations in late August, as well as a third conversation he has with Perry March in the first week in September. The typed statement indicates that in the final conversation, Perry confided to his law partner that Janet was missing, and claimed that he had traveled to both Chicago and Quebec City, two places Janet enjoyed, passing out photographs of his wife in hopes that someone would have seen her. During the same conversation, Perry also explained that the reason he had asked for a referral of criminal defense attorneys was that he felt they could refer him to a good private investigator.

The typed statement that Geracioti will provide to authorities also notes that during the conversation in early September, when Geracioti asks if he can help in any way, Perry replies, "Find Janet . . . or find her body."

On August 28, Perry finally does call a private investigator. It has now been thirteen days since his wife left. Thirteen days, and not a single clue has surfaced. Not one.

Janet has simply vanished.

That afternoon, Perry March and Larry and Carolyn Levine jointly walk into the Nashville offices of Henry E. King, private investigator. After the cursory introductions, Mr. King gets right down to business.

"Have you contacted the police?"

"We didn't want the media involved," Perry says. The Levines do not contradict him.

"Do you have any idea where she may be?" the investigator probes.

Perry answers without hesitation. "She loves Quebec City and Cozumel."

"What about money?" King asks. "Has she used any of her credit cards?"

"Not that I know of," Perry says. "But she does have some cash. She made several cash withdrawals over the last few weeks." He looks at some notes and reads off the figures, "A thousand dollars, four hundred dollars, six hundred dollars, and another four hundred dollars."

"In the last few weeks? You mean since she left?" King asks.

"No, no, all before she left," Perry says. "And then there was an insurance refund check she cashed for six hundred and forty-three dollars on August thirteenth. That's two days before she left."

The investigator jots down the figures on his pad and quickly adds them up—over $3,000, in cash.

"Could she be using any other name?"

"Possibly Marchant," Perry offers. "She once told me that if my name had been Marchant, instead of March, she would have married me sooner." His lips form a faint smile as his words fade. Larry and Carolyn glance at their son-in-law at the same time, but both remain silent. Neither joins him in smiling.

King gets up from his chair and walks toward Perry. "I would like to speak with the Levines alone, if that's okay."

"Sure. I understand," Perry says. "You can ask them anything. It's fine. Ask them anything."

The moment is understandably awkward. Perry gets up and leaves the office, shutting the door behind him. King returns to his chair and gets right back at it. He turns to Carolyn.

"Were they having marital problems?" the investigator asks.

"They had been seeing a marriage counselor, a psychiatrist," Carolyn says. She feels bad betraying her daughter's secrets, her problems. She thinks about her conversation with Janet on the night of the fourteenth, about the appointment with Lucinda Smith, but she doesn't add to her response.

"Did your daughter use drugs?"

"Not that we know of," Larry answers.

"No, certainly not," says Carolyn.

"She has two small children to care for," Larry adds. "I can't see her doing drugs."

King again leaves his chair. Going to his office door, he cracks it open and asks Perry to rejoin them. Once Perry is settled, the investigator addresses them collectively. "I will be glad to help you if you want to retain my services, but the best advice I can give you is go to the police immediately, and report her missing."

"We have one more investigator to meet with, so we couldn't do it before tomorrow," Larry says.

After their meeting concludes, King, an experienced investigator, dictates a statement outlining their conversation for his files. Later the typed statement will be given to police. When detectives review it, King's last paragraph jumps out at them: "I find it very disturbing that they have not contacted police. If your loved one is missing, I would want to move as fast as possible."

Chapter 6

#M956251899

The Nashville Criminal Justice Center is a busy, bustling place. It is located on James Robertson Parkway in the heart of downtown, only blocks from where James Robertson himself stepped foot onto the shores of the Cumberland River and founded the city of Nashville in 1779.

Unlike many cities in the United States, Nashville, Tennessee, has a metropolitan form of government. In 1963, what had been formerly two separate and somewhat overlapping governmental entities, the city of Nashville and the county of Davidson merged into one metropolitan governmental body. The idea was for a more streamlined model of governmental affairs that would benefit the residents of both the city and county. Decades later, many Nashvillians would argue that with a council made up of forty elected representatives, the desired goal of a smoothly operated governing body may not have actually been achieved.

In the area of law enforcement, the Nashville Police Department and the Davidson County Sheriff's Office maintained their separate identities, but not their same powers. The sheriff's office, which had previously handled all the

law enforcement activities in the unincorporated areas outside the city limits, became responsible for managing all
correctional facilities located within the city and county,
along with overseeing the service of all civil litigation
process. The remainder of all law enforcement matters fell
under the jurisdiction of the chief of police. The position of
chief of police was instantly a very powerful one, with a
huge and ever-growing responsibility as the city grew in
population from just over six hundred thousand in 1963 to a
million in the next three decades.

In January of 1996, Emmett Turner, a metro police officer with over a quarter of a century on the Nashville police
force, was named chief of police. Little did Chief Turner
know that just eight months into his tenure, the highest-
profile criminal case in Nashville's history was about to
come through his door.

If you are a citizen of Nashville, Tennessee, and the criminal justice system invades your life, 200 James Robertson
Parkway is the place where your journey will begin. The
complex is a one-stop shop for everything amiss in the
human condition—homicides, larcenies, rapes, robberies,
burglaries, aggravated assaults, domestic violence, motor
vehicle theft, and missing persons.

On August 29, exactly two weeks after Janet March was
last seen, Larry Levine, Perry March, and Janet's brother,
Mark, walked into the Nashville Criminal Justice Center to
officially report her missing. Two excruciating weeks have
generated every level of human emotion—concern, which
grew into worry, which then became dread, followed by denial, and now finally acceptance of the fact that something is
horribly wrong. No one knew where Janet was or when her
family would see her again. As Henry King stressed the day
before, until this pivotal step was taken, the investigatory
powers and full resources of the Nashville Police
Department could not spring into action and pursue the mysterious disappearance of Janet Gail Levine March.

In a world where statistics are maintained for every aspect of human life, on August 29, Janet Levine March joins

the official statistics of the national databases as Missing person—NCIC #M956251899. Providing each physical detail of a missing person has to be almost unbearable for family members, but they are the required details that must be conveyed to the police investigator, information that may allow an officer in some distant city to discover a clue that could put this nightmare to an end, and bring Janet home. Maybe she is in a hospital, hours or days away, the victim of an accident, and is physically unable to communicate with those who are desperately waiting to hear her voice.

Father and husband provide the necessary information: *female, white, 33 years old, DOB 02-20-63, 5'4", 104 lbs, brown hair, brown eyes.* And then there is the required photograph, in hopes that someone somewhere has seen her or will see her—this beautiful young woman with thick hair, high cheekbones, lovely full lips, and bright lively eyes; this mother, this wife, this sister, this daughter. The completed missing persons report will also include Janet's Social Security number, her Tennessee driver's license number, and a description for her 1996 gray Volvo 850 with Tennessee license number 844-CBD. There will also be the disturbing standard language that appears in all such reports, a warning to officers around the country that they may be dealing with a person in a delicate emotional condition: *Victim's welfare and mental health are in question.*

Larry prays that those piercing words do not apply to his daughter.

After the painful ordeal, Larry Levine and Perry March, whose lives have just been changed forever, leave the Nashville Criminal Justice Center together.

It is a snapshot we will not see again.

CHAPTER 7

Break in the Case

A week after Janet March is reported missing—three weeks after her disappearance—finally, a break.

Detective Tim Mason's pager goes off as he raises a cup of steaming black coffee to his lips. Mason, with experience in both homicide and missing persons, and his supervisor, Detective Sergeant Billy Smith, have just sat down at McDonald's on West End to have a cup of coffee and go over their schedule for the rest of the day. They have been at it since before eight. Mason checks the number flashing on his pager and heads for the pay phone.

"Some local residents at an apartment complex called in," the dispatcher tells him. "There's a car parked behind one of the buildings. They think it belongs to that missing woman. The lawyer's wife—March."

"Janet March?"

"Right."

Digging for his notepad and pen, Mason says, "Give me the location."

"Brixworth Apartments on Harding Road, next to Vine

Street Christian Church," the officer says. "Just down the road from that ritzy private school."

Mason makes a notation. "Secure the scene. We're in route. Call ID."

At ten thirty Mason and Smith arrive at the Brixworth Apartments. Mason checks his notes for the names of the residents who called in the sighting, James Murphy and Thelma Bennett, Building 131. Some residents of this quiet, private apartment complex are milling around outside their front doors, while others peer out of their windows, curious and concerned that their environment is being invaded by the police. It is just not something they expect to see in this area of Nashville.

The official name of the complex is the Brixworth at West End. The developer must have felt that by incorporating "West End" into the name, he could justify charging rents that were much higher than he could have received for the same apartments had they been built in other areas of Nashville. The units are by no means architecturally unique, but they have been nestled comfortably onto a site that backs up to Ensworth Avenue, where mature trees shade the street and spacious older homes date back to the 1940s and 1950s. On one side of the complex and across Ensworth is the Vine Street Christian Church, occupying several acres with its sanctuary and educational buildings. On the other side is the Windsor Towers condominium complex, built in the 1960s, one of Nashville's few highrise residential developments in this part of town.

This tiny pocket of city landscape, lying within a fashionable portion of West Nashville, with its luxury condominiums, private schools, and churches, projects a sense of urban refinement, but the footsteps of criminal mystery have crossed this ground before. Directly adjacent to the Brixworth complex, on the property where the Windsor Tower Condominiums are located, once stood the plush private residence of John and Jean Wilson, Nashville socialites in the 1950s. One evening Mrs. Wilson killed her husband by running a samurai sword through him. When the trial was held, her legal defénse team somehow was able to convince a Nashville jury that the death of John Wilson had been an unfortunate accident, resulting from a late night of bedroom frivolity, the samurai sword having been prominently displayed on the wall above the bed. Even after the verdict of acquittal, rumors spread through the nearby wealthy pockets of Nashville that Jean Wilson had castrated her husband in his own bed, and then called her best friend to come help her clean up the evidence before the police arrived.

On this summer morning, at the apartment complex, the detectives are approached by a short, stocky, middle-aged woman. "Are you Detective Mason?" she asks. "I'm Thelma Bennett." Mason extends his hand and introduces Sergeant Smith. The man standing next to Mrs. Bennett steps forward and identifies himself as James Murphy. He may be a little older than the woman, probably in his fifties.

Introductions completed, Mason begins the interview. "How was it you happened to notice the vehicle?"

"It's been here around two weeks," Ms. Bennett begins. "I thought it belonged to a girl from Virginia. She moved out the weekend after August fifteenth, and I had understood she was leaving a car and coming back for it. People are coming and going all the time around here. Lots of corporate rentals, so having a car parked for several days or even a week isn't that unusual."

"So what changed your mind about whose car it was?" Mason asks.

"The newspaper story," she answers. She looks at James Murphy for confirmation.

"We both saw the story about the missing March woman," he says. "They mentioned the type of car she was last seen driving. Once we saw that, we realized it was probably her car, so we called the police."

"Do you know if anyone else saw anything?" Smith asks.

"I'm not sure," says Murphy. He glances at Ms. Bennett. "Have you heard anything?"

"Not really."

"We appreciate your alertness," Mason tells them. "Let us get your apartment numbers and phone numbers in case we need to follow up."

"Have they made any progress in finding the poor woman?" Ms. Bennett asks.

"A lot of people are working on it," Mason says. "Something will turn up soon." He shifts his attention to the Volvo.

Smith takes their information and says, "We'll be in touch if we need a formal statement. Thanks, folks."

Smith notes that the vehicle has been backed into the parking space. "Somebody didn't want the plates to be seen," he comments to Mason.

Mason checks his notes. They include the Tennessee tag number taken as part of the missing persons report—*844 CBD*. He makes his way to the rear of the vehicle; the tag numbers match his notes. The description of the car—*1996 gray Volvo 850*—seems to match as well. He glances in the left corner of the front windshield to see if he can read the VIN number. The glare is too strong, and he doesn't want to touch the vehicle until it has been dusted for prints. The veteran detective's trained eyes continue to scrutinize the Volvo. He notes the layer of pollen on the vehicle, the pile of leaves against the tires, indicating the car has been there for quite some time.

"Did you notice that the driver's-seat position is pushed forward? It appears that somebody very small was the last driver," Smith points out.

"Or someone wanted it to appear that way," says Mason.

A variety of possessions are visible through the glass, including a child's car seat in the back and a pair of white backless shoes on the floorboard. The detective knows it could be days before the lab boys dust for prints. The car needs to be towed to a more climate-controlled environment, where the moisture collected from being outside for a long time can begin to evaporate, making fingerprints more discernible.

After making a series of notes about the vehicle that will later find their way into his report, Mason suggests they canvass the buildings to see if they can come up with any more information. They divide up the buildings. Since the Volvo is parked in front of Building 131, in space number six on the outside back row, they start there, heading out to do some good old-fashioned police work—checking the area for witnesses. Before he starts knocking on doors, Mason takes a minute to call for a tow truck to remove the car to the 501 Building, the metro forensic lab. "Put it on hold for homicide," he says.

Of the twelve units in each building, few doors open to the detectives' knocks. It's the middle of the morning and many of the Brixworth residents appear to be at work. But there are a few residents at home. Paul Jerman of Apartment 135-3 confirms what Thelma Bennett had stated, that the Volvo has been there for approximately two weeks. Doug Arnold of Apartment 135-7 says he thinks the car has been on the property before, but he's not sure how long it has been there this time.

Other residents including Gina Cox, Kathlyn Bryant, Susie Misner, Marcia Ellison, Bob Funk, Malek al-Omery, and Dr. Claude Workman inform the officers that they had never noticed the Volvo at the complex.

After canvassing all four buildings, Mason and Smith return to their car and drive through the rest of the complex. They wind between the two-story buildings until they reach a separate entrance onto Ensworth Avenue. From the main entrance on Harding Road, one would not even know this other entrance exists. Mason makes a note to check with the apartment management to determine if that back entrance is open at night. He also wants to ask what private security they may have in place patrolling through the complex after regular hours.

By the end of the day, what Perry March told Henry King he did not want to happen has occurred. The news of the discovery of Janet's Volvo makes its way to the media, and the story follows the missing persons item that appeared a few days earlier. The barrage of headlines announcing each and every development of the case will continue for the next several months. What has been a private matter since August 15 is now an intensely public one.

CHAPTER 8

An Army of Police

Within days the investigators step up their activities on a variety of fronts, and their main focus is Perry. Detective David Miller, a member of the criminal investigation division, who was previously assigned to working solely on missing persons cases, heads up the investigation. He is a twenty-year veteran of the force whose receding hairline and generally kind appearance are more reminiscent of Robert Duvall than the stereotype of the rugged homicide detective on TV. Miller is somewhat of a loner, not overly interactive with the other guys on the homicide squad, but he is excellent at what he does. In 1996, there were 1,244 missing persons reported in Nashville-Davidson County. Detective Miller found or reconciled every one of them except Janet March.

When Larry Levine, Mark Levine, and Perry March walked into the Nashville Criminal Justice Center on August 29 to report Janet missing, the case became David Miller's. He follows his own rules on how to run an investigation, but the route he ultimately chooses on the March investigation will end up forcing him completely off the case.

The investigators request that Perry take a polygraph examination. At first he agrees, but after consulting with a Nashville criminal defense attorney, Perry informs police that since he is currently taking medication, he has been advised not to participate in such an examination. The attorney Perry has elected to consult as things heat up is Lionel Barrett, one of the names on the A-list of criminal defense lawyers he'd been given in late August by his law partner Michael Geracioti.

On September 9, the same day Perry March is conferring with legal counsel, investigators in the criminal investigation section receive a call from Bill Ozier, a managing partner with the prestigious Nashville law firm of Bass, Berry, and Sims. Ozier reports that Bass, Berry, the firm that hired Perry upon graduation from law school, was forced to fire their young associate in 1991 because of an incident involving sexually explicit letters he had written to a paralegal. The investigators make an appointment to meet in the next few days with Mr. Ozier to investigate more fully the details surrounding this incident, and to see if copies of the sexually charged letters are still available. Although it occurred five years earlier, Miller's experience tells him there just may be a connection to recent events.

The next day, investigators contact Janet's physician, who confirms that prior examinations indicated no signs of physical abuse.

On September 10 Perry consents to a police search of Janet's Volvo and his Jeep Cherokee. The contents of the Volvo sedan are itemized and the inventory becomes an early document in a case file that will ultimately grow to contain multiple volumes and thousands of pages: *a purse with $11 in cash, a $50 bill in the glove box, a passport for Janet Levine March, sunglasses, a suitcase, a checkbook, a dead battery for a pager, a bag containing some clothes, CDs and a CD player, makeup, and a hairdryer, white* *backless ladies' shoes, a baby seat, and from the trunk a stroller.*

The investigators ask Mrs. Levine to come and review the items found in her daughter's car. As a mother, she finds what is missing the most curious. There are no bras, no deodorant, and no toothbrush, items her daughter—or any woman—would normally take on a trip. Carolyn can scarcely take it all in: It looks like a bag a man had packed.

Later that day, faced with Perry's refusal to take a polygraph examination, investigators ask him to give them a formal statement. He complies with their request. The handwritten statement ends up being almost six pages in length and covers the period of August 13 to August 17—the two days before Janet left, the day she was last seen, and the two days after. It includes the following particulars for August 15, the day Janet disappeared:

Thursday I went to work at 8:15. I came home around 4:30 because Janet wanted for me to get the kids to sleep so we could talk. When I got home, the cabinet repairmen were working. I came in, took the kids and played with them. We went to the grocery, came back, and I fed them dinner. I helped the cabinet men finish the faucet sink. After the cabinet men left, I bathed the kids, and put them to sleep.

Janet was working on her painting when I came downstairs. After a while she came out and asked if we could discuss some things. I—we sat at the kitchen table, and talked. After about 1/2 hour, she grew frustrated and asked me what I was going to do to make up to her these last 12 days that I was on vacation from household duties. I said we agreed on Tuesday.

She became upset, and said I wasn't trying very hard, so maybe I should go to the Hampton Inn again. I stayed calm, and told her I needed to know if she wanted me to go or if she didn't. She said go. I got up, went to the phone and reserved a room at the Hampton Inn with my credit card, guaranteed. When I hung up, she became very upset, and said "no more vacations on my time with our money." She grabbed my credit card and wallet out of my hands, and ripped up the card. She took my drivers license and cash out, handed that to me and she said she had a different idea tonight. She walked to my study, and started working on the computer. The computer had been on when I came back home earlier.

After a while, she left my study and went upstairs. She came down a while later with her small bags. She had three small bags, her gray overnight bag (Samsonite?) which she always used for short trips, which I used on a few hotel nites the week before. She had her black leather(?) back-pack, which is her carry on bag. She had her open canvass shopping bag which looked like it had her toiletries and blow drier in it. She went to the stereo and took some CD's I think, and then handed me her "12-Day Vacation Note" and told me to read it and sign it. I did. She then said something like "Your turn, see ya" and left. She drove off.

I waited a while, and then I called my brother and sister and told them that Janet had left with bags. They said just chill out and let her calm down. I waited some more time, and then I called the Hampton Inn to see if she took my room, since we already paid for it. She had not gotten there, so I called the Vanderbilt Plaza, thinking it might be where she went.

I think I called both the Hampton Inn and Vanderbilt Plaza a few more times. She wasn't there. I started to worry about her, so finally I waited till about midnight to call her parents to see if she went there. Janet did not like me to in-volve her parents, so I waited. At midnight or so I called them, and they said she wasn't there. They said don't worry and call them when she came back. Janet had left like this before, so we all settled down to wait. She had never stayed out before, nor packed.

The intense scrutiny is taking its toll on Perry. By the time he is finally finished with investigators after several hours, he places a call to his psychologist, Dr. Thomas Campbell, stating he must come in for an appointment in regard to decisions about the children. His mother-in-law arrives for the appointment as well. Perry informs Dr. Campbell that he needs to get away for a while from all the police harassment, and he has decided he should take the children to stay with his brother, Ron, in Chicago for an extended period. Visibly upset, he breaks down and cries during the appointment. As he hurries to his car, his anger reaches the surface and he yells out at his mother-in-law, "Tell Larry I didn't bury Janet in the backyard."

On September 12, Perry does indeed leave for Chicago with Sammy and Tzipi. Earlier that day, he'd consented to a search of his home, waiving an earlier demand that he be present when the police search the house. The search is another major newsworthy story for the TV stations. The media attention that Perry was so desperate to avoid for himself and his children will continue for months—daily fare on the local menu of nightly news.

The initial search by a team of police investigators turns up some items that police want to check more closely—a blue dress shirt with a stain, a white bath mat with a stain, two hairbrushes, and thirty-three different books found in the home including titles such as *Love Is Never Enough*, *Love and Marriage*, and *Mr. Murder*. One thing conspicuously missing from the March home, however, is the hard drive on the couple's Ambra home computer. It has been literally ripped out of the computer.

Following the search of the Blackberry Road residence, the Nashville police officially declare that the case of Janet Gail Levine March is no longer being considered a missing persons case.

This is now a formal homicide investigation.

With a possible murder to solve, Detective Miller and his team of investigators move into full gear. In less than a week, the investigative team interviews a wide array of witnesses, including Marissa Moody. She tells about the scheduling of a playdate for her son, Grant, with Sammy on August 15 and recalls the events that unfolded when she was at the March residence on August 16. Her statement specifically includes a reference to the rolled-up dark rug she saw—the rug on which Sammy was bouncing up and down—and to the fact that it was not present when she returned to pick up her son that afternoon.

The investigators also meet with Deneane Beard, the Marches' housecleaner, and take a formal statement from her. She reviews with investigators her activities at the Blackberry Road home on the dates of August 16, 23, and 30. Her statement includes the information that the evening before her scheduled arrival at the home on August 30, Perry called her home, as he had done in the early morning hours of the sixteenth and again on the twenty-third, to ask what time she would be arriving. During their conversation on the thirtieth, Perry informed Mrs. Beard that Janet had some errands to run, and that his dad, Arthur, would be letting her in the house. She informs police that Arthur March did indeed let her into the residence on that morning, and then he left the Blackberry Road location. Then around ten that morning Mrs. Levine arrived with Tzipi, and while she was there, Deneane inquired about the cleaning supplies she had requested in the list she left for Janet on August 16.

Even though Janet had been officially reported missing to the Nashville police on the previous day, Mrs. Levine replied to the housecleaner's question by stating, "Just make up another list and I will see that Janet gets it."

Was it a hopeful prayer that she was pronouncing, or was this a mother determined to keep up the proper image and not betray her daughter's secrets? Either way, she simply could not allow herself to publicly admit the details of the situation.

The police interview the children's part-time nanny, Ella Goldshmid, who informs them that she did not witness anything unusual before Janet disappeared. In her formal statement she says that Janet was a devoted mother who always put her kids first, and that if she planned to be out of town, she would give Ella two weeks' notice. The children's nanny also tells police that on August 30, Perry and Carolyn disclosed to her that Janet was missing. They were both visibly shaken, she says.

Investigators also take statements from the two construction workers, John Richie and John McAllister, who were at the March home to install kitchen countertops on August 15 and were the last two people outside her family to see her. John McAllister informs police that Janet met them at the door at approximately three thirty and that Perry came home while they were working. John Richie in his statement indicates that Perry brought them a tool they needed to fix a leaky faucet. He says they completed their work for the day and when they left around five, everything looked normal, and Perry was outside playing with the children.

On September 15, John L. Templeton contacts police and informs them that some workers on Crater Hill, adjacent to Blackberry Road, noticed a foul odor coming from an area near the pump house during the week of September 8. In response to this information, over a period of two days, September 15 and 16, the police secure consent search forms from seven of the Marches' neighbors, so that the investigative team can physically search the nearby properties.

That same morning, Detective Miller meets with Larry Levine, who turns over two documents to the police. The first is a set of his daughter's dental records. Though this type of information is routine for the veteran detective, Miller is all too aware that it has to be gut-wrenching for Janet's father, who knows police will need the dental records only if they find her body.

The other document is a letter from Mr. Robert Levine of Levine Group Insurance. The letter states that the Union Central Insurance Company issued a life insurance policy on the life of Janet March for $250,000. Her husband is the sole beneficiary. No provision is made for the two young children.

After already putting in what feels like two days' work on this single September day, Detective Miller asks

Detective Mason to accompany him to the March residence. The purpose of the visit is to interview Perry's father, Arthur March. Arthur is ex-military, craggy-faced, with a gritty voice. The two experienced detectives find him easily likable and very talkative, a guy who says what he thinks and has an opinion about everything. After informing them of his birth date—January 15, 1928—and his official address—Apdo. 544, 45920 Ajijic, Jalisco, Mexico—he indicates that he's in Nashville because his daughter called and asked him to come and help Perry after Janet left. He tells them that he has not been in Nashville for a few months. "I came for a short visit in May," he says.

"You have a daughter, as well as your son Perry?" Detective Miller asks as they settle in the living room, a spacious room with hardwood floors and few accessories.

"Kathy. She's a dentist. And another son, Ron. He's an attorney. Both in the Chicago area."

"Is Perry the oldest?" Detective Mason asks.

"Right."

"So were Perry and his wife having marital problems?" asks Miller.

"I knew they had problems, like everybody has problems," Arthur says, "but I was never told anybody was going to move out."

"Why do you think they were having marital problems?"

Arthur raises his forefinger and shakes it emphatically. "Because Janet, she was a little JAP. You know? Jewish American Princess. And Perry always let her get whatever she wanted. He doesn't have any balls. In fact, he's a wimp."

Miller pauses. He exchanges glances with Mason while Arthur lights a cigar.

"How did you get along with your daughter-in-law?" Miller asks after a minute.

"We tolerated each other," Arthur says.

Miller looks at his watch. He can't believe it's just two thirty. It has already been a long day. He makes motions to go; Mason follows. But as they depart, Perry's loquacious father injects a few more comments about his son's past. He tells the detectives that by the time Perry was thirteen, he had earned a black belt in karate, and he continued with martial arts in high school and college. Arthur beams when he says his son is fluent in four dialects of Chinese.

Mason ponders this information. A black belt in karate who is a wimp? He wonders which statement is true—or are they both true?

The detectives shake Arthur March's hand, thank him for his time, and say they will be in touch if they need anything further. They do not know it on this day in September 1996, but the talkative Arthur March will indeed have lots more to say.

Detective Miller believes that Perry has not been completely forthcoming about all he knows concerning his wife's disappearance. He convinces his captain that they need to search the March residence again. On September 17, he presents a formal application for a search warrant to search 3 Blackberry Road to Davidson County judge Michael Mondelli. In his application, Detective Miller states that *there is probable and reasonable cause to believe that Perry March is now in possession of certain evidence of a crime to wit: the body of Janet Gail Levine March, Female White 02/20/63, and any unnamed evidence pertaining to the disappearance and/or murder of said person.*

In his sworn affidavit attached to the application, Detective Miller alleges that *Perry March has refused to take a polygraph examination; he has not cooperated fully with the investigation of his missing and/or murdered wife; he has been untruthful with Detective Tim Mason as to previous acts of violence as has been reported by his previous employers as well as other information about financial and domestics incidents with the missing or murdered victim; and the personal computer used by Mr. March at residence had hard drive removed so evidence could not be extracted.*

What Detective Miller fails to disclose in his affidavit is that prior to the consent search of the March home of

September 12, he had placed a call to the law offices of Perry's attorney, Lionel Barrett.

"I'm calling out of professional courtesy," he had told Barrett. "We're about to search the residence of your client Perry March."

"I see," Barrett said, managing to contain his satisfaction at getting this heads-up.

"Just keeping you up to speed, Mr. Barrett. I wanted to let you know that the investigation is expanding."

"So it appears, David. Thanks for the call."

The line went dead. Barrett pushed the intercom and buzzed for one of his secretaries. "Get me Perry March," he yelled. "Now!"

On September 17 Judge Mondelli also approves a search warrant for a police search of the law offices where Perry worked at Levine, Mattson, Orr, and Geracioti.

With the Mondelli-approved search warrant in hand, and with the previously secured consents to search from the seven neighbors of the Marches, the entire homicide unit of the criminal investigation division arrive en masse at 3 Blackberry Road on the same day. To supplement their efforts, a helicopter with heat-sensitive monitoring equipment is brought in, along with cadaver dogs. A cadre of recruits from the Police Academy will also be at the scene to flare out and search the many acres that make up this secluded pocket of exclusive Forest Hills. In fact, there are so many police that the Red Cross sets up a water station at the nearby Hillsboro Church of Christ.

When the police arrive, they find Perry and his brother, Ron, the attorney from Chicago, outside, smoking cigars, as if they had just stepped away from the social chatter of a cocktail party for some fresh air and a smoke. Perry leaves Ron to monitor the activity of the police.

After hours at the scene, according to their written reports generated from the search, investigators will leave with a varied sampling of possible evidence that includes: *a pair of jeans, a knife, a shovel, lint from the dryer, fibers from the hallway, fibers from the basement stairs, fibers from the second floor stairs, fibers from the vacuum, several soil samples, a rug pad, a trowel, a glove, a boot, fireplace ashes, and vacuum sweepings from the dining room and basement.*

One member of the investigative team, Nashville police veteran Johnnie Hunter, will later summarize their efforts that day for the media: "In my twenty-five years of experience, I don't know of any other crime scene we've ever covered any closer than this one."

CHAPTER 9

Good-bye, Nashville

While the huge team of investigators, detectives, and police recruits scour the inside and outside of 3 Blackberry Road for hours on September 17, 1996, Perry is preparing to remove himself and his children permanently from Nashville. In a period of just one month, his life in the city he has called home since 1988 has been turned completely upside down.

Perry's face has been all over the newspapers. The nightly television news feeds the citizens of this gossipy Southern city every new tidbit about Janet and Perry; Nashvillians are eager for each morsel, like a nest of birds waiting for their mother to return with their next meal. Neighbors are being asked if their beautifully manicured yards can be dug up. Perry's social acquaintances and clients are being quizzed by police. He has been fingerprinted and photographed at police headquarters. Helicopters with special heat-seeking equipment are flying over his home, buzzing down like giant vultures in search of their next prey.

Perry calls Larry Levine and yells, "Use your influence! Call off the police!"

Larry says, "I don't want to, Perry. They're searching for Janet. And even if I wanted to, I couldn't make them stop."

"I know how much you care about your grandchildren," Perry says. "What if you couldn't see your grandchildren anymore? Then would you call off the police?"

"I can't call off the police, Perry!" Larry says.

Not only has the Blackberry Road house been scrutinized, but Perry's new apartment at University Square Apartments and his law office have been searched by police as well. He has severed ties with his father-in-law's firm, Levine, Mattson, Orr, and Geracioti. There is simply no aspect of his life that has not been completely affected.

He has had all he can take. On the same day that police are combing his home, Perry is making some critical phone calls.

The first is to University School. Ms. Marty Bishop, in the school office, answers.

"I would like you to have all the files and papers regarding my son, Samson March, available to be picked up this afternoon," Perry says, sounding more like a lawyer than a parent.

There is a distinct and noticeable pause before Ms. Bishop responds. "I'm not sure I understand, Mr. March."

"I'm taking Sammy out of your school permanently and I want any applicable papers concerning his time there ready for me when I pick him up this afternoon." Perry's tone becomes impatient. Those who worked with Perry in the Nashville legal community were familiar with his highly mercurial behavior; he could be dismissive and combative, all at once.

"Would you like to speak with the headmaster?" Ms. Bishop asks.

"No. What I want is for you to have my son's files ready this afternoon when I arrive."

Before the puzzled Ms. Bishop can offer any other possible suggestion or course of action, she hears the dial tone.

•   •   •

For Samson, the all-important beginning of school has been anything but normal. He has started kindergarten without the comfort and support of his mother, and now, after less than a month, he is yanked out of school. Unbeknownst to this innocent child, there have been troubling undercurrents surrounding his attendance at University School during the short time he has been enrolled. The check that Perry March wrote on July 22, 1996, made payable to University School of Nashville and marked "for Samson," was not honored by the bank. In a peculiar financial arrangement, the account at Union Planters was only in the name of Janet March, but Perry was the person who signed the check, with his own distinctive and yet almost indecipherable scrawl. The repeated routing of the check between Union Planters and the depositor's local bank, First American, continued all the way up until August 19, when Union Planters finally refused to process the check after several prior refusals to honor.

Perry makes another call on September 17.

"Bo, I need a favor," he says.

Andrew Saks, called "Bo," is puzzled by the call in the evening but feels obligated to help his friend.

"Bo, you know I loved Janet," Perry says.

Saks knows his friend has been under intense pressure, but he is unsure how to respond to the comment about Janet, so he doesn't. He asks, "What favor do you need, Perry?"

"I need to move some things out of the house. Think you could lend me a hand? It won't be just the two of us. My brother, Ron, will be there to help—and some others."

"When exactly do you need my help?" Bo asks.

"In the morning," says Perry. "Sorry for the short notice, but I need to get the kids out of this media circus, and the damn cops are harassing me every day. I'm going to sue every one of those bastards."

After a long silence, Bo replies. "Okay, I'll help you for a few hours."

The next day, September 18, Perry, with the help of his

brother, Ron, Bo Saks, and two other friends, Elliott Greenberg and Todd Friedenberg, pack a rental truck. Perry and the children are relocating to Wilmette, Illinois, outside Chicago, the city where his brother practices law, and a place Perry has known from his youth. The packing and moving of the personal effects from Perry and Janet's life together will continue over the next few weeks.

In early October, Michael Gilpin, owner of A-1 Economy Movers, is contacted by Barbara Smith, a woman Arthur March will later refer to as "my lady," about loading and moving some additional items from the home in Tennessee to Illinois. Mr. Gilpin will later tell police that during the moving process he never met Perry or his father, Arthur; he dealt exclusively with Barbara Smith. Mr. Gilpin is paid for his services with a check drawn on the same account as was the check issued to the University School. This check, like the one to USN, is not honored by Union Planters Bank. Gilpin finally receives his money from Perry, but only after Gilpin returns to the Blackberry residence, where he loads up some remaining items and moves them to a storage location. He does not release the items until several weeks later, after finally receiving the funds due him.

Perry March's life is in a state of constant turmoil, and he is scrambling.

Certain items remain at 3 Blackberry Road after Perry and his children relocate to Illinois. Maybe they were overlooked, or maybe they were among the items Mr. Gilpin held until being paid in full. One particularly notable item is a manila envelope containing two sexually explicit letters and a condom wrapper. It is an omission that will come back to haunt Perry.

When police later interview all the individuals who assist in the loading of personal property, each will be asked if he saw the rolled-up Oriental rug that Marissa Moody reported seeing on August 16 when she dropped off her son at the March residence. Every single interviewee will have the same response: No.

At some point during these weeks of mid-September to early October in 1996, Perry's father, Arthur, assists Perry with moving.

The full implications of Arthur's actions while in Nashville will not be realized for almost another decade.

CHAPTER 10

Dead Ends

By late 1996 the March investigation has lost whatever momentum it may have gained after the discovery of Janet's Volvo on September 7. Laboratory evidence from the clothes, soil samples, and other items taken from the exhaustive search of the March residence have not produced anything definitive. Helicopters with heat-seeking equipment have made repeated flights over the March residence, nearby parks, and Radnor Lake, a nature sanctuary nestled within the city only a few miles from Blackberry Road. Portions of larger regional lakes and also the Cumberland River have been dragged and searched by divers. Public and private parks have been combed by both officers and cadaver dogs. Construction sites all over Nashville have been searched, especially those where concrete was being poured in mid to late August. Scores of leads and telephone tips have been individually tracked down, yet none place the police any closer to finding Janet, dead or alive.

Between September and December, several other detectives and investigators have now been assigned to interview witnesses and follow leads, regardless of how unrelated they may first appear. In addition to detectives David Miller and Tim Mason, detectives Danny Satterfield, Brad Corcoran, Kent McAlister, and Mike Smith become actively involved in the investigation. Sergeant Johnnie Hunter, usually limited to his role as forensic investigator, is asked to conduct follow-up interviews with witnesses who have given earlier statements.

On December 6 at about six p.m. Sergeant Hunter places a call to Diane Saks, one of Janet March's close friends. He introduces himself and they exchange a few pleasantries. "I hope I haven't caught you at a bad time," he says.

Her reply is congenial. She seems like a nice lady. "Our files indicate that you spoke with Detective McAlister on September fourteenth, and then Detective Miller on October third," he says. "I'm just following up, calling to see if you've thought of anything else or have any other information that might be helpful in the March case."

He doesn't expect much from these routine calls, so he perks up when Mrs. Saks says, "You know, this is really odd. I'm so glad you called, Sergeant. I've been debating whether or not I should contact the police about something."

Hunter tries to tune out the noise around him—a buzz of voices, a phone ringing, the whir of a printer. He picks up a pen. "About exactly what, ma'am?"

"Well, you may think it's crazy"—she hesitates at first, then continues with more authority—"but some of us that were Janet's friends—we contacted a psychic."

The investigator maintains a level voice, the result of years of experience responding to witnesses, but there is a noticeable pause before he says, "Go on."

"She tells us she was able to make contact with Janet— you know, her spirit."

"I understand, ma'am."

A lot of things have changed in the quarter of a century since Johnnie Hunter became a cop, including a more general acceptance of the use of psychics. "The department has used psychics in the past," he says. What he really wants to say is that the way this case is going, they could use all the help they can get.

"Should I tell you what she learned from Janet?"

"Yes. I'm making notes as we speak, if that's okay."

"Well—the psychic—her name is Pat Morton." Mrs. Saks's voice is more of a whisper now, as if she doesn't want anyone else to hear what she is about to say, or as if by repeating it, she is somehow causing poor Janet to relive the hell she is about to describe.

"She says Janet told her that on the night of August fifteenth, she and Perry argued about Perry taking money from Janet's wallet, and Perry became angry and violent—and he killed her by breaking her neck, and then he rolled her up in something and put her in the back of his Jeep and disposed of her body somewhere along the Natchez Trace, possibly Bowie Park." By the time she finishes, Hunter can hear her breathing in rapid bursts, like a winded jogger.

"Mrs. Saks, are you okay?" he asks.

"It's just all so terrible to talk about," she says.

"I understand, but I'm glad you shared it with me."

Sergeant Hunter listens. All he hears is shallow breathing. He waits, allowing Mrs. Saks to proceed at her own pace. "I'm sure you're familiar with the Natchez Trace, but what about Bowie Park?" she asks finally.

"I believe it's in the Fairview area," Hunter says. He also recalls that the park covers hundreds of acres. If Ms. Morton is a real psychic, couldn't she be more specific?

The Natchez Trace Parkway is a limited-access, two-lane federal highway that stretches 444 miles from Natchez, Mississippi, to just south of Nashville. The route traces and commemorates an ancient trail that connected the southern portions of the Mississippi River to the salt licks in what is now central Tennessee. Over the centuries, the Choctaw, Chickasaw, and other Indian tribes marked their path along the route. Between 1785 and 1820, the trail was used extensively by the "Kaintuck" boatmen who floated the Ohio and Mississippi rivers to the bustling markets in Natchez and in New Orleans. Upon reaching their destination, they would sell their boats along with their cargo, and then begin the long trek back on foot to Nashville, and from there to points beyond.

When the federal highway project was finally completed, decades behind the original schedule and tens of millions over budget, it was hailed as a scenic route where modern-day travelers could hop on in either Natchez, Nashville, or limited-access points in between, and traverse this portion of the southeastern United States without the noise and visible pollution associated with so many of America's interstate highways.

Sergeant Hunter knows that at least for that portion of "The Trace," as it is usually referred to, which can be accessed just south of Nashville, there are basically three local groups who regularly use the two-lane highway: elderly couples who don't mind abiding by the fifty-mile-per-hour speed limit on a Sunday afternoon after they have stuffed themselves with too much country ham, fried chicken, and too many homemade biscuits at the Loveless Café, only a stone's throw from the federal highway; teenagers who like the remote route's privacy for activities that require a secluded spot; and married men and women who seek the same refuge as the teenagers, but with someone else's husband or wife. Hunter wonders if he will have to add a fourth group—husbands who have murdered their wives and are looking for a remote gully in which to dump the body.

"Will you send someone to look for Janet's body in Bowie Park, Sergeant?" Mrs. Saks's voice brings Hunter back into the moment, in his office that is crowded with too many files about too many open homicide cases.

"We follow up all leads, ma'am. I'll relate our conversation to the rest of the team working on the case, and I'll get back to you if we find anything." He adds, "If there's anything else you want to share with me or any of the investigators, you call us. And please tell the rest of Mrs. March's friends the same thing."

"There's not a day that goes by that I don't think of Janet," Diane Saks says.

Sergeant Hunter will contact Captain Mickey Miller about his conversation with Mrs. Saks, but he already knows where this is going. Even though he doesn't have much faith that the information will lead to anything in a park of hundreds of acres, he will have to check it out.

By December 9, both aerial and cadaver-dog searches are completed at Bowie Park and Nature Center. The park encompasses 722 acres. In fact, investigators do unearth some bones, but lab results quickly confirm that they are from a large animal.

Just days later, on December 11, Sergeant Hunter receives a call about a second location suggested by psychic Pat Morton. This time she has teamed up with another psychic, Kathleen Finn. Hunter wonders just how accurate a psychic can be if, in a matter of only a few days, she's having mental images of Janet March's body in two different locations twenty miles apart. Trying to rein in his skepticism, the veteran cop is doing what every investigator has done and will continue to do in this frustrating case: he follows every lead until it is productive or a dead end. On December 13, with the assistance of Tennessee Highway Patrol trooper Larry Lewis and his cadaver dog, Kemo, police search this latest area of strong interest, a large public park within the Nashville city limits. It turns out to be another dead end.

Pat Morton and Kathleen Finn will not be the last psychics who contact friends of the Levines or the police directly with persistent and detailed visions of the location of Janet March's body—ranging from a motel in Santa Fe, New Mexico, to a shallow ditch just miles from Blackberry Drive. As is true in the search of Bowie Park, investigators in Tennessee and in various other states, with a combination of frustration and hopeful promise, will check out the psychic visions. The results are always the same—no evidence of the remains of a human corpse.

Some callers who say they have premonitions or can contact the spirits of the dead are certain of the location, but have few other details. Others, like Sally Phillips from

Bristol, Tennessee, who speaks with Detective Tim Mason, are extremely detailed as to the events, but not the exact location of the body. Sally Phillips states to police, "I saw two people, and . . . both were small, and one was well versed in the martial arts." According to her mental visions, the man often put pressure on the woman somewhere around the collarbone, but no one knew because it did not leave any marks. Mrs. Phillips went on to add, "Two men were involved and one would lie for the other, and the body was placed in an Oriental rug with fringe on the end." She also reports seeing "a large, long beige, tan, or yellow van that had been used to haul the body to a forest preserve near a stream, where she was in a shallow grave but no longer inside the rug."

There has been so much on television and in the press about the case that it is nearly impossible for the police to separate what someone like Mrs. Phillips has read from what she has envisioned. There is, however, one intriguing detail contained in the recitation of her premonitions that none of the other psychics include—the involvement of two men—an evidentiary aspect of the Janet March homicide investigation that will surface in a most dramatic way, but not for almost another decade.

The disappearance of Janet March is the biggest news story in Nashville, and everyone wants a piece of it.

Even incarcerated felons from around the mid South, who view the frequent news reports while watching television in the recreation rooms of their prisons, decide they should get in on the act. They understand how the system works, and as the months of 1996 drag on without a break in the case, they know that the Nashville police will be increasingly willing to cut deals for information about Janet. Also, they hope to cash in on the reward that friends of the Levines have established for information about the whereabouts of Janet—now up to $50,000.

One such enterprising inmate is James Kennedy, who is doing time in the Turney Center in East Tennessee. He lets it be known to authorities that he has valuable information about Janet. Prisoner Kennedy presents a most bizarre scenario. He indicates that months earlier he was transported to Nashville to attend a court hearing, and that while at the courthouse he met Janet March. They became pen pals, he says; she wrote frequent letters to both him and his cellmate, James Clark, describing her marital problems, telling how her husband was drugging her and having her followed. The last correspondence was alleged to have arrived at Turney Center on August 5 or 6. The actual letters are never produced.

As the March case drags on and on with no real progress, James Kennedy will by no means be the last inmate whom an investigator feels compelled to interview. Nor will the prisoners, claiming to have the one tip that will break the case wide open, be limited to those in Tennessee institutions. During their years as homicide investigators, Miller, Mason, Hunter, and all the others have encountered human behavior that defies the imagination. Why should the March case prove any different? As strange as any lead might initially sound, and as questionable as the source might be, every lead must be thoroughly pursued. By the end of 1996, four months after Janet March's disappearance, the Nashville police have logged literally hundreds of man-hours chasing down leads and tips, leads that have led nowhere.

And then there are the "sightings" of Janet. Early on in the case, the police began to receive multiple calls from citizens of Tennessee (as well as other states) who are confident that Janet is still alive, because they have seen her. Even her own friends report they may have seen her after August 15. One of Janet's friends informs investigators that on August 27, while at the kids' soccer practice, she spoke with Perry and thought she remembered seeing Janet as well.

In the first week in September, police are informed by Missy Scovel, one of Perry's clients, that a friend of hers is sure he saw Janet while vacationing in Destin, Florida, a frequent vacation spot for Nashvillians. Barbara Smith, the friend of Arthur who meets the movers in September at the Blackberry Road residence, is later questioned by police and informs them that on August 24, while dining at the Gerst Haus, a local restaurant frequented by the courthouse crowd and especially police investigators and prosecutors, she remembers seeing Janet with friends.

Investigators check out every single one of these sighting reports, but nothing pans out.

In October, Nashville police receive information from Kentucky authorities that one of their citizens, James Howard, remembers assisting a woman he is sure was Janet along I-65, which runs north out of Nashville into and through Kentucky. Mr. Howard indicates that the woman he assisted informed him she had recently moved to Franklin, Kentucky, and was using the name Suzanna Fewduezer. Tennessee investigators go to Franklin, Kentucky, to pursue the possible sighting, but they determine the woman is not Janet. It will happen again almost a decade later; Franklin, Kentucky, will reemerge as a significant link in connection with this homicide investigation.

These four alleged sightings will not be the last that Nashville authorities will receive in the months—even years—that follow.

By early 1997, after hundreds and hundreds of man-hours, almost no tangible evidence has emerged that will solve Janet's mysterious disappearance. Although they lack the hard physical evidence they are after, police construct what they believe is a plausible theory about exactly what happened on August 15, and why.

From Perry's own written statement, the authorities know that the couple argued that night. From the statements taken from Janet's friends; Janet's brother, Mark; and Janet's mother, Carolyn, it has been clearly established that the couple was experiencing marital problems. Janet confided to one of her close friends that she and Perry had engaged in sex only three times in the last year. The couple had been seeing Nashville psychiatrist Dr. Thomas Campbell over a period of several weeks. And it is obvious that even though they resided in a home and private estate worth well over a half a million dollars, cash flow was tight, as evidenced by the bounced check to the University School for their son's tuition.

Investigators also followed up on the call in early September from attorney Bill Ozier, managing partner at Perry's former firm, Bass, Berry, and Sims. They have interviewed the paralegal who was the victim of the sexual harassment actions that led to Perry's dismissal in 1991. Although the events occurred five years earlier, investigators learned that in August of 1996, Perry March was still communicating with the victim about his inability to pay the balance of the $24,000 he was obligated to pay under a negotiated settlement agreement.

The police theorize that on the summer night of August 15, Janet found a copy of the letter her husband had written just two days earlier, asking his victim for more time to pay the money he owed. They surmise that this was the first time Janet learned of the sexually charged events involving her husband in 1991. A heated argument ensued. At some point the argument escalated to a physical confrontation, and based upon the complete absence of any blood found at the scene, the police conclude that Perry, who was trained in karate, struck his wife a blow that proved fatal.

With a dead body on his hands, Perry had to quickly produce a story to explain Janet's absence to his children the next morning. Thus he created the story of her demanding a vacation, and then typed the to-do list to support the story he fabricated. He then called one of her closest friends, Laurie Rummel, as well as his brother, Ron, and his sister, Kathy, both out of state, and told them Janet had left him, to inject more credibility into the story he knew he would ultimately have to tell.

And then, in a daring move, he called Janet's parents at midnight to inform them that she had left. But what if they had felt compelled to come over to the Blackberry residence to see for themselves, or to confront their son-in-law? It was almost three full hours between the time Perry called his siblings and the time he called his in-laws. Three hours to cover up his actions and hide his wife's body. Perry knew the Levines were aware of his and Janet's marital problems, so it was not illogical that she would drive away from the house after an argument. In fact, it was a scenario Mrs. Levine appeared to fully accept when she told Perry during their midnight conversation, "Don't worry, she'll be back."

However, this is where the police theory seems to break down, or at least deviates from one certain course. If police believe that Perry March used the dark red Oriental rug in which to roll up his wife's body, would he have left it out in plain view the next day, to be seen by Deneane Beard when she came to clean the house, by Ella Goldshmid when she came to care for the children, and by Marissa Moody when she dropped off her son to play with Sammy?

As the famous phrase associated with the Watergate hearings goes, "It all depends on what he knew and when he knew it."

Did Perry know Marissa Moody was stopping by on the morning of the sixteenth? Not according to statements made by Mrs. Moody herself, who says that she spoke only with Janet the night before, and that Perry's actions, or actually the lack of them, convinced her that her arrival that morning was a surprise. Perry *was* aware that Deneane Beard was coming to clean the house the morning of the sixteenth, because he called her at home to confirm when she would be arriving. And yet Mrs. Beard informed the police that Perry did not know how to spell her name, even though it appears on the August 15 to-do list, as item number three: "Pay Deneane and Ella." Did Perry simply tell the housecleaner that he did not know how to spell her name to give his story about the to-do list more credibility, or did Janet really type the list? And if it were Janet who authored the list, as Perry claims, would she have included in the last sentence the parenthetical phrase "in response to Perry's cowardly, rash, and confused vacation"? Or is that the language of someone attempting to artificially inject a basis for the existence of his own vacation? In the words of Shakespeare: "[He] doth protest too much, methinks."

So why was the Oriental carpet rolled up and in the home just off the doorway leading from the kitchen? If it had been used to hide Janet's body, was she still in the rug when Marissa Moody saw Sammy bouncing up and down on it? If not, why was the rug still rolled up and inside the house, visible to all? And if, as Mrs. Moody related to police, the rug was gone when she returned a few hours later, did that mean that Perry had somehow disposed of Janet's body while his daughter, his son, his son's playmate, and the nanny were all at Blackberry Road? Or did it mean, as Perry ultimately claimed, that the rolled up rug simply never existed?

And what about the fact that Janet's Volvo was not found for two weeks, yet was only a few miles from the March residence? The police theorize that Perry may have moved his wife's Volvo on the night of August 15, so that when the kids asked about Mommy the next morning, he could show them that she was truly gone because her car was not there. But how could he get it to the Brixworth Apartments and still be back at home by midnight to call the Levines? Or was he taking another brazen risk when he called them? He might be able to explain that Janet was not there should they decide to come to the house in the middle of the night, but there would be no logical explanation he could offer them if her Volvo were still present. So he either moved the Volvo before midnight, or he gambled that the Levines would not be so taken aback by their daughter's abrupt departure that they would actually come over in the middle of the night.

Finally, as part of their overall theory, the police return to the fact that the employees of Universal Tire in Nashville confirmed that five days after Janet disappeared, Perry had all four tires replaced on his Jeep Cherokee—tires that one of the employees described as still having twenty thousand miles of wear left. Whether Perry made the trip between nine thirty and midnight on August 15 or late in the predawn hours of August 16 or a day or two later, the police feel confident that his purchase of new tires was specifically designed to remove any evidence of where the older tires had been, when he used his Cherokee to dispose of his wife's dead body.

By early 1997, Chief Emmett Turner concludes that if his detectives are going to finally get a real break in this most frustrating case, maybe they need some outside help.

CHAPTER 11

The Grave Seekers

On February 8, 1997, Jerry Nichols, Al Nelson, Milica Wilson, and Clark Davenport arrive in Nashville. The day is typical of winter in Tennessee. The bleak sky is swirled with slate-gray clouds. The temperature hovers around freezing, but the dampness in the air makes it seem much colder. These four individuals from diverse backgrounds, who are in Nashville at the request of the metro homicide unit, are all affiliated volunteers with a nonprofit organization, NecroSearch International. The name is derived from the Greek word for death, *necro*. They specialize in locating the dead.

They have come to search for Janet's body.

Detective Mason and Sergeant Hunter meet the plane when it arrives and welcome the volunteers, but there is no denying that they have mixed feelings about involving outsiders, even ones who come so highly regarded. Mason and Hunter have been in the trenches of homicide investigations for years, and they are good at what they do. To bring in outside help, especially a complete team of trained investigators, is like taking a direct blow to the solar plexus, but they know they are not really making progress in the March case. Something has to happen.

The political heat within the department has been turned up several notches, and the entire homicide unit is feeling it. For Mason, now lead detective in the case, the flame is particularly hot. Detective David Miller, who was the point man on the investigation from the time it started as a missing persons case, has been removed as lead detective. The official reason is not documented, but the word around the homicide unit is that the call to Lionel Barrett put him at odds with the brass, and then when he was exceedingly open with the *Nashville Scene* about the police theory in the case and the status of the investigation, it was the proverbial last straw.

The *Scene*, Nashville's most gossipy rag sheet, is a free publication that appears weekly in doorway racks at businesses throughout the city. The newspaper is a road map to everything Nashville—from piercing political commentaries, to an inside look at the arts and music scene in Music City, to ads for everything from million-dollar homes to half-hour massages. It is reporting with an edge.

Miller does not protest his removal as lead investigator. He knows his attempt at professional courtesy with Lionel Barrett about the search of the March residence, and his candor with the newspaper are not the reasons the investigation has stalled. His experience tells him that the lapse in time from August 15 to 29 was simply too great an evidentiary burden to overcome. Too much time to alter the crime scene.

On this raw February day, Mason is hoping he fares better than his predecessor.

NecroSearch, headquartered in Colorado, was founded with one goal in mind—to assist law enforcement agencies in locating clandestine graves. In performing their physical searches around the country, they rely upon a combination of many different sciences and investigatory techniques: anthropology (the identification of human remains vs. nonhuman remains); entomology (a branch of zoology studying insects in search of information about the timing and duration of taphonomic pressure); serology (the study of body fluids: blood, saliva, and semen); geophysics (the use of remote sensing methods and equipment such as ground-penetrating radar, sonar, electromagnetics, metal detectors, and thermal imaging); meteorology (the study of the impact of weather conditions, temperature, humidity, barometric pressure, and precipitation on scent preservation); remote sensing (the use of airplanes, helicopters, and even unmanned aircraft as nondestructive investigatory resources); botany and plant ecology (the identification of plant fragments, age-dating of roots and stems, and the condition of vegetation as relates to surface disturbance); psychology (the assessment of the behavioral profile of a suspect as indications of grave location and even depth); in addition to the more traditional tools of criminalistics including fingerprints, shoe prints, tire prints, drug identification, DNA analysis, and the use of cadaver dogs.

To aid in their search, Jerry Nichols and Al Nelson have brought along two of their trained cadaver dogs, bloodhounds Yogi and Duke. Clark Davenport operates the GPR (ground-penetrating radar) and Milica Wilson, who has reviewed most of the case file history before arriving, is working with the Nashville investigative unit to identify additional locations that should be searched.

After getting all of the gear and the dogs into vehicles, amid the stares and whispers of other travelers, the group exits the airport. They confirm the schedule for the next two days and immediately go to work. The physical search begins with the site of a Nashville synagogue still under construction. The dogs and their handlers spend approximately an hour in a sweep of the exterior ground while Clark Davenport scans the inside of the structure with the GPR unit.

Nothing develops from this initial search.

The next location is a property not far from the synagogue. After another hour of searching, the results are the same—no helpful clues.

That same afternoon, the NecroSearch team is taken to a

pump house on property contiguous to the March residence. They are informed by the local detectives that the pump house was under construction during the time Janet disappeared. In fact, the Nashville police understand that the concrete floor in the pump house was poured shortly after August 15. Clark Davenport enters the small structure with the GPR unit while Al Nelson and Jerry Nichols initiate their search on the outside. The two veterans of these searches direct the bloodhounds to focus on the perimeter of the pump-house foundation.

The GPR search turns up nothing definitive. At one point Yogi attracts the group's attention by lying down at the southwest corner of the pump house, giving his handler an indication of decomposing human scent at that location. But Jerry Nichols knows from many prior searches of construction sites around the country that the scent his trained bloodhound has picked up may not be that of a body. Construction workers routinely leave trash, urine, or even blood from injuries at construction sites.

Al Nelson's dog, Duke, also indicates the decomposing human scent around the foundation of the pump house. After months of dead ends, the Nashville investigative team begins to hope they may finally be onto something. It would all make sense. The pump house is so close to the March residence that it would have afforded Perry a convenient location for dumping his wife's body, even if only temporarily. This site would be something feasible within the pressurized time frame under which Perry found himself operating on the night of August 15, knowing his kids would wake in just a few hours expecting to see their mother.

Detectives quickly arrange for equipment to be brought in. When they canvassed the neighborhood months earlier, authorities secured written permission from all of the Marches' neighbors to excavate portions of their property if doing so might lead to the discovery of Janet's body. The incident cast an ominous cloud over the neighborhood—in fact, over the entire city. It has now been almost six months since Janet's mysterious disappearance. The Nashville community wants to know what really happened to the beautiful and talented young artist.

While workers begin removing a portion of the pumphouse floor, the NecroSearch team walks the short distance to the March residence. Yogi begins to gravitate to the back door and back porch. Again he lies down, indicating the presence of decomposing human scent. A few minutes later Duke and his handler, Al Nelson, arrive from searching a wider area around the massive home. Duke also shows direct interest in the back porch.

Was Janet's body dragged or carried across this porch? Was it stowed there temporarily? Possibly inside a rolled-up rug?

Jerry Nichols takes his trained bloodhound into the dirt crawl space. The dog does not react. However, once inside the house, Yogi indicates an interest in the walk-in closets of the Marches' bedroom. The large dog approaches Perry's closet with his head low to the ground. Like a stealthy hunter, he creeps into the closet and lies down. A moment later he goes through the same routine in Janet's closet.

It is a chilling scene.

Did something horrible happen in this room? Did Perry hide his wife's body on the floor of their walk-in closet while his two young children slept down the hall, until he could remove it from the house?

By the time Jerry Nichols and Al Nelson return to the pump house, an area of the concrete floor has been removed, along with some of the gravel underneath. Both dogs go again to the southwest corner and lie down. The Nashville investigators all hover around the pump house.

Mason's eyes lock with Hunter's. The pump house was searched several times months earlier. Did they miss something? At this stage in the investigation, they are ready to ignore prior mistakes, even their own, if they can find the body. Are they about to see the decomposed remains of Janet March?

The answer turns out to be no.

It has been a very long day for everyone. Mason and

Hunter decide they are simply at another dead end. Dead ends have become familiar territory.

The following day, the NecroSearch team is taken to Percy Warner and Edwin Warner Parks, areas of the city that represent to Nashville what Central Park does to New York City. Comprising 2,684 acres, the two parks are frequented by over five hundred thousand people annually. They offer a broad array of recreational activities, including picnic areas, miles of scenic roadways, hiking, bike and horse trails, a cross-country course, athletic fields, and even a nine-hole golf course.

To locate Janet's body within such a huge area seems like an impossible task.

To cover as much ground as possible, the bloodhounds and their handlers ride at a slow pace in the back of police SUVs, and whenever the dogs give any indication, the handlers exit the vehicles and walk into particular areas within the parks for a more detailed search. For the first three tedious hours, nothing of any real interest surfaces.

Shortly after noon, the investigatory team stops at an old cemetery, where slaves from the Old South were buried around the time of the Civil War. Although the ground cover has grown over most of the area and the stone markers are for the most part missing, the graves themselves are still clearly determined by a pattern of repeated depressions in the ground. Jerry Nichols lets Yogi search the area. The dog seems to be overloaded with sensory input. He lies down in one impression, and then moves and lies down in another. Even though bodies were buried at this site over 130 years earlier, the bloodhound knows he is in the presence of decomposing human scent.

The passage of six months is obviously not going to act as an impediment to locating Janet's body. The Nashville homicide unit learned from initial conversations with the NecroSearch team that they have, in past investigations, found skeletal remains of homicide victims as long as a decade after the murder. Mason can't even think in those time frames for the March investigation. But Mason can sense that the higher-ups are already running out of patience. The presence of the team from Colorado is clear evidence of that. Detective Mason and his investigators need to narrow down the search to the correct location. ·

But on February 9, 1997, Nashville's Warner Parks prove not to be that right location.

After driving the NecroSearch team back to the Nashville airport at the end of their two-day search, Mason and Hunter return to their offices at the Justice Center. Neither has much to say.

As far as the Janet March case goes, they are right back to where they started.

Nowhere.

CHAPTER 12

No Body, No Cause of Death, No Time of Death

The failure of the NecroSearch team to produce any definitive results in the Janet March case proves symbolic for the Nashville metro homicide unit for the remainder of 1997. The investigation continues to stall. Detective Tim Mason is moved to the murder squad, no longer lead detective on the March case.

Yet maybe something more fundamental than who was leading the investigation was the root of the homicide unit's problem in making real progress. Did the investigative unit take the wrong approach with Perry from the outset? Even if they thought that as the husband he was the prime suspect, did they apply the wrong psychology in their approach to him? If they had been less adversarial initially, and treated him more like a victim, could they have learned crucial facts that now seemed to have vanished forever? If Perry had felt less threatened in the first few weeks of the investigation, would he have been more open about what took place on August 15? Would some crucial information have slipped from his lips?

Captain Mickey Miller, who, for the first few months, was

only peripherally involved, now takes over the day-to-day operations of the March investigation. Yet this police veteran of twenty years is no more successful than David Miller and Tim Mason in putting the pieces of this real-life puzzle together.

By late 1997, from the media's perspective, focus in the Janet March case has shifted from the missing and presumed dead to the living. A multistate visitation battle has begun between Janet's parents and Perry, over the future of the two youngest victims in this developing tragedy, Tzipi and Sammy. For Perry and his two young children, Illinois is now home, and that is just one jurisdiction where the first battles are taking place in what will become a long-drawn-out visitation and then custody war—a war that will ultimately find its way to the United States Supreme Court.

The expanding drama of Janet March has shifted from the physical to the procedural. Instead of remote parks, private lakes, pump houses, and Blackberry Road, the flurry of the activity is now inside the marbled halls of courthouses. Instead of psychics, grave seekers, and homicide investigators, the search for the truth is now directed by men in pinstriped suits, using endless piles of documents instead of ground-penetrating radar and cadaver dogs.

Larry Levine uses his decades of legal experience, directing it all against one adversary—his son-in-law. Since the opening act in this legal drama, the deposition of Perry during two days in November of 1996, Janet's father has been operating full flame, with a controlled fury. In addition to active custody litigation over their two grandchildren, Larry and his wife, Carolyn, are also parties in probate litigation filed in Tennessee over the distribution of their daughter's estate. They have also filed a separate wrongful death lawsuit against their son-in-law in Nashville, attempting to prove in civil court that he was responsible for the death of their daughter, Janet, and accordingly that they and her estate should be awarded tens of millions of dollars in damages as a result of her wrongful death. And at the same time, Levine's law firm, Levine, Mattson, Orr, and Geracioti, initiates legal battles with their former associate over legal fees totaling $23,000 that they contend Perry diverted to his own use after severing his ties with the firm only weeks after his wife's disappearance.

What started off as a criminal investigation into the mysterious disappearance of a beautiful young Nashville housewife from a well-to-do-family has now evolved into a multifront legal battle dominating the legal dockets of several courtrooms in two states. It is attorney versus attorney, not as counselors for their respective clients, but as the litigants themselves. For the Nashville media, the March case has become a cottage industry. The internal battles of a prominent family are unfolding for all the world to see.

The multiple legal battles drag on throughout 1997 and into 1998. More courts become involved as one side or the other seeks relief in appellate courts from one ruling or another.

By the spring of 1999, Perry has had all he can take of the endless skirmishes, and the costly bills associated with all of the legal issues. He needs a completely fresh start, and he wants his children's daily lives to return to some semblance of normalcy. His abrupt relocation in 1996 to Chicago has not allowed him to escape the spotlight or the scrutiny. Also, he senses that he has imposed about all he can upon his attorney brother, Ron, and his dentist sister, Kathy, for counsel and financial support.

Perry needs to make some money. His notoriety as the center of a criminal murder investigation, a contentious custody battle, and a dispute over legal fees—all at the same time—are continually publicized in the media. His ability to make business contacts has completely evaporated. He needs to go somewhere where his past will not precede him—and he needs to make it much more procedurally difficult for the Levines to pursue their multiprong legal attack.

In Ajijic, Mexico, Arthur March is living the good life. Ajijic is a place where, in Arthur's words, "the sky is blue, the beer is cold, and the Mexicans are warm." He has made his home in this little fishing village on Lake Chapala since the mid-1990s when he retired from a part-time pharmacy career.

He is able to live on his government pension from thirty-two years in the army and the reserves—on vacation every day of his life in this sunny paradise.

But Perry's troubles eventually intrude on Arthur's idyllic retirement.

On May 28, 1999, Carolyn and Larry Levine have a court date in Chicago. It is another skirmish in the battle over the March children, a battle that will escalate as the Levines' fight for custody of Sammy and Tzipi.

But today they are simply seeking the visitation rights they believe grandparents are due. The hearing is for permanent visitation.

Perry's brother, Ron, arrives in his official capacity as Perry's attorney. But he is without his client. It is one of those ironic twists that before the night of August 15, the night that changed everything, Carolyn and Larry often faced Ron across a table piled high with food, at one of the many occasions they enjoyed with Perry's family members. Recently, they have faced Ron only across the aisle in court.

Ron March announces to the court that Perry has moved to Mexico. He seems as surprised by his own words as the Levines.

"He's supposed to be in this courtroom today for this hearing," the judge says. "And what about the children?"

In a muted voice, Ron says, "They are with their father, Your Honor."

His announcement is a call to war.

When the Nashville authorities learn of Perry's relocation, it is like someone has driven the last nail in the coffin.

Their one and only suspect is now in another country, outside their jurisdiction, and they still have not discovered Janet's body. Without a body, how can they prove there was even a homicide?

For all practical purposes, almost three years after the disappearance of Janet March on August 15, 1996, the investigation of one of the most celebrated cases in Nashville history is at a complete and seemingly permanent dead end.

PART TWO

CHAPTER 13

The Ghost of Marcia Trimble

Nashville rings in a new year: 2002.

The March case no longer dominates the Nashville head-lines and newscasts, but the citizens of the city have not for-gotten. Many still talk about Janet March, and as often as not, they say her name in the same breath with the name of Marcia Trimble, another celebrated and unsolved case in the Athens of the South.

Marcia Trimble was a nine-year-old freckled-face girl who left her home on a mild February afternoon in 1975 to deliver some Girl Scout cookies before dinner, and never re-turned. Nashville was a much slower, sleepier city in 1975, and the Green Hills section, where the Trimbles lived, was a *Leave It to Beaver* kind of neighborhood. After the most massive search in the city's history turned up nothing for thirty-three days, the body of Marcia Trimble was found on Easter Sunday, less than two hundred yards from her home on Copeland Avenue. Her body was discovered under a crumpled wading pool in a neighbor's cluttered dirt-floor garage. She had been sexually assaulted and strangled.

Just as in the March case, a suspect was identified early

in the investigation, a teenage boy named Jeffrey Womack. Yet it was four years later before Womack, who was fifteen at the time of the murder, was arrested. The police had statements from other children who placed Womack and Trimble together on the date in question, and rumors circulated through the city that authorities also had incriminating statements made by Womack. However, the case was dropped in 1980 due to a lack of evidence after Womack successfully passed two polygraph tests, and after DNA experts could not match semen samples to any of the over eighty DNA samples gathered by police during their investigation.

The *Tennessean* revisited the Marcia Trimble case with a story on February 25, 2001, the twenty-sixth anniversary of her disappearance. The article was titled, "City Lost Its Innocence with Marcia Trimble Murder." The newspaper article quoted Metro Police Captain Mickey Miller, one of the many investigators still working on the unsolved Janet March case: "In that moment, Nashville lost its innocence. Our city has never been, and never will be the same again. Every man, woman, and child knew that if something that horrific could happen to that little girl, it could happen to anyone."

For Larry, Carolyn, and Mark Levine, Miller's words resonated with the painful truth: their lives had already changed forever.

By 2002, the fact that the Trimble case has never been solved still haunts not only the police department, but the entire Nashville community, as well. Nashville, it seems, has become a city that lacks the ability or the focus to solve the tough cases.

CHAPTER 14

Moving On Without Janet

There have been enormous changes to the urban landscape in the six years since Janet March vanished. The city is booming as corporations around the country begin to identify Nashville, with its "right-to-work" policy and its comparatively inexpensive home prices, as an excellent place to set up shop. With each new month there is an announcement of new jobs coming to the city.

Before leaving office in September 1999, Mayor Phil Bredesen, the key player in the 1997 negotiations that resulted in Nashville's first professional sports team, added another jewel to his deal-making crown using the same technique that enticed the Houston Oilers to relocate its professional football franchise to Music City—a massive package of land and tax incentives. This time the total value was $166 million, enough to attract one of the world's top-tier computer services companies, Dell Computer. While based in Austin, Texas, where it employed over twelve thousand people, Dell decided to open its first facility outside of Texas. Even with the political fanfare that accompanied its move, Dell, with its projections of over a thousand new jobs the first year, was still a comparatively minor player in Nashville. This was a city where health care was king, with Vanderbilt Medical Center employing over ten thousand people and Columbia/Hospital Corporation of America employing over six thousand.

By 2002, Nashville has for the most part shaken off any economic worries that followed the attacks on the World Trade Center and the Pentagon on September 11, 2001. New homes rise up from the ground at an astonishing pace. Major real estate developers from around the country open local offices to monitor their latest residential projects. In November 2002, Phil Bredesen parlays his successful record as economic deal-maker to an election as the forty-eighth governor of Tennessee, an office he failed to win on his first attempt as the Democratic nominee in 1994.

Many changes have occurred in places far away from Nashville as well. Shortly after arriving in Ajijic, Mexico, Perry March met a young Mexican woman, Carmen Rojas, and in less than a year they were married. He also proceeded quickly on the business front, by forming an alliance with an American-educated Mexican attorney and entrepreneur, S. Samuel Chavez. Chavez was close to Perry's age, and, being Mexican and having a law degree, he appeared to be the perfect partner. A fastidious individual, with a neatly-trimmed mustache and dark hair slicked back from his balding head, Chavez projected an air of authority and sophistication.

From the outset, their personalities and ambitions clicked and there was excitement to their joint entrepreneurial endeavors. The growing expatriate population allowed them to target their business' growth to serve the property, insurance, security, financial, and medical needs of this generally affluent group.

There have been changes in the Janet March investigation, as well, but none of them positive. Since 1996, three different lead detectives, David Miller, Tim Mason, and Brad Cochran, have all been given a shot at the case, with the same results—no body and not enough evidence to make an arrest.

Two new detectives will get their chance. Murder is something these two police veterans know a lot about.

CHAPTER 15

The Cold Case Unit

February 16, 1997, is a Sunday, and for Nashville murder squad detectives Patrick Postiglione and Bill Pridemore, the day starts off great. Postiglione spends a leisurely Sunday morning at home, relaxing with the newspaper and his second cup of coffee, when he gets the call from his captain. The message is brief but urgent. Pridemore is where he always is whenever his job permits—on the golf course at Old Hickory Country Club, getting ready to line up a putt. Most people don't play golf in February, but Bill Pridemore is not most people.

The phone call he receives is just as short and direct as the captain's call to Postiglione: "Two dead kids in a freezer."

The call comes exactly one week after the team from NecroSearch International flew out of Nashville International Airport, just a few miles from the Old Hickory Country Club, after spending countless hours scouring various sites in West Nashville for Janet's body. Pridemore and Postiglione hadn't been involved with the Colorado-based investigators. They'd had way too much on their plate to be called in to run the March investigation. And their plate just became more crowded.

There are two dead kids in a freezer.

Postiglione and Pridemore have been partners in the Nashville Metropolitan Police Department's murder squad since 1988. For years their cubicle offices were directly across from each other, close enough so they could slide their chairs into the narrow hallway and confer with each other on the latest break in a murder case. To a first-time visitor the cubicles looked like the space of any office worker, with personal photos and plaques.

On Postiglione's wall is a photo of him, his brother, and his dad at a St. Louis Cardinals baseball game, and several pictures of the Three Stooges. "I like to keep some levity in the place," he likes to say. When you're dealing with dead bodies every day, occasional levity may be a necessity in maintaining your sanity. "It sounds strange, I know," Postiglione tells people outside the police force, "but with an average of almost a murder every three or four days, we could stand over a cold dead body and eat a fresh hot pizza."

In Pridemore's cubicle, which is remarkably neat and organized, there is a picture of his wife, and a photo of him sitting in a chair with his Labrador retriever. For a moment you might think you've entered the office space of an adjuster for one of Nashville's many insurance companies, but then you see the blown-up mug shot of O. J. Simpson looking back at you with a contemptuous smirk. A daily reminder not to let the bad guys get off.

Just down another short hallway is the conference room with a large white board on one wall, littered with names and numbers, references to the ongoing investigations of murder cases. They are written in erasable Magic Marker. When you deal with murder, new names are constantly being added.

Before joining the murder squad, Pridemore and Postiglione both served in the homicide squad, though not as partners. To the layman, the homicide squad and the murder squad would seem by definition to have the same duties, but in the world of law enforcement, at least in Nashville, that is anything but the case. The homicide squad is referred to in police department lingo as the "Band-Aid squad." The detectives assigned to this squad handle not just homicides but anything and everything that even approaches an attempted homicide. If two guys get into a fight at a bar, they call the homicide squad. If one guy pulls a gun on another and in the squabble one of the combatants is shot in the foot, they call the homicide squad. And if there is a drug-related shooting, where the known shooter is still at the scene or officers have a clean address, they call the homicide squad.

In contrast, the murder squad investigates homicides where there is no known suspect. Obviously a position on the murder squad calls for someone with investigative skills—someone who can analyze the evidence and follow it until it leads to a suspect. Postiglione and Pridemore have honed their craft with years of on-the-job training.

With an average of over a hundred homicides a year in Nashville, they have had lots of practice.

Before attaining their positions with the murder squad, both Postiglione and Pridemore paid their dues working in the patrol division. Yet they arrived at the Academy from two completely different backgrounds.

For Pat Postiglione, coming to Nashville with an Italian name was tough. His father was second-generation Italian and his mother Irish. He grew up in New York City—in Queens—and later in Nassau County, and then Suffolk, Long Island, speaking Italian with his father. His hair is black and he keeps it trimmed short. He is thin, angular, and weighs no more than 160 pounds dripping wet, keeping his weight exactly the same with regular games of racquetball. He looks more like an accountant than a homicide detective, meticulously dressed, with everything neat and in its place. His analysis of murder cases mirrors his demeanor: each detail examined carefully, methodically, all the evidentiary pluses and minuses in the correct column.

His fastidious appearance gives the impression he just

had a shower. Maybe working with dead bodies does that to you. You just can't take enough showers.

After graduating from Northport High School in 1969, he joined the navy Seabees and served overseas in Diego Garcia and Guam in support of the Vietnam War effort during his two years of active duty. His job was as a bomb hauler, transporting bombs from navy ships through the jungle to the waiting air force for loading onto B-52s, as they littered North Vietnam with thousands of bombs in an effort to try to bring the elusive and persistent Viet Cong to their knees. Pat participated in four or five bomb runs a day, each load consisting of about forty thousand pounds of explosives. He did not know it at the time, but his years in the navy would be good training for him as he learned how to deal with the parts of life others don't want to face.

How to deal with death every day, and not let it drive you mad.

In 1977 Pat visited Nashville on vacation. Apparently, Johnny Cash and Waylon Jennings played well in New York Italian neighborhoods. Pat noticed one day while reading the local paper, then called the *Nashville Tennessean*—the same paper where his picture would appear prominently decades later with the resolution of one big murder case after another—that the Nashville Police Department was hiring. He was then working for his father's heating and air-conditioning business, but for years he had carried around a dream of being a police officer.

Pat decided to apply, and in 1980 he was hired. His brother Danny would also join the Nashville police force in 1981. Another brother, Ronnie, spent twenty-one years with the New York Police Department. Pat's wife, Margaret, was also a police officer with the Nashville Police Department for six years, assigned to the South Precinct and the criminal warrants division.

The Postiglione family bleeds blue.

Bill Pridemore knew he wanted to be a policeman from the time he was ten years old. That was in 1963, and Billy was living in public housing with his mother in Kingsport,

Tennessee, an industrial town in the northeastern tip of the state where the largest employer was Eastman Chemical Company. The industry's massive operations cast a constant stench over the city, which lay trapped in the bottom of a natural valley. Billy's father and mother had grown up in a small town in the Appalachian Mountains of southwest Virginia. With few employment opportunities, his father had joined the army, and before Kingsport, Billy had only known army housing. But his parents had divorced and now it was Billy; his brother, Paul; two younger sisters, Sharon and Debbie; and their mom, Mary, who was attending night school to learn data entry.

Billy didn't have many possessions, and on a day in 1963, he was mad at the world. Someone had stolen his bicycle. He saw a Kingsport policeman drive through the neighborhood and flagged him down. Instead of just ignoring a poor kid from the projects, the officer let Billy ride in his patrol car as they scanned the neighborhood for the missing bike. And on that afternoon, the officer solved the crime, and Billy Pridemore was once again able to ride the streets of Kingsport.

After Kingsport it was Cincinnati, Ohio, where the family lived in the inner city and his mom worked two jobs. And then there was a stepdad and a new little brother, but this marriage lasted only a year or two, and then it was off to Dayton, Ohio, now the six of them. While working at Wright Air Force Base, Mary met and married her third husband, John Tuinei, an air-force career man. After a transfer to Offutt Air Force Base in Omaha, Nebraska, the family ended up in Nashville, the city where Billy's newest stepfather elected to retire.

That was 1971, and Billy was a senior at a new school, Stratford High. A tough position for any teenager, but especially rough for a kid in a Southern city that was experiencing its first year of court-ordered busing. Billy didn't like school and looked for part-time work, which he found with one of the new growth companies in the South, United Parcel Service. After graduating from Stratford, Billy took a few courses at a local community college, but finally he gave up school and went to work for UPS full-time.

But Billy Pridemore had not given up his dream of being a policeman.

By now he had grown into the stocky, barrel-chested man he is today, with a physique like that of an offensive lineman. A man you would want on your side in a barroom fight. A man who would not take shit from anyone, and yet is kindhearted and quick to tease his coworkers. His childhood dream finally came true when he graduated from the Nashville Police Academy in May of 1976. It was now his turn to help others; in his own way, he was ready to pay back the cop who helped a ten-year-old kid find his stolen bike.

On this chilly February day in '97, two decades have passed since he joined the police force, and there are several more inches on his waistline and a lot less hair on his head, but, like a lineman, Pridemore still keeps pushing away at whatever obstacle lies in his path until he gets to the truth.

Postiglione and Pridemore will go on to solve the murders of Steve Hampton and Sarah Jackson, the two dead kids in the walk-in freezer. The shooter turns out to be a man named Paul Reid.

They will not be Reid's only victims.

The two veteran detectives use DNA evidence from the blood of a murder victim in a multiple murder at a Baskin-Robbins in Clarksville, Tennessee, some forty miles northeast of Nashville, to locate their shooter. It is evidence that they secured on the bottom of Paul Reid's shoes that ties him to that bloody crime scene as well, evidence they gathered after serving a routine search warrant on his residential address.

Unlike the March case, no one called Paul Reid's attorney to inform him the police were coming.

Thanks to the relentless investigatory efforts of an Italian kid from New York and a kid from the projects in Kingsport, Paul Reid receives death sentences in 1999 and 2000 for the capital murders of seven fast-food restaurant workers: the two kids shot to death in the freezer at Captain D's, the two

Baskin-Robbins workers from Clarksville, and three McDonald's employees, also in Clarksville.

The Paul Reid case will not be the only high-profile murder cases that these two partners would crack. Two investigations are related to the music industry in Nashville, the main tourist draw in a place known worldwide as Music City.

The first music-industry-related murder was that of Kevin Hughes. Hughes was a student at Belmont College, a campus within a stone's throw of Nashville's famed Music Row, a pocket of the city where, over the last half century, everyone from Hank Williams to Elvis Presley to Willie Nelson to Neil Diamond to Kid Rock have recorded songs. Belmont has one of the nation's most highly acclaimed programs for music management, and in many instances the college assists its students with intern positions in the city's vibrant music industry.

In1989 Kevin Hughes had an internship with Cash Box Promotions. While trying to soak up all he could about the music industry, the eager intern came across a dark side of the business—a new twist to the old "pay for play" scandals that first surfaced in the industry when Dick Clark was a young disc jockey in Philadelphia. The observant college student discovered that in the constant struggle to have a hit record, the ever-so-important chart numbers were being manipulated by independent record promoters. Fearing the promoters were about to be exposed, Richard D. Antonio gunned down the young intern on Music Row as Hughes left Evergreen Records.

Then there was the case of Tom Steeples in March of 1994. Steeples murdered Kelly and Rob Phillips, a young married couple from California, lured to Nashville with dreams of becoming the next George Jones and Tammy Wynette (before Tim McGraw and Faith Hill became stars). Steeples somehow met Kelly and Rob, entered their motel room and, after raping Kelly, beat them both to death. Steeples was actually out on bond at the time, awaiting trial for the murder of Nashville bar owner, Ronnie Bingham, whom he had killed and then set on fire before leaving to attend a family bowling event in the city.

Not all cold case murder investigations are high-profile ones. There are the single murders in the seedy parts of town—like the case of Donna Bacot, a prostitute found strangled in a motel room on Dickerson Road. "We knew it was not a normal homicide," Postiglione says, "by the way the body was displayed and with a pillow over her head." The motel clerk told the detectives that a man had signed for the room, using a Dallas, Texas address. They didn't have security cameras in this part of town. Postiglione and Pridemore concluded it was a bogus name and address, but they had dealt with a lot of criminals, and even murderers stuck to familiar things. Believing their suspect had killed before, they decided to start calling detectives in the major Texas cities to see if they had come across a similar murder scene. Nothing panned out. So they narrowed the focus to major cities in Tennessee, but again found nothing similar. Then an investigator in Chattanooga suggested they call a detective in Ohio based upon a recent conversation the two had had.

Cincinnati detective Ed Zivernick informed them that they had an ongoing motel murder investigation of a strangled woman with a pillow over her head.

"What do you have?" Postiglione asked.

"We have some DNA," Zivernick answered.

"We've got some blood from a shirt that was not the victim's," Postiglione said.

They had a match. Michael Scott Magliolo, the manager of a McDonald's in Jasper, Texas, liked to take long road trips, pick up prostitutes, and murder them. "After the Janet March case, the public may think we only spend countless hours on cases of the missing daughter of a prominent Nashville family, but we treat every victim with the same respect and the same commitment," Pridemore explains.

By the time Postiglione and Pridemore were assigned the Hughes case, now known as the Music Row Murder, it is 2000, and they are fresh off the Paul Reid convictions. While still officially assigned to the murder squad, their actual investigative roles have been narrowed. Instead of investigating all crimes where the killer is unknown, the two veteran detectives begin to concentrate more of their efforts on the old unsolved murders—the "cold cases."

Nashville law enforcement brass do not hold their usual press conference to announce this latest effort in solving crime. Instead, the formation of the Cold Case Unit is happening behind the scenes. The initial unit, which consists of Terry McElroy, Grady Eleam, and Dean Haney, works out of the DA's office. In February 2002 Pridemore will be assigned to the unit, joining Sergeant Charlie Griffin, Al Gray, McElroy, and Eleam. Postiglione will be in charge of both the Cold Case Unit and homicide in 2003, continuing to work on the "mystery murders" as well as cold case investigations.

By working out of the DA's office, the unit is housed in separate quarters away from the heartbeat of law enforcement, the Nashville Criminal Justice Center at 200 James Robertson Parkway, the same location where Larry Levine, Mark Levine, and Perry March walked in to report Janet's disappearance on August 29, 1996.

The powers behind the creation of this new investigative squad—Davidson County attorney general Torry Johnson (the person Mike Geracioti called seeking the reference of a good criminal defense lawyer for Perry's alleged client), Deputy District Attorney Tom Thurman (who successfully prosecuted the Paul Reid cases and would end up being the prosecution's point man on the Janet March case), and Police Chief Emmett Turner (who had been on his watch only a few months when Janet disappeared)—wanted to keep the whole thing low profile. Such a position actually makes sense: What police department wants to publicize that it has high-profile murder cases that it has failed to solve? Cases like that of nine-year-old Marcia Trimble, found dead in fashionable Green Hills in 1975, Kevin Hughes, gunned down on Nashville's famed Music Row in

1989, and Janet March, who mysteriously disappeared from her affluent Forest Hills estate in 1996.

Postiglione and Pridemore are assigned the Music Row Murder case in 2000. Although the crime had occurred eleven years earlier, by 2001 they have their man—Richard D. Antonio (a.k.a. Tony D). It is not the latest DNA science that proves to be the difference in the case, but rather good old-fashioned police work. A ballistics match is made from a projectile found in Chattanooga, the city that years later would be called upon to provide the prospective jurors in the Perry March murder case. The cold case detectives then secured testimony from an individual who stated that Tony D. was the person who stole his pistol on March 9, 1989—the same day Kevin Hughes was gunned down in cold blood on Music Row.

With their prompt success in the Music Row Murder case, Postiglione and Pridemore are next assigned to be lead investigators in the Janet March case. They will be the fourth set of lead detectives.

They will not be able to duplicate their earlier investigative magic.

CHAPTER 16

Just Who Were Janet and Perry?

Although the March case file has been around for six years, to cold case detectives Bill Pridemore and Pat Postiglione, this is a brand-new investigation.

During the two decades before the creation of the cold case unit, they worked scores of homicides, but the Janet March mystery is by no means one of their *normal* murder cases, if murder can be called normal. It is the first time in all their years on the force that they do not have a body. No body means no way to pinpoint time of death or to even know the cause of death. For homicide detectives, a body means the possibility of an autopsy, and an autopsy can be the voice of the victim speaking to them.

But they have their theory on the cause. They have already concluded, from the lack of any trace of blood at the March home, that Perry March strangled his five-foot-four-inch, 104-pound wife.

They know from experience that the best way to catch a killer is to know all you can about the victim in addition to the suspect or suspects. In this case, there is only one viable suspect. They are convinced that the more they know about

Janet and Perry—what made them tick—the better their chances that one clue will lead to cracking the case. Reviewing the scores of witness interviews, they start to piece together the two personalities.

They start with Janet March, born Janet Gail Levine on January 20, 1963, and raised in a privileged home in Nashville's Jewish community. Her parents, Carolyn Rosenblum and Lawrence Levine, also met at the University of Michigan. Carolyn from Nashville, Larry from New York. Larry attended U of M as both an undergraduate and a law student. In 1960, the same year he was admitted to the bar in New York, he and Carolyn married. They lived on Long Island, where Carolyn taught school. But the South beckoned the Southern girl. In 1961 they moved to Nashville, and Larry began to lay the foundations for his successful law practice. They settled in a comfortable house on Vaughn's Gap in West Meade. It was here on this winding road, in a neighborhood of trees and lush lawns, with other Jewish families as neighbors, that Janet and her brother, Mark, grew up.

She lived a charmed life.

Janet attended the elite and artsy University School of Nashville, graduating in 1981. She was pretty and popular, elected president of her junior class, vice president of her senior class, and prom queen. She was a "Commended Scholar" and participated in the student council and the Academic Creative Theater. A photo in her yearbook shows her in a skit called "The Twilight Zone." An eerie prophecy?

Janet had plenty of boyfriends, and was always surrounded by her girlfriends. She was one of a tightly knit group of Jewish girls who grew up together—six of them, according to Diane Saks, one of those girls who continued to be Janet's close friend after they had families of their own.

Janet left Nashville to attend the University of Michigan, her parents' alma mater, to major in political science and art. There she met Perry March. Southern girl meets intense, determined Jewish young man from the North—her parents had to smile at this. Her roommate, Stacey Goodman, introduced Perry and Janet. Goodman, now a physician in Nashville, would give an interview after Janet's disappearance, saying Janet would never leave her children. She went on to testify against Perry March, telling the court that after her interview, he threatened, "I'm coming to get you!"

But in those college days, they were all friends.

Janet put great stock in relationships. She was always close to her parents and her brother. After she and Perry moved back to Nashville and married, hardly a day passed that she didn't see or talk with her mother and father. Even as a young wife and mother and working artist, Janet made time for her friends. They went on trips together. About once a week, they had girls' night out, often at the Bound'ry near Vanderbilt. She belonged to a book club with Marcy Eskind, Tamelyn Feinstein, Lori Fishel, Gabi Friedman, Betsy Hoffman, Simone Meyerowitz, and Laurie Rummel.

Janet's friends described her as witty, caring, and remarkably talented. She had her first art exhibition in 1989, and her art career was just starting to flourish when it was cut off sharply on August 15, 1996. Janet was sensitive, a dreamer. Friends also said she was a private, reserved person. She could be a little ditzy sometimes, often forgetful or late. But in some ways she was predictable; when the girlfriends took shopping trips to Chicago, Janet always shopped in the same stores and dined in the same restaurants.

And yes, she could be difficult.

Perry was quoted in an interview with the *Nashville Scene* as saying he was drawn to her "beauty, her soft voice and her Southern accent, her whimsical and artistic personality, and her offbeat, but perceptive, sense of humor." But he also complained to Laurie Rummel that Janet was spoiled and used to getting everything she wanted. Some of the contractors who worked on her dream home described her as self-centered and hard to please, demanding that work be performed to a certain precision, or else she would call her father or husband who were lawyers. *Spoiled*—not just

Perry's word. On the other hand, Mitchell Barnett, the architect on the Blackberry Road house, had nothing but praise for her, saying she was one of the most creative clients he ever worked with.

"Sounds like a lot of women I know," Pridemore says. "She had her moods."

Pridemore muses over the word *difficult.*

"Seems like everybody that was close to her loved her, but she had an artist's temperament," he says.

The detectives turn to the files on Perry.

Born January 14, 1961, in the industrial town of East Chicago, Indiana, not far from Chicago's notorious South Side, Perry Avrum March was the son of Arthur and Zipora March, themselves a study in complexities. Zipora Elyson March was born in Israel, her mother an immigrant from Ukraine. Arthur met Zipora on a trip to Tel Aviv, married the dark-haired beauty, and brought her back to East Chicago. In photographs of Perry's mother as a young woman, she bears an uncanny likeness to Janet March.

In 1970, when Perry was only nine years old, Zipora died at their home in what was widely rumored to be a suicide. A half-empty bottle of Darvon capsules was found in her bedroom. According to Arthur, a doctor prescribed Darvon because she had a cut on her head, and she had an allergic reaction to the painkiller. The death certificate calls the death "barbiturate overdose" and also states "home accidental death."

"Darvon's not a barbiturate," Pridemore notes.

"When did you get your medical degree?" his partner asks.

Pridemore grins, picks up his coffee mug, and drains it. "Honest to God, I remember hearing somebody talking about it, saying 'home accidental death' might have meant 'don't ask, don't tell.' "

Postiglione makes notes. This tidbit is like so much else in the case—you get a couple of facts and they beg a dozen questions.

Zipora left three children. The oldest was Perry, a small boy with large brooding eyes. The detectives are familiar with the siblings, Ron and Kathy, whose names have cropped up a number of times during the investigation. Entertainment attorney Ron has represented Perry in various court appearances. Kathy is a dentist. Both live in the Chicago area.

And then there is Arthur.

Postiglione and Pridemore scan the notes about Perry's father, who was born Arthur Wayne Marcovich in 1928. Arthur's father was a Romanian immigrant, a self-made man who eventually owned several businesses. Arthur went to Ohio Northern University and earned a pharmacy degree. After college, he served in the army. Although he boasted of great feats during a glorious military career in Korea, Burma, Africa, and Germany, his brief active duty found him serving as a pharmacist. Most of his thirty-two years of service were spent in the Reserves. When he retired in 1988, he was a lieutenant colonel. The detectives will learn first-hand that Arthur liked to be referred to as "the Colonel."

He came home to work in his father's pharmacy after the army. He also Americanized his name: Marcovich to March. Not because he was ashamed of his Jewishness, he insisted. It was just easier. In the late 1950s, he traveled to Israel, met and married Zipora. Back home in East Chicago, they began raising a family, but their marriage was cut short when Zipora died.

After his wife died, Arthur and the children moved to Michiana, Michigan, on the Lake Michigan shoreline, where they had previously taken their vacations. He took care of his kids, hung out with his army buddies on weekends, and never remarried. Arthur was known in Michiana for his eccentricities. According to the *Nashville Scene*, there are stories that he rode through town in a horse and buggy and appeared outside on the coldest Michigan days wearing a T-shirt and no coat.

Over the years, Perry repeated Arthur's claims about his military life and inflated them. At various times he boasted that his father was a Green Beret, CIA, FBI, or Special Forces. That he had killed over three hundred men. The detectives also see notations that Perry told people his cousin was in the Mossad and that Perry himself had been approached to join the CIA.

Postiglione shakes his head. "It's like he needed to mythologize his family and their exploits. Make everything larger than life."

"He lived in a different reality," Pridemore says.

It must have been hard being Arthur March's son, the detectives agree.

When they meet him in 2005, they will learn that in Arthur's own gruff, crude way, he is an engaging personality, and a man who will go to extraordinary lengths for his family—but with Arthur, things are not always exactly what they seem, even in the case of family loyalties.

At thirteen, Perry was a black belt in Soryu Kan karate. Though he was Jewish, he went to a Catholic prep school, La Lumiere School, where he made excellent grades and loved sports. He played tennis, lettered in soccer and wrestling, and studied karate.

Perry chose the University of Michigan because he liked their Asian studies program and eventually became fluent in four dialects of Chinese, but the fact that he could get instate tuition was no small factor. Unlike Janet Levine, he had to think about money.

Perry was reportedly intelligent, hard-driving, and successful in whatever he pursued. He was a member of the Honor Student Council. But everything wasn't rosy for Perry at U of M. A coed claimed he assaulted her in a fit of jealousy. Perry denied the charges. He was quoted in the *Nashville Scene* as saying, "She was a slut. I fucked her for a few months." His version is that he dumped her. The woman denied ever having sex with him. She never made a report of the incident to police.

In 2006 Arthur will tell Detectives Pridemore and Postiglione that Perry was "mentally ill because he didn't have a mother." He will also tell them that Perry had psychiatric counseling in college, a fact that police are never able to confirm.

If there were warning signs, signaling future problems, Janet didn't see them.

Perry has indicated the two were "inseparable." Janet's friends confirm that she was deeply in love with this bright, ambitious young man. Six months after Perry moved to Chicago, Janet followed, and they lived there for two years. Janet finished part of her senior year at the Art Institute of Chicago, and Perry worked for a brokerage firm. But like her mother, who brought Larry back to the South with her, Janet wanted to come home, so she encouraged Perry to apply to Vanderbilt Law School. He was concerned about the cost. Not to worry, Janet said, her parents would pay his tuition.

And so, back in Nashville in 1985, the lives of Janet and Perry and Janet's parents began to intertwine. The Levines provided the duplex in the Vanderbilt area where Janet and Perry lived, even deeding it to Janet as her own property. This residence was nothing like the typical student apartment; it was a spacious dwelling nestled on a hillside. The duplex offered one side for their living space and the other for Janet's studio. The Levines always encouraged Janet's artistic talents. From all indications, they encouraged Janet in every aspect of her life.

"I wonder what they really thought about Perry—from the get-go," Pridemore muses. "He was Jewish and smart, but not a bit like the Levines."

"Yeah, but that's now—that's since Janet disappeared. You don't know how it was back in '86 or '87," Postiglione counters. "Larry treated him like a son, put him through law school, took him into his law firm. I tell you one thing, if Larry Levine ever had any suspicions that Perry was a jerk, I don't care how much he loved his daughter, he would've held back on his wallet. And Carolyn, you know, people have said she was like a surrogate mother to Perry."

"She felt sorry for him because of what had happened with his mother."

The detectives agree that whatever feelings Larry and Carolyn nurtured in their hearts for Perry, they wanted Janet to be happy, and Perry seemed to be the ticket to Janet's happiness.

And the Levines were generous with Perry's family. Early in 1986, the bank foreclosed on Arthur's house in Michiana, Michigan. The Levines bought the property and let Arthur live in it rent-free for a considerable period. Later, when Arthur more or less showed up on the Levines' doorstep, Janet's parents took him in until he could find a place to live. They loaned him money and helped him get the necessary training to be a pharmacist in Tennessee.

With the Levines, it was all about family.

The story goes that Janet got tired of waiting for Perry to propose marriage, so she proposed to him on bended knee in Percy Warner Park. When Pridemore and Postiglione come across this notation, they exchange a glance, both remembering that Percy Warner Park was the site of one of the extensive searches police conducted for Janet's body.

Perry and Janet married in 1987 in a beautiful wedding, surrounded by adoring friends. In photos from those years, they are smiling and affectionate. It is easy to imagine the dreams they had. They look happy, connected, eager for the future.

Meanwhile, Perry excelled in law school, serving as associate editor of *Law Review*. An animated fast talker, he earned a reputation for an aggressive style in negotiations exercises. According to Willie Stern from the *Nashville Scene,* one of Perry's former classmates said that the other law students joked about his intensity and his obvious focus on money, calling him "the classmate most likely to be indicted for securities fraud." He graduated in 1988 from Vanderbilt Law School, and although he received attractive offers from New York firms, he elected to stay in Nashville. This was Janet's home, and now it was his home. A well-connected, extremely bright young lawyer, Perry must have believed his future had no limits.

When he was given his first job by blue-blood Bass, Berry, and Sims, he and his Vanderbilt classmate Bennett Ross were the first Jewish lawyers ever hired by the firm. With several well-to-do Jewish clients, Bass, Berry had received some pressure to hire Jewish lawyers. After a while coworkers began to speculate that he was on track to becoming a partner. Perry referred to himself as a "go-to guy." He did pro bono work for the Jewish Community Center. According to Willie Stern's article, Perry boasted that partner James H. Cheek III referred to him as "Nashville's next Jewish consigliere," suggesting that he would succeed Harris Gilbert as "Nashville's most prominent Jewish attorney."

"Some irony there," Postiglione points out. "Gilbert represented the Levines after Janet disappeared."

One of the lawyers who knew Perry at Bass, Berry described him as one who would "never crack under pressure," who could "sleep and never worry." Hard-driving, high energy—he was a guy who couldn't stand to lose, a tremendous competitor in the so-called friendly tennis matches on Sunday mornings at Whitworth Racquet Club. His aggressive style had generally worked for him, but it did not appeal to everyone who met him across the courtroom in Nashville—or to everyone who socialized with him and Janet. Some described him as angry and manipulative. The detectives key on one word that was used frequently in the witness interviews to describe Perry March: *deceptive*.

Still, Perry did not impress everyone in that manner. His last secretary at Levine, Mattson, Orr, and Geracioti was Alivia Watson. The only black person in an all-white atmosphere, she got along well with Perry during the short time that she worked for him—from July 15 to August 23, 1996. Perry left after that date, but in a letter to him she wrote, "You are the best boss I ever had."

The words *difficult* and *deceptive* jump out at the cold case detectives. It supports what they have already theorized. A deceptive husband is confronted by a difficult wife—a recipe for a heated argument, which, in this case, detectives believe led to murder.

Carolyn Levine stated that for the last six years of marriage, Janet and Perry had experienced marital problems. After only two years of marriage, she said, Janet told her Perry had mental problems.

Witness statements indicate that the death of Perry's mother might have been an issue on the table. Diane Saks knew that Janet was troubled about Perry's mother's death. Janet told her Perry had lied about that case.

Laura Zinker, Janet's close friend since 1988, said that when Janet visited her in May of 1996 they had some long conversations about Perry and Arthur. "Janet believed [Arthur] was responsible for the death of Perry's mother," Laura stated. She said Janet told her she was afraid of Arthur and that he had been arrested for pulling a gun on someone in a Kroger grocery store parking lot.

Laura also said, "When Janet was with Perry, she was a different person. He dominated her." She said, "I knew Janet was dead when she missed Sammy's birthday party. After the party, Gabi Friedman and I both said, 'Janet is dead.'"

The detectives spend some time reviewing the letters that Perry wrote to the young paralegal at Bass, Berry. The language is, on the one hand, sexually graphic, like passages in a porn novel, but on the other hand it is full of ponderous poetic declarations, the kind a lovesick schoolboy might write. And then there are the passages like "I feel like the lucky leprechaun who has seen the rainbow" and "I feel like a puppy whose master has finally come home to play."

Postiglione shakes his head. "Who *is* this guy?"

Both detectives agree he had some serious problems in the sex department.

A number of statements in the file indicate that Perry was seen with other women.

"Tracy at Déjà Vu, and another dancer they called Lita," Pridemore says, flipping through one of the three-inch binders in which they are organizing their information.

"Didn't somebody see him with a blonde at the Belcourt Cinema?"

"And a brunette at the Bound'ry."

"Shit. The guy wasn't trying to keep his women a secret."

"He wanted Janet to know. It was another way to try to intimidate and demean her," says Postiglione.

In the months prior to Janet's disappearance, Perry had been seen working out at the Jewish Community Center for long periods at a time.

And he spent time with his client, Paul Eichel, and bragged about his connections to the club scene in Nashville.

Postiglione turns page after page, trying to get a fix on Perry March, a *real* fix on him. Perry March, desperate to fit into Janet's world, the Levines' world, the wealthy Jewish social circles. That layer of respectability. Yet there were so many other layers—deeper, darker ones.

Pridemore knows that look his partner gets, when he's so sucked into the case, he can barely come up for air. Pridemore's reaction is different, a craving for physical activity after so much mental work.

Postiglione is mentally walking around the edges of what Joseph Conrad examined in *The Secret Sharer*—a true doppelganger, yet unlike most, who struggle to stifle or suppress their other selves, Perry seems eager to embrace his "dangerous side."

Postiglione lingers over a copy of an invoice dated June 14, 1996, flowers delivered to Janet March at 3 Blackberry Road. Perry had ordered mixed roses and white daisies.

Something about a woman and flowers. Postiglione knows how a woman melts when the florist delivers that bouquet. He imagines the florist at the door, Janet's wide sparkling eyes. He wonders, *Did she think everything was going to be all right?*

CHAPTER 17

"Janet Loved Him"

Larry Levine did not like to lose.

By 1991, when he welcomed his son-in-law into the family law firm, Larry Levine had been a practicing attorney for thirty years, and was the senior partner in a legal practice that he had turned into one of the city's busiest midsize firms, with a steady base of insurance defense cases and business litigation. Several of Nashville's best civil courtroom attorneys at one time or another learned the ropes as associates with Levine's firm.

By 1996, after thirty-five years of legal battles, Larry Levine was finally starting to slow down. He had sold a good percentage of his controlling interest in the firm to younger partners and was spending more and more time with his two grandchildren. In fact, there was seldom a day that he did not stop by Janet's home, or that Janet did not bring the children by for a visit to her parents' house just a few miles away on Vaughn's Gap Road.

Larry Levine's passion for practicing law ranked second only to his deep love for his family.

Each year of their daughter's marriage, the Levines gave

her $20,000 as a gift, $10,000 from each parent, the maximum annual tax-free gift permitted by the Internal Revenue Service. The Levines were not embarrassed by their unabashed love for their daughter; and if Janet loved Perry, then they would love him, too.

The Levines were generous with Nashville as well. They were frequent contributors to a wide range of charitable causes, especially within the close-knit Nashville Jewish community. Pictures of the couple taken at social and charitable events show Mrs. Levine always impeccably dressed, a perfect smile framed by the natural beauty and high cheekbones she passed on to Janet. Mr. Levine was always close to her but appeared less relaxed, the light reflecting off his oversize glasses. Larry Levine was not a fun-loving, back-slapping social gregarian. He was a serious, focused man who deeply loved his family and his faith, and who applied to his charitable works the same commitment he did with everything else in his life.

Many within Nashville, and especially within the city's Jewish community, viewed the Levines as influential and powerful people. They had developed a broad base of equally influential and successful friends in the social and civic circles of Nashville. They lived comfortably, but with almost a complete absence of ostentatiousness, residing in the same home since 1961. Larry Levine worked hard, methodically building a lucrative legal practice. By the 1990s he was ready to loosen the reins, sit back, and observe the full blossoming of his daughter and son.

The events of August 15, 1996, changed everything.

When Perry elected to leave Nashville with almost no warning, taking Sammy and Tzipi and relocating to Illinois near his brother and sister, he blamed the endless scrutiny by the news media following Janet's disappearance. He said it was so intense that it was harming his children. To all who saw them together, Perry was always an attentive parent. It was common for him to fix dinner for his children and put them to bed after coming home from the office.

For the Levines, this unexpected and abrupt move out of state is another dagger in their hearts. It has been only a month since the inexplicable disappearance of their beautiful daughter. Now their grandchildren are removed from them as well. This generous and loving couple, who have spent so much of their lives and fortune to nurture and protect Janet and her entire family, have all of it taken away within a period of just a few weeks.

They simply will not stand for it.

Larry Levine turns to the one place where he is the most comfortable: the courtroom. A brutal twist of fate has brought this veteran attorney—a man on the verge of retirement—the most important case of his legal career, a case he will pursue on multiple fronts for the next decade, in a series of legal filings in courts at the trial and appellate levels in both Tennessee and Illinois.

For Larry Levine, life is now centered on seeking justice for one client—his daughter and her memory.

First he files on his own behalf and on behalf of his wife a petition with the Tennessee courts seeking grandparent visitation with little Sammy and Tzipi. When Perry moves with the children to Illinois, Larry Levine's legal maneuvers follow him. Along with the issue of grandparent visitation, Janet's father also initiates legal filings in the Probate Court of Davidson County, Tennessee, seeking the appointment of a conservator or receiver for Janet's property. Although Janet has not been declared legally dead, the Levines fear the worst. In their hearts, they have come to believe that the same person to whom they have been so generous for so many years, the same person they've loved like a son, knows exactly what happened to Janet on the night of August 15.

The home in Forest Hills is now vacant. The Levines want to be sure the design project to which their talented and artistic daughter devoted so much of her life will be properly protected. They are extremely proud of their daughter and all she accomplished with the Blackberry Road property. As the story of Janet and Perry March plays out almost daily in the media in 1996, and the aerial photo of the stately stone residence flashes on the TV over and over again, most of Nashville will come to assume that the Levines have been responsible for all the details behind this unique development and construction project.

In reality, it was Janet who was responsible for most of it.

In 1992, Janet and Perry were living in their Harpeth Trace condo with their son, Sammy, and they had plans for more children. Janet, already known around the city for her paintings, drawings, and book illustrations, longed to apply her artistic skills to the design of a dream home, a home where she and Perry could raise their family and live happily ever after. She began to drive around Nashville searching for just the right piece of property and came upon a unique wooded tract of approximately ten acres hidden away behind one of the many hills of Middle Tennessee. The site was in the exclusive city of Forest Hills, a large enclave in the western portion of Nashville, where large homes rest upon manicured lots. The property was completely nestled away from the surrounding homes, waiting to be discovered by someone who understood its potential.

Without any prior background in real-estate development, Janet knew she had found her dream site. She tackled the project with all her energies. First she appeared before the powers that be within the city of Forest Hills and obtained permission to subdivide the ten-acre tract into smaller tracts of one to two acres each. She hired a road contractor to construct a new road, opening up the beautiful wooded valley to the possibility of several new home sites, and in a relatively short time proceeded to secure buyers looking to build in such an exclusive part of Nashville. Janet retained the best and largest tract for herself, and with the proceeds from the sale of the other lots was able to pay for a prime site in one of Nashville's nicest residential areas.

With site development complete, Janet now turned to what would become her labor of love for the next two years. First she set out to find just the right architect, one who would be receptive to the multitude of design concepts that flooded her brain. She formed the perfect alliance with local architect Mitchell Barnett. He would later publicly pronounce that Janet was the most involved client that he had ever worked with. She knew exactly what she wanted—a French country house—and she applied her passion for perfection to every minute detail. She visited the site daily, sometimes more than once a day, watching the various crews at work, making sure the various components of the lengthy construction project were perfect realizations of her vision. Barnett would also state that from the inception of the project, he invited participation and involvement by Perry. He sometimes called Perry's office to remind him of progress meetings. Perry attended no more than four or five meetings over the three-year duration of the project, and he rarely visited the job site. He made it clear to everyone involved in the construction: "This is Janet's project."

Apparently Janet and the Levines took Perry at his word.

As the project grew more and more expensive, the Levines loaned Janet a considerable sum. To secure their loan, they placed a mortgage of record against 3 Blackberry Road for $240,000. It did not require Perry's signature. He was not even listed as a co-owner of the property. The house was solely in Janet's name. Later the Levines would increase their real-estate loan to their daughter to $300,000.

One of the features of the house was an area that contained future living quarters for her parents, should their age or health necessitate such an arrangement. Janet never planned to live anywhere else.

In July 1995 the Marches moved into their five-thousand-square-foot home. Janet was able to enjoy her artistic creation for eleven months—less than half of the time she had spent overseeing its design and construction.

While many of the battles that would consume the lives of both the Levines and Perry centered around the disposition of Janet's estate and the issue of custody of Samson and Tzipora, the one thing that Larry Levine wanted most of all was the truth.

What really happened on the night of August 15, 1996?

Janet's father gets his first real opportunity to attempt to discover the truth on October 15, 1996, in a civil deposition held in Nashville in connection with visitation rights for his grandchildren.

Headlines the next day in the *Tennessean* read "Perry March Takes Fifth." The front-page article goes on to recite that when asked on various occasions if he was involved in the disappearance or death of his wife Janet, that under advice of counsel, Perry strongly denied any such involvement, but refused to answer certain questions as to particular details of what transpired on the night of August 15, relying on the constitutional privilege afforded all Americans not to incriminate themselves under the Bill of Rights.

The private war between Larry Levine and Perry March is now a very public one.

It will be a very long and contentious war, lasting an entire decade.

Just over a month later, Perry March is sworn in and placed under oath again for a deposition. For two long days, November 20 and 22, 1996, Larry Levine sits across the table from his son-in-law in the conference room in a downtown Nashville law office. Beside Perry are his brother, Ron, and Lionel Barrett, acting as Perry's legal counsel, at a deposition scheduled in the case of Janet Gail Levine March, Probate Case 96P-1702. Representing the Levines are Jon Jones, an attorney from Cookeville, Tennessee, about seventy miles east of Nashville, and Harris Gilbert, one of the most respected Jewish attorneys in Nashville—the attorney many said Perry most wanted to emulate. Larry Levine, Jon Jones, and Harris Gilbert are old friends and colleagues. All have been practicing law for decades and all are known to be tenacious in their questioning.

The questioning of Perry will end up lasting two days. As with many depositions, especially in important cases, not only does a court reporter take down every word that is spoken, but a video camera also tapes the entire deposition.

It is a videotaped appearance that Perry seems to almost

enjoy. He appears cocky and at times even arrogant. He is poised, never completely rattled by whatever is asked him, confident that he is the one in control.

Throughout the deposition, he uses his memory strategically—precise on some matters and sketchy on others.

At one point Jones asks, "Did you ever strike Janet?"

Jones considers Perry's demeanor, the haughty angle of his chin, the incredibly long pause before completing his answer.

"Mr. Jones, to the best of my recollection, I have never struck my wife," Perry says. "It has always been something that I am proud of. I never struck my wife."

His answers do not seem convincing to Jon Jones—or to Larry Levine.

After two grueling days of verbal combat, Perry and his brother leave together and begin to negotiate the heavy afternoon Nashville traffic. Perry feels he has performed well and that Larry Levine and his hired bulldogs, Jon Jones and Harris Gilbert, have not landed any punches. He feels confident about these two days that are now behind him.

Almost ten years later, on April 19, 2006, and again on August 11, 2006, Perry will be proven wrong.

In 2002, when the mysterious disappearance of Janet March is very old news, just another tragic case that the Nashville Police Department cannot seem to solve, the national media comes calling. The award-winning CBS television show *48 Hours* arrives in Nashville with all its microphones and cameras as part of what will become the first of four investigative pieces on the Janet March case that will air between 2002 and 2005. For CBS, the Janet and Perry March story has all the elements of a Shakespearean drama. Lesley Stahl announces to her national audience during one of the episodes, "I will say this is as good a mystery as you will ever see—in fiction or in real life."

"Mrs. Levine, please move closer to your husband."

The room is filled with cables and lights, crew members rushing around tending to last-minute details. There are so many people and the lights are so bright, Carolyn can barely catch her breath. It is like a small army has descended upon them. Yet she is poised. Anxious but brave. Larry is, as always, intense.

The pain on their faces is unmistakable, but they are committed to their cause. They are doing this for Janet.

People with less inner strength would have simply said no to the invitation of CBS News to appear on national television. It has now been six years since their daughter's mysterious disappearance. The police have never found any trace of her or her body. In fact, they have located no direct physical evidence that a crime had been committed on the night of August 15, 1996. The United States Supreme Court has rejected the Levines' final appeal in the multiyear custody battle with their former son-in-law over the March children. Carolyn and Larry fear they may never see their grandchildren again. They may lose them, as they've lost Janet, now that Sammy and Tzipi reside in Mexico with Perry and his new wife, Carmen.

Grief knows no calendar, not when a person's child disappears. There will surely be awkward and probing questions about why they did or did not do certain things. This is what television journalists do; they dissect people's lives in excruciating detail before a national audience of millions. It is like surgery without anesthesia. Yet the Levines know they must be here on this day. They have a message that they must convey, a message they will voice with each breath until there is justice.

Justice for Janet.

"Mr. Levine, do you think that Perry March is responsible for your daughter's disappearance?" correspondent Bill Lagattuta asks.

"Unconditionally positive."

"And this is the same person that you paid to go to law school, the same person you welcomed into your family, and the same person you welcomed into your law firm?"

Larry Levine pauses before replying. The camera zooms in on his tortured face. His eyes cannot hide the sadness that engulfs him. The last six years race across his memory at the speed of light, images of Janet and Perry, Sammy and Tzipi. This tough-as-nails attorney who is never at a loss for words in the courtroom can offer up only three in response to Lagattuta's probing question.

"Janet loved him."

CHAPTER 18

A Change of Jurisdictions

The front-page publicity following the intense two-day deposition in November 1996 convinces Perry that he cannot return to Nashville. The city that has been his home for his entire professional life, where all his clients are, where he was married, and where his two children were born is simply too tainted an environment for any kind of normal life.

Lawrence and Carolyn Levine have turned it into a battle zone.

His dream of opening an office and pursuing his own practice where he is the partner, not an associate, will never come about in Nashville. But he knows he's smart—so much smarter than the guys he's had to work for at Bass, Berry and at his father-in-law's firm—so why not just set up a new life here in Illinois? Maybe he could join his brother Ron's law practice. Perry realizes that the first step to making his new plan work is to secure all his files from the offices of Levine, Mattson, Orr, and Geracioti. But he can't simply stroll in and casually collect the voluminous product of years of legal work without placing himself in a position to be served with a court order regarding visitation with Sammy and Tzipi.

Levine, Mattson, Orr, and Geracioti is known within Nashville legal circles, especially among the younger attorneys in the city, as a place that has a generous income program for its associates. In most law firms, associates are paid a fixed annual salary and are assigned cases or matters within the firm from a collective client base that has been built and nurtured by the partners. In the Levine firm, however, an associate can earn additional income by means of a fee-splitting arrangement that encourages associates to bring new business to the firm. It is a design that seems to be a win-win situation for both the associate and the firm. Associates see the potential for more personal income and the firm's partners see the potential for participating in fees generated from new clients.

Yet the slope can become slippery when an associate elects to leave the firm. One would anticipate that since attorneys make their living preparing documents concerning disputes, the Levine firm would have a clear and workable written policy regarding the division of clients who have been brought into the firm by its associates. But Brian Brooks, a young associate with the Levine firm from 1980 to 1986, found the arrangement to be anything but workable.

For a variety of reasons, Brooks elected to form his own firm with some other young attorneys. To be sure that he could take the files with him that had been generated from clients he had brought to the firm, he followed a radical course. With the help of some friends, he entered the offices of the Levine firm in the middle of the night and cleared out his entire office, along with all his current files. When asked later why he felt forced to follow such a clandestine approach, Brooks replied, "I knew Larry Levine would change the locks on the doors and lock me out of my own office."

When Perry left Nashville in early September of 1996, he simply stopped coming into his office at Levine, Mattson, Orr, and Geracioti. Based upon the emotions that were swirling around the March and Levine families, the level of communication was not what would be considered the norm between members of the same law firm when personal issues force one of them to take an unexpected and extended absence. Superimposed on this awkward working environment was the fact that everyone in the firm not only knew Perry's wife was missing, with all the frightful implications that come with such a realization, but also that he had elected to leave the firm after being turned down for partner.

And while Perry had physically relocated himself to Illinois and was never to be seen again inside the offices of the Levine firm, he continued to work on legal matters for clients based in Nashville. Two in particular to whom he devoted time and energies in the late summer and fall of 1996 were his close personal friend and client, Elliott Greenberg, and his business client Paul Eichel.

Prior to Janet's disappearance on August 15, Elliott Greenberg had asked for Perry's legal assistance in the multimillion dollar sale of his family's business, Tennessee Mat Company. Over a period of several months, both pre- and post-August, Perry advised his friend and client about certain legal details surrounding the sale of the business for a price exceeding $20 million. Perry was not sending out monthly statements itemizing his hours of involvement, as is customary. Rather, the two friends had an understanding that when the sale was concluded on a basis acceptable to Greenberg, he would pay Perry an amount that they both thought was fair. That amount, which turned out to be twenty thousand dollars, was paid through two checks made payable directly to Perry, not to the firm, on October 8 and October 22, 1996, one for five thousand dollars and one for fifteen thousand dollars.

Paul Eichel, with his multiple business entities, was another Nashville client Perry continued to advise after relocating to Illinois. From time to time, Perry would send Eichel a statement or call up and tell Eichel's bookkeeper what amounts were due for various legal services rendered. Upon presentation of these written or oral invoices, Eichel approved the issuance of a check on October 8, 1996, for three thousand dollars.

As with the payment from Elliott Greenberg, this check was written to Perry March personally, and not to the firm.

As the humid days of a Nashville summer gave way to a cooler fall and then a crisp winter, the issues surrounding Perry's clients, his case files, and the fees he was due became more contentious. Perry formally demanded in writing the release of all his files from the law firm. A partner within the firm wrote to all of Perry's clients notifying them that Perry March was no longer a member of Levine, Mattson, Orr, and Geracioti and asking what fees, if any, they had paid Perry March directly. The issue of which fees Perry deserved was not going to be easily or quickly resolved. As 1996 rolled into 1997, it looked like the application of the fee-splitting arrangement for associates with the Levine firm would end up in a civil courtroom, with wealthy lawyers arguing over the spoils of their collective efforts.

Larry Levine, however, views the entire matter in a much different light. Based upon actions that he will later initiate, Perry's pressurized life is about to become much more complicated.

When Perry moves out of Tennessee with Sammy and Tzipi, the issues surrounding the visitation of their grandchildren by the Levines follows him to Illinois. Once a petition was before an Illinois court, the judge appoints Ralla Klepak as a guardian ad litem to represent the legal interests of Samson and Tzipora March, as they are both minors. Klepak, a veteran of the domestic relations courts in the Chicago area, frequently represents the interests of minor children in custody and visitation disputes. Her position as guardian ad litem means that she will from time to time meet with the children outside the presence of either their father or their grandparents. Given that Sammy, the elder, only turned six in August 1996, her discussions with the children are limited in their scope and depth, but one of the things that comes up in Klepak's discussion with Sammy is his memory of the events of August 15.

It is not uncommon for the written reports of a guardian ad litem to be filed directly with the judge overseeing the case, rather than first being presented to the parties themselves or their respective counsel. In the case of the March children, neither Perry nor the Levines knows exactly what the court is being told. Neither know that during their periodic interviews, Sammy talks with Klepak about his memories of the night his mother left.

Many years later the exact details of these discussions between a six-year-old child and his guardian ad litem would come to full light, and in the most dramatic of settings.

Perry is adamant in blaming the Nashville media for his decision to move to Illinois, yet when he wants to get his side of the story out to the world, he is not shy about inviting the media back into his life. On October 1, six weeks after Janet's disappearance, he grants a televised interview to Annette Nole Hall, a reporter with the NBC affiliate in Nashville, WSMV, in which he states, "Without a shred of evidence, the police and my in-laws have taken away my house, my livelihood, my community. But you'll see, I'll be vindicated."

In 1997 Perry's life in Illinois is not an easy one. He is in a dispute with his previous law firm over possession of legal files and division of fees, continues to battle his in-laws over their demands regarding his children, is embroiled in a separate dispute with the Levines over the disposition of the Blackberry Road property, and is attempting to make a new life in a new location.

And on top of all these pressures, he continues to be the main focus of a homicide investigation.

And yet Perry finds time to begin writing a novel. In fact, he asks his good Nashville friend Robert Heller, who maintained contact with Perry via e-mails and telephone calls, to critique it. One can only imagine that when Heller receives the first several chapters for review, he is stunned by its title and subject matter.

The name of Perry's novel is @*murder.com.*

The story involves the murder of Violet DiCoccio, a brilliant young dark-haired woman, who is extremely computer savvy, and who holds an important position with the Federal Reserve Bank. The novel opens with sights and sounds coming from a computer monitor inside Violet's apartment, her body lying on the carpet next to the desk chair in her study. The detective assigned to the case is Gideon Laval, a thirty-nine-year-old lieutenant, who is a veteran of dozens of homicide investigations.

Years later cold case detectives Postiglione and Pridemore will review in great detail the pages of @*murder.com* as part of their renewed homicide investigation of the Janet March case. These real-life detectives will find that many of the passages in the first thirty or so pages of the novel have an eerie familiarity.

The novel opens with the examination of Violet at the crime scene by Dr. Lars Almgren, chief deputy county coroner. Perry writes:

> Strangulation appears to be the obvious cause of death. Small diameter cord or rope. No skin break. No visible fibers evident on the outside of the wound that I see right now. No other signs of trauma or struggle. It looks like a very forceful and clean choke . . . Based upon the absence of any signs of struggle from the victim, and the clean line around the strangulation mark, I doubt she had but a few seconds to ever realize what was happening before her brain shut down.

On page eight, Perry describes how the murder victim in his novel is found at her apartment:

> Violet herself was lying on the smooth pile carpet, crumpled and soft-looking. She lay on her back, left leg tucked beneath her, head facing the ceiling, hands to her throat, eyes open and bulging. Classic strangulation expression . . . The subtle reek of decay was just starting to become apparent in the corridor outside the study. Textured on top of the

cadaverous stench, a more embarrassing smell loomed; Violet had spoiled [sic] herself and stained the carpet.

In 1992, just four years before Janet's disappearance, one of the top-grossing movies of the year was *Basic Instinct* starring Michael Douglas and Sharon Stone. Stone plays a character named Catherine Tramell, a novelist and a suspect in a murder that is eerily similar to one depicted in her current novel. Was it mere coincidence that in 1997 Perry was writing about the murder of a beautiful dark-haired woman while at the center of a homicide investigation of his wife, Janet, a beautiful dark-haired woman? Was it life imitating art? Or was it evidence of unbridled arrogance? Perry seemed to project a malicious joy in his arrogance, regardless of the setting.

It will not be the first time that Perry will display what appears to be a detachment from reality.

On page seven of his novel, Perry says of the principal detective, Gideon Laval: *This is Gideon's strength. He comes to befriend the victim, post-mortem.*

Those same words will apply equally to cold case detectives Postiglione and Pridemore.

Chapter 19

Absentee

By late 1996, everything concerning the house at 3 Blackberry Road had turned into a contentious nightmare.

For the Levines, Perry's abrupt relocation and his removal of Sammy and Tzipi from Nashville changed everything. After the October 15 deposition followed by two more days of grilling depositions in November, the dispute quickly became an all-out war.

Having someone accuse you of murdering their daughter will do that.

Of course it surely did not help when Perry screamed at Carolyn on the afternoon of September 10 as they walked to their respective cars after leaving the offices of Dr. Campbell: "Tell Larry I did not bury Janet in the backyard."

Larry Levine wanted to be sure his missing daughter's property was under the protection of the court—the property consisting primarily of the expansive home and surrounding acreage at 3 Blackberry Road, the house she had designed and labored over for almost two years, the house where Nashville police believed she had been murdered.

All states within the United States have probate laws that

set forth the rules and regulations regarding the disposition of someone's estate when he or she dies. Yet, in late 1996, there had been no determination that Janet was dead. The Levines were living in a legal purgatory. On the one hand, they held out hope that their daughter was still alive, lying in a hospital somewhere, possibly the victim of an accident, unable to communicate. On the other hand, based upon the pointed and direct questions they had posed to their son-in-law during the depositions and the legal maneuvers they were now pursuing, the Levines must have felt in their Shakespearean "heart of heart" that Janet was dead. After August 15, 1996, Larry Levine was being ruled by deep passions—a passion for truth and a passion for justice. At the same time he knew the courts would allow him to proceed with matters involving his daughter's property in a manner tempered by reason.

Janet and her dream home were also in their own purgatory, a legal one. She had not been declared dead, nor had it been determined that she was alive. But of course the legal system had faced this situation before, and it had created long ago a label, a term, a legal doorway through which matters, like those involving Janet's home and other property, must pass.

Janet was, under the law, an "absentee."

The legal definition of the word *absence* is "the state of being absent, removed, or away from one's domicile or usual place of residence." According to *Black's Law Dictionary*, "absence is of a fivefold kind: a necessary absence, a probable absence, a necessary and voluntary absence, an entirely voluntary absence, and an absence cum dolo et culpa (with grievous fault)."

Months had gone by. Janet was surely "away from usual place of residence." The house at 3 Blackberry Road was empty—there were no family dreams being pondered behind its majestic stone walls, no child's footsteps tapping down its wooden staircase, no beautiful art being created within its spacious rooms. Its mistress was gone.

For Janet's parents and for her children, her prolonged

absence was neither "necessary nor voluntary"; rather, it fell into the last of the five categories. Further on in the definition of *absence* in *Black's*, there is a separate subsection titled "Presumption of Death Created." When Janet did not attend Sammy's sixth birthday party of August 25 in Dragon Park, the party she had lovingly planned, her good friend and birthday guest Gabi Friedman would later tell *48 Hours*: "I knew Janet was dead. Because she would never, ever not come to her son's party."

In the core of his heart, Larry Levine must have known it, too. He had to protect what had been so central to Janet's life, 3 Blackberry Road. His grandchildren's future was at stake. An unexpected move by Perry forced his hand. On October 30, 1996, Perry filed in the probate court of Davidson County a Petition for Summary Relief seeking the transfer to him of two bank accounts totaling $4,770.19, held by the Union Planters Bank in the name of Janet Levine March. When the Levines learned of the Petition, they filed just a week later, on November 6, their own Intervening Petition arguing that Perry was not entitled to these funds because he may have been responsible for Janet's death, and they also asked that a conservator be appointed for their daughter's "absentee" estate. The judge presiding over the case was Frank G. Clement Jr., son of Frank G. Clement, who served as Tennessee's governor from 1953 to 1959 and again from 1963 to 1967. While Judge Clement bore an uncanny resemblance to his father, he had a much more temperate personality and did not possess his father's famous oratorical skills.

In January of 1997, Perry elected to take his own offensive approach in response to the Levines' probate filing and the court-ordered appointment of local attorney Jeffrey Mobley as conservator and/or permanent receiver for Janet Gail Levine March, Absentee. He filed a legal pleading with the probate court in Case 96P-1702. It reads as follows:

> Perry A. March, husband of Absentee, hereby claims an undivided interest, absolute and uncontested in all of the

Property of his wife, Absentee Janet Gail Levine March, including, but not by way of limitation, all real property, personal property, tangible property, intangible property, contingent or actual in nature and extent.

As Janet's husband, Perry was submitting his position that under the laws of Tennessee, their marriage "created an undivided interest among and between themselves in each other's property," and he wanted his full share. In the March marriage, at least as of August 15, 1996, the most valuable marital assets were not in their joint names, but rather in Janet's name only.

When Janet conceived her development plan for the Forest Hills tract, the deed from the sellers, J. J. Foley Jr. and wife, Harriet H. Foley, dated June 17, 1992, conveying the acreage in return for payment of $150,000, was not to Janet and Perry March as husband and wife, but was only in the name of Janet Levine March. However, just one year later, when Janet found a buyer for a portion of the acreage she had purchased and then developed into large estate lots, Perry, as Janet's husband, was reflected as a co-seller of Lot 1 to purchasers Stephen W. Ward and wife, Helen S. Ward, in consideration of their payment of $225,000.

In 1994, when Janet was ready to commence the construction of the house on Lot 2 of the property she had acquired in 1992, her parents made her a personal loan of $240,000. They protected their financial position by filing in the register's office of Davidson County, Tennessee, a deed of trust or mortgage putting the world on notice that they were the first lien holders against the property. In recognition of the fact that although their son-in-law's name was not on the deed to the property, he had a marital interest in the land and the house that was to be built upon it, the Levines made sure that Perry joined in the execution of the deed of trust. On August 31, 1995, the Levines filed an amended deed of trust documenting that they had increased their mortgage against the dream home project to $300,000.

Perry again joined in as a signatory to the legal instrument.

Perry's name had not been included on the deed of either of their two previous properties—neither the duplex near Vanderbilt University, nor the condominium in West Nashville. From 1989, with the gift of the duplex to its sale in 1991, and then the purchase of the condo in Harpeth Trace in 1991 and its sale on December 19, 1995, and then with the purchase of the Forest Hills property and the subsequent sale of a portion, there is nothing of public record that reflects that Perry invested any of his own money in any of their residences.

Yet he was determined to receive his marital interest in all of Janet's real-estate investments.

Recognizing that as first mortgage holders against the Blackberry Road property, the Levines were in a position of control, possibly even a position that trumped his marital interest, Perry took additional steps to protect his position. On March 17, 1997, he filed his own lawsuit in the chancery court of Davidson County, styled a "Complaint to Quiet Title to Real and Personal Property." The named defendant was Jeffrey Mobley, the local attorney who had been named as the conservator and receiver for Janet, or as she was now formally referred to, "Janet Gail Levine March, 'Absentee.'" Perry also filed in March of 1997 a *lien lis pendens* (a lien pending litigation). This legal instrument is specifically used to put the public on notice that there is a pending suit that may affect the title to the property against which the lien has been filed. To further clarify his position, Perry included in his *lien lis pendens* his position that the Levines were about to orchestrate what he felt was a fraudulent foreclosure sale against 3 Blackberry Road in their capacity as mortgage holders, in an attempt to unlawfully divest him of his marital interest.

Perry wanted to be sure that any prospective purchaser would know that on some basis they were going to have to deal with him before they received clear title to Janet's home.

Perry's legal tactics proved sufficient to encourage the Conservator Mobley to reach a settlement regarding the disposition of any proceeds generated from the sale of 3 Blackberry Road.

On June 12, 1997, Jeffrey Mobley executed a special warranty deed conveying to Roger A. Schecter and wife Carina Schecter the Blackberry Road property for which they paid $726,600. In return for a payment of $73,000 in monies and personal property, Perry released all his claims against Blackberry Road. The Levines' mortgage was paid in full, and after the deduction of all the costs, expenses, and legal fees that had been associated with the disputes regarding title and ownership, the sizable balance was tendered to the probate court to be held pending further orders of the court as to who was entitled to these remaining proceeds, with the interest of the two March children, Sammy and Tzipi, paramount in Judge Clement's mind.

Blackberry Road had a new mistress—a mistress who moved into a house where there may have been a murder.

CHAPTER 20

"They Are Kidnappers"

People say that children are resilient. Sammy and Tzipi March are poster children for resiliency.

By 2000, at ages nine and five respectively, Sammy and Tzipi have experienced the mysterious disappearance of their mother, a move to Illinois, a move to Mexico, a new language, and a new family—dramatic changes for their young lives to absorb.

Yet they appear genuinely happy. Their traumatic past has not impaired their performance at school. They are bilingual, and their excellent grades put them near the top of their respective classes. Sammy plays the cello and loves horseback riding. Tzipi takes ballet lessons.

"I have never seen them happier," their grandfather Arthur likes to say.

It has been a year since Perry brought Sammy and Tzipi to Ajijic, Mexico. Upon their arrival in the Lake Chapala region, Perry and the children moved into a spacious home with an attractive young Mexican woman, Carmen Rojas, and her three children. For twelve hundred American dollars a month, they are able to rent a house with bright tile floors, open terraces, large windows that let in the mild breezes, and a pool. The children can swim every day in this temperate region. They play in the water like little otters, splashing, laughing, showing off for Carmen's three small children, Daro, Thomas, and Cinty.

Ajijic is home to a large and ever-growing expatriate population, most of them Americans and Canadians. The expats are all attracted by the same thing: the ability to stretch their budgets. One can secure an extremely comfortable lifestyle at a reasonable cost. Retirees on pensions, like Arthur, can afford luxuries here that they could never afford in the States. As Arthur is fond of saying, "The sun is warm, the women are hot, and the beer is cold."

Within months of his arrival, Perry began to assemble a Mexican business conglomerate with Samuel Chavez, and they hit the business streets of the Lake Chapala region running. Together, March and Chavez undertake a series of business ventures, primarily directed at the wealthy and growing expatriate population of retired Americans and Europeans living in the Lake Chapala region. Their joint businesses included C & M Insurance, C & M Development, Chavez and March Legal and Financial Services, Guardian Security Services, Premier Properties, and PriMedical, seeking physicians and patients as investors, with a minimum investment of $1.25 million.

Business opportunities were not all that Perry March was seeking in Mexico. He needed a brand-new life, and with Carmen and her children, he had found it.

But the idyllic Mexican paradise that Perry had created for himself and his new family was about to be torn apart.

When Perry left Nashville behind in September of 1996 and relocated with his two children to Illinois, he barely escaped the implementation of a court-ordered grandparent visitation that was issued days earlier by a Davidson County, Tennessee, court. Denied their rightful visitation, the Levines quickly changed jurisdictions and filed a series of visitation-related petitions in the Illinois courts. Again they were awarded certain court-ordered visitation as the children's grandparents. However, Perry March did his best to obfuscate and impede the implementation of the court directives at every turn. The Levines were publicly accusing him of being responsible for their daughter's disappearance—or worse, her murder. From Perry's perspective, how could one realistically anticipate any civil dialogue during a series of court-ordered exchanges? The competing emotions that surrounded the central underlying connection between all these parties—Janet—were simply too strong; it was impossible to expect any effective pattern of orderly visitation.

Illinois was not far enough away; Perry's relocation did not remove him from the persistent inquiries and demands of the Levines. He was sure that a small historic village in the mountains of the Lake Chapala region of Mexico would prove different.

He was wrong.

After Perry's shocking flight to Mexico with their grandchildren in tow, the Levines did not remain idle. Larry Levine rarely remained idle. He geared up the pleading machine one more time. What he sought was a court order granting him and his wife visitation with Sammy and Tzipi. Larry Levine convinced a Cook County, Illinois, judge to award him and his wife an extended "grandparent visitation" of thirty-nine days. It was a "catch-up" visitation for months of missed weekends after Perry moved to Mexico.

The June morning in 2000 starts out like every other day in the land of eternal spring. Sammy and Tzipi are brightly dressed, groomed, and eager for another day at school. By nine a.m. they are seated in their classrooms at Oak Hill Academy.

Without any prior notice to their son-in-law, Larry, Carolyn, and Mark Levine fly to Mexico, in possession of a state court order granting them the thirty-nine-day visitation. They appear ex parte before the Mexican authorities and present the official document from the Cook County court.

The procedural strategy works.

The Mexican authorities accompany them to Sammy and Tzipi's school. The Levines have done their homework and know exactly where to go. After a discussion with the school authorities, arrangements are made for Sammy and Tzipi to be released to their maternal grandparents.

The two March children are taken from their classrooms and handed over to their grandparents, whom they have not seen for months. The children have to be bewildered by the events as they are unfolding. What about their father? What about their friends at school? What about their grandfather Arthur and their new stepmother, Carmen? When will they be coming back to Mexico? But the Levines have no intention of returning to Ajijic to secure clothes, toys, or other belongings. Their plan is to dash to the nearest airport and depart Mexico as quickly as possible.

During the hours of discussions with the Mexican court, the Mexican authorities, and the local school officials, word has somehow leaked about the arrival of the Levines into the country, and it filters back to Arthur March, who springs into action. A significant part of Arthur's background is his military service—thirty-two years in the United States Army. While he was at times stationed in various countries throughout the world, he never saw combat service, but this does not inhibit Arthur from projecting the bravado of an ex-military man. In fact, he prefers to be called "colonel," a rank he attained through his lengthy service in the reserves.

He knows the Levines will be leaving the country quickly. There is no time to find Perry. It's up to him to stop them from stealing his grandchildren.

Arthur grabs his pistol and races to the school, ready to do whatever should prove necessary to prevent his grandchildren from being ripped from their Mexican home. By the time he arrives, he is too late. The Levines have just left, and they have Sammy and Tzipi. Arthur knows they will try to leave the country immediately, and he must intercede. A race ensues through the back roads of the Mexican country-side. The Levines' car bounces along the poor roads at a high rate of speed, Carolyn clutching Sammy and Tzipi in her arms. Arthur is not far behind, forcing his vehicle to its maximum with only one goal in mind—rescuing Perry's children. Years later, Mark will recall the scene: "It was like a bad movie."

As their driver speeds toward Guadalajara, the Levines get a call from the FBI agent, who tells them Arthur has men waiting there for them. "Get out of the country any way you can," the agent says, "but whatever you do, do not go to the Guadalajara airport."

So the driver heads for Manzanillo, and soon the Levines, with Sammy and Tzipi, board a plane and lift off into the Mexican skies, beginning their long flight back to the United States. They would later publicly pronounce that on this day, "We thought Arthur March was going to kill us."

When they arrive back in Nashville, it is the first day of the Levines' court-sanctioned thirty-nine-day visitation with their two grandchildren. Yet it will be nearly a year before Sammy and Tzipi see their father—or Mexico—again.

Perry is in a rage over the unforeseen and unnerving events of the day. His hatred for the Levines contorts his face as he shouts, "They are kidnappers!"

CHAPTER 21

Sex, Lies, and Videotapes

When the Levines suddenly and unexpectedly take the children away, it's another reminder to Perry of how life can turn upside down in a blink of an eye. When his mother died, overnight a carefree little boy turned into a too-serious child burdened by sadness and loss. That was his first experience with heartbreaking tragedy, but he endured. He is, if anything, a survivor.

And he knows how suddenly fortunes change. Take, for example, the painful time in 1991. One day he was at the top of his game; the next, he was disgraced. But he survived. He held his own with the most prestigious law firm in Nashville—and he was able to leave unscathed despite the sexual harassment allegations by Leigh Reames. One thing he has learned about himself: he has a tremendous capacity to land on his feet.

Perry March's first job, right out of law school in 1988, is with Bass, Berry, and Sims. The hard work at Vanderbilt Law School has paid off. The American Jurisprudence award in his property-law class and his position as associ-

ate editor of the prestigious Law Review, *along with his excellent grades, have stood out on his résumé. And he knows he nailed the interview. He is smart and confident, and it shows. The night after the interview, he tells Janet, "I know I'll get an offer." Even his father-in-law is impressed when the news that Perry is hired becomes official.*

Perry knows his mother would have been proud of him.

Days start early *at Bass, Berry, and Sims. Everything has to be in its place. The well-crafted appearance must be maintained at all times. Unlike some law firms, where there is a discernible sense of at best organized chaos—phones ringing, messengers darting off to have important papers signed, attorneys heading to the elevator with ties askew, files sliding from their arms—Bass, Berry, and Sims conveys an overwhelming calmness, an air of confidence that is almost tangible. The walnut paneling is highly polished, the artwork properly illuminated, the Oriental rugs in perfect symmetry. This is the environment that offers an unspoken promise to each of hundreds of clients who come with their problems, pressing needs, and concerns: although the world may be a hostile place that can threaten the security of your business or financial interests, here at Bass, Berry, and Sims, we are never in a hurry. We can deal with any problem or crisis, for we have the talent, the knowledge, and the resources to resolve any issue. Put your confidence in us. If you have the money, we can solve any of your legal problems.*

At seven a.m. Perry looks up as his secretary opens his door. They exchange good mornings. She asks if he'd like coffee, but he's had two cups already. As usual, he's been in the office since six thirty. Every hour counts at Bass, Berry, and Sims, for every hour is a billable hour, and billable hours are the standard by which all associates are judged. The more billable hours, the more opportunity for a bonus at year end.

The secretary doesn't know much about her new boss, just that he is a graduate of Vanderbilt Law School, has an undergraduate degree from the University of Michigan, is married to the dark-haired beauty whose picture sits on his desk, and is Jewish. She has never worked for a Jewish attorney before. As she understands it, he is one of only two at Bass, Berry, and Sims, but the place is so big that she doesn't know much about the lawyers who work in other sections.

"Shut my door and hold all my calls," Perry says, without making eye contact. He has turned his attention back to the important-looking documents neatly arranged in stacks of varying heights on his desk.

As the secretary closes the heavy door, Perry slides a folded piece of paper across his highly polished desk into his middle drawer. He has a most curious smile on his face.

Perry reaches for *the tallest mountain of files on his desk. There are also stacks of files on his credenza and on the floor along one wall. Each pertains to a different corporate client, a different deal or dispute. He likes what he does, rubbing elbows with the region's rich and powerful business clients. He is now in his third year at Bass, Berry, and Sims, and things are going well at the office, and at home, too, most of the time. Janet's art and illustration work is catching on around town, and Perry adores their first child, Sammy. He loves having a son.*

He cannot imagine leaving his child, like his mother left his life when he was only nine.

People who knew him then would be surprised to see him today. He really has everything, yet there is a restless yearning in his soul, a craving for something else. There are times when he steps out of himself. Best to stay busy, he knows. He turns on his dictation machine and proceeds with what will be the first of at least twenty letters along with various legal pleadings he has to knock out that day. Bass, Berry, and Sims' corporate clients are demanding, but they pay well.

Ever since 1922, the firm has handled the business affairs of the most powerful and wealthy in the Nashville business community. It was within this storied tradition that Perry found himself when hired in 1988, fresh from graduation, as a young associate for the corporate law division. He had hit a home run with his first at bat.

By 1991, he would strike out.

"Why are you up *so early? It's pitch-black outside." Janet's voice—fuzzy and fussy—reminds Perry of the way Sammy whines when he's tired.*

"No earlier than usual," Perry says. "Go back to sleep."

"You leave at dawn and never get home before eight o'clock."

"Janet, you know I'm doing what is expected at the firm. I have to post a certain number of billable hours." He manages a patient, deliberate tone, masking the annoyance he feels. Janet, daughter of a powerful attorney, should know these things. Thoughts of her parents and the pressures associated with being Janet March's husband anchor him back in reality. "You know I would rather stay in bed with you." He leans over and plants a kiss on top of her head, his lips brushing her thick, dark hair.

"Don't wake Sammy," she says, still pouty.

Moments later, as Perry lets the shower's hot soothing water cascade over him, the delicious fantasies begin to excite him. It is not Janet that he's thinking about.

It starts off *almost as a game. Her fair complexion and her red hair are so different from anyone he has yearned for before. He begins to scribble romantic poems to her after work, but he doesn't have the courage to approach the young paralegal. He doesn't dare. He has a wife and a young son, and she has a husband, and while he is making an excellent salary, it costs a lot for them to live the lifestyle that is expected of an up-and-coming Jewish couple. He doesn't really have any substantial assets of his own. The real money comes from Janet's family. He simply can't risk jeopardizing the situation.*

But he can't stop. On some days, he steps into the firm's law library and there she is, doing research for one of the partners. The word around the firm is that she is very bright, but it is not only her intelligence that attracts him. He often finds himself totally distracted, staring at her between the rows of leather-bound books. Within seconds he has to alter his position within the stacks to hide the visible signs of his arousal.

Then he takes the leap. Something that expresses how much sexual passion he feels for her. Anonymous, of course. It's not what he wants, not what he feels, but it has to be that way—anonymous.

Perry types, barely able to keep up with the mental images that flood his brain. He pours out his heart to her— page after page. Finally, he folds the plain white paper and slips it into his center desk drawer. He slides it under a box of checks and other personal papers and then locks the drawer.

For three straight afternoons, he makes his way to the firm's library. It is the perfect cover. He is simply another enthusiastic associate verifying the law for his important clients. Finally, on the third day, she comes in. He can smell her perfume from across the room. He stares at his files and does not make eye contact. She doesn't even know he is present. There are at least eight others in the library, several associates and several law clerks, all male. It is perfect. She will never know who left her the note. After a few moments, she rises from her desk and disappears into the endless rows of books. Briskly, he walks over, reaches for the folded note inside his right front pocket, brings it to his lips, and kisses it. He leaves the letter and is out of the library, back to his office, in a flash.

It will be another hour before she is ready to leave. Gathering up her research and papers, she finds the note. She furrows her brow as she reaches for the stark white paper and unfolds it. She begins to read the typed words:

"I want to inhale the essence of you." She refolds the note, and then reopens it and forces herself to read on: "The pure animal sexiness of your body grips me," she reads silently. "If I were granted a single wish in life, I would not hesitate for that to be to devour you . . ." When the note be-

gins to describe in the lewdest of details Perry's fantasies of
oral sex, she shrieks, flinging the note to the floor. A chill
runs down her spine for a moment, as if she has been groped
in her sleep. For a brief moment, she wants to vomit.

It takes a while before she can even touch the note again,
but finally she composes herself and stoops to pick it up. She
will need it for evidence.

At exactly nine the next morning, she appeals to the managing partner's secretary to interrupt his already-busy morning. Perhaps it's the dark circles under her eyes. Perhaps it's
her shaky voice. Something convinces the secretary that her
boss needs to hear what this young woman has to say, and
he needs to hear it now.

It is a first for the firm. Sure, there have been rumors of
liaisons, even affairs. When young, bright, intense profes-
sionals are thrown in with other young, bright, intense pro-
fessionals for eight to ten hours a day, things can happen.
But never the possibility of a sexual harassment claim. It is
simply not an option at Bass, Berry, and Sims. A slight crack
begins to form within the wall of calmness. The managing
partner knows that this has to be handled exactly right. One
of their own has become a client. Or has she? A plan is conceived.

Perry forces himself to wait nearly two weeks after the first
letter on July 19 before composing the next anonymous note.
She has not approached him. There is no indication that she
has a clue who her silent admirer is.

Perry knows he should let it go, but he can't. He thinks
about her constantly. Every morning in the shower he sees
her face and then slowly undresses her in his mind, working
his way down her body until he arrives at the moment of release. He has forced himself to wait as long as he agreed;
now he has to communicate with her again. Even though he
now knows in his heart it is over, he can't fully admit defeat.
He needs his fix. Sitting alone late at night in his office, he
begins to type.

The note, again typed on his computer and printed on

nondescript plain white paper, is part apology, part good-bye, part hopeful wish:

> *The purple was so vibrant, I wanted to reach out and touch it; the look in your eyes was conclusive. I am so sorry for your decision, and for disturbing you. I am sad and embarrassed. I am gone, but if ever you should reconsider or wish to communicate, then check out from the library the Tax Management Estates, Gifts, and Trusts Portfolio #134-4th titled "Annuities" . . . When you check it out, insert a library check out card, signed by you in its place. I will periodically notice if it is gone. If so, I will contact you to let you know how to reach me, anonymously.*

This second letter to his lovely fantasy lover is only twenty-five lines, but it offers a broad window into the mind of Perry March. When dealing with others, his words always seem to be dripping with sincerity, wrapped in an eloquence that somehow elevates their impact. Yet at the same time he is always holding back, cautious, unable to be completely truthful.

> *One final thing . . . before I leave you forever. I have thought long and hard about this, but I decided I must tell you this in order to be fair to you and the others who have been affected by this selfish act of mine. A number of "facts" contained in my prior letter were intentionally false. I did this to keep my secret better, but now realize that your "short list" of candidates is probably a list you will never truly trust or be easy with.*

Days pass and then for Perry the unthinkable occurs. The library card with her name on it is there. Exactly as he had instructed. He can barely contain his excitement, his lust. He hurriedly composes a third letter. It begins in the same deeply romantic vein as the first, yet the tone is reminiscent of a love-struck teenager, afraid to approach a beautiful cheerleader about the upcoming prom:

I can barely type this. My hands are unsteady, and my thoughts are whirling in a maelstrom of emotions. I wonder if you realize the impact of your simple message. I felt as if my heart stopped beating . . . I feel like the lucky leprechaun who has seen the rainbow and knows what lays beyond . . . You have acknowledged me! I feel like a puppy whose master has come home to play.

The letter quickly turns lustful:

The thought of my tongue buried within you excites me more than anything else in the world . . . to taste you is my day dream . . . never has a woman so occupied my mind, never have I longed to be with someone this much.

It is after seven thirty p.m. and everyone in his section has already called it a day. By the time he gets to the third page, Perry is so aroused, he can barely stand it.

Again he folds his composition in half and places it inside his locked middle drawer. Now for the right moment.

The right moment presents itself the very next day. Again the office library is the perfect place. Perry walks among the other office workers, all preoccupied with their own tasks, briefly pausing to pull down a volume to give the appearance of a dedicated researcher. He sees the paralegal, Leigh Reames, in the corner of the library, deep in the stacks, concentrating and oblivious to his presence, her briefcase and purse atop one of the worktables all the way across the room. He makes his way to her abandoned workstation and leaves his third letter.

This time when Perry makes his move, Big Brother is watching. The firm has hired a security company, which has installed secret cameras in strategic locations. After the delivery of the third anonymous note, they have him—right there on videotape—each furtive movement as Perry March leaves the anonymous note, with a strange, wild look in his eyes.

•   •   •

The end comes quickly. Perry March is forced to resign. He agrees to a financial settlement with Leigh Reames, the terms of which will not come to light until five years later, after Janet's disappearance. Bass, Berry, and Sims makes the calculated decision not to report their young associate to the authorities. They will not have to publicly admit that even with their careful and deliberate hiring practices, they could have made such a serious misjudgment in hiring Perry March.

Even with the written settlement of the matter, couched in the best legal provisions the city's legal talent has to offer, it will not be the last time Perry composes a letter to this beautiful woman at the center of his sexual fantasies. But this letter has a different purpose, and it is also addressed to her husband:

> *I am sorry for the delay, but I now can give you a firm pay-off date. I am establishing my own firm, and have financing in place to cover your outstanding obligation. I will pay you, in full, on or before October 1. Cash flow is tight right now as my expenses are building for this, but I will also pay as much as possible before the final payment.*
>
> *I need a pay-off number from you, assuming an October 1 payment date. Please calculate what you believe I owe in principal, interest and penalty, and indicate your willingness to accept it in full satisfaction of my obligation to you. Please reaffirm your obligation of continuing confidentiality, as well. Please send this information to my office, marked "Personal & Confidential."*
>
> *Thank you.*

This letter is dated August 13, 1996, two days before Janet March's disappearance.

CHAPTER 22

Right Person, Wrong Theory

In mid-2004, as Postiglione and Pridemore sit down inside a conference room in the district attorney's office to once again labor over the seven volumes of police files that make up the March investigation, the lyrics from Bob Seger's rock-and-roll classic "Night Moves" seem close to describing their situation: "working on mysteries without any clues."

Perry March has been the only viable suspect in Janet's disappearance since as early as mid-September 1996. From the perspective of the police, no other person has ever entered into the "orbit of opportunity." Yet these two homicide veterans know that the worst thing they could do as they attempt to establish a case that Deputy District Attorney Tom Thurman deems worthy of prosecuting is to have the right person but the wrong theory as to how the crime occurred. They have both sat through too many trials and witnessed too many jurors latch on to discrepancies in a prosecutor's case and return with a hung jury or—even worse—an acquittal. They have to be sure the proof introduced at trial paints the most logical theory of the criminal events in ques-

tion, a theory they can support with the most consistent line
of evidence.

Thurman and his two cold case detectives know that after
eight years, time is running out. With so many years elapsed
since the date of the crime, witnesses' memories are fading
fast. All a good criminal defense attorney needs is just
enough of an evidentiary blur to create reasonable doubt in
the minds of a few jurors. Without a body, the prosecution
must work with what they have—what is contained inside
these seven bulging three-ring binders filled with endless reports, witness statements, and the dozens of leads that to
date have not panned out.

In 2004 the prosecution team has no way of knowing that
scores of new pages of evidentiary matters are yet to be written in the March case. For now all they can do is go through
the voluminous paperwork one more time.

Start, once again, at the beginning.

It is like building a house—the whole structure has to be
built upon a solid foundation. Postiglione and Pridemore decide to see just how strong their foundation is.

Some issues in their investigation are beyond dispute.
Janet and Perry were having marital problems. The detectives have the testimony of Janet's parents, brother, and
friends, and, if necessary, they can elicit the expert opinion
of Dr. Campbell, the psychiatrist of record. They have the
information taken down by Detective David Miller on
August 29 when Janet was reported missing.

Pridemore opens up volume I and finds the initial offense
report. At line forty-two, under "Possible Cause of Absence,"
it reads "Domestic." Adjusting his reading glasses, the detective turns to page two and tells his partner, "Listen to
this." Postiglione looks up from across the long conference
table filled with dirty cups and half-eaten sandwiches.
Pridemore reads aloud the first few sentences of the narrative conveyed on that date:

Victim and her husband have recently been having domestic
problems. Victim asked her husband to move out and he

complied. An attempted reconciliation was made and the victim told her husband that she was going on an extended vacation.

At the very end of the narrative, the home and work numbers for Jimmy Lawson appear with the notation "former boyfriend." The police have left no stone unturned. In a macabre twist, Mr. Lawson's business was Lawson's Ready-Mix, a concrete-pouring company. The Nashville police spent hundreds of man-hours examining construction sites around the city where fresh concrete had been poured within a few weeks of August 15, 1996. It was most likely that Mr. Lawson's company provided some of the fresh concrete to construction sites police searched for Janet's body.

"What do you make of the reference in the offense report to her former boyfriend, Jimmy Lawson?" Pridemore asks.

"I think it was intentionally planted by March for effect," Postiglione says, without hesitating. "There's nothing to it. Just something else to raise doubt or give some credence that she left intentionally."

"Yeah, but there's nothing in the files that Larry Levine objected to that being made part of the official report or that he thought it was contrived."

Perry's own statement given to police a few weeks later further acknowledges the marital disharmony.

Pridemore flips through the pages of the first volume until he is staring at Perry's six-page handwritten statement given to the police on September 10, 1996. Appearing immediately behind Perry's statement is the report from a handwriting expert and analyst from Arizona that Detective David Miller elected to consult with. Although the cold case detectives have been over the report several times before, Pridemore begins to read to his partner the opening paragraph from the analysis one more time:

Deceptive people put more at the beginning than they do at the end of a statement. His subjective time is off. There are 147 lines in his statement. Before the incident he has 69 lines. During the main issue he has 43 lines, and after the incident he has 35 lines.

Pridemore stops and looks up, "Do you buy this report?"

"I think they know what they are doing," Postiglione says.

The analyst has numbered each line of Perry's statement and offered a line-by-line analysis. Pridemore runs his finger down the numbered lines and reads aloud from the ones he finds especially revealing:

"After I put the kids to bed, she wanted to discuss our issues."

Discuss = unpleasant conversation, it is a very harsh word . . . indicates he did not want to discuss it at all.

"She became upset and said I wasn't trying very hard, so maybe I should go to the Hampton Inn again. I stayed calm. I told her I needed to know if she wanted me to go or if she didn't. She said go."

He makes a point to say he remained calm. I would say that is very untrue . . . they were in a very heated argument. Janet obviously wants him to leave and he doesn't want to go.

"I got up, went to the phone and reserved a room at the Hampton Inn with my credit card, guaranteed. When I hung up, she became very upset and said no more vacations on my time with our money."

They have been arguing about him wasting their money.

"She came down a while later with her small bags . . . she said something like 'your turn, see ya' and left and drove off."

If you notice throughout this section he is just saying what she said. He does not tell us at all about what he said or what he is doing. He is coming up with this story if I had to guess.

"Janet had left like this before, so we settled down to wait . . . I went upstairs. I took my son to the toilet and I checked on my daughter."

He has referred to "the kids" the whole statement and he changes his language to "my kids." "My kids" shows possession that the kids are just his kids now. I think he changes his language because he knows Janet will never be back.

"It will all depend on whether March takes the stand," Postiglione says.

"I can't see him taking that risk," says Pridemore.

"Normally I would agree with you, but with this jerk—" Postiglione shakes his head. "He's such an egomaniac, he'll want to be in the limelight at every turn."

"I hope the SOB gets the chance."

The veteran detectives believe that the fact that the couple was experiencing money problems will be beyond dispute. Although it is clear from the public records that Janet's parents had loaned her $300,000 toward the cost of the construction of the Blackberry Road dream home, and Perry was engaged in an active legal practice from which he earned an excellent income, cash flow seemed to be a genuine issue in August of 1996.

Pridemore again flips through the pages of the voluminous case files. After a few minutes, he huffs to his partner, a little frustrated: "Where did Terry put the copy of the school check?" The files had already been compiled when Pridemore and Postiglione were asked to take over the investigation. Detective Terry McElroy was in charge of organizing them. The detectives know the case files are not as organized as they would like them or that Prosecutor Thurman will demand they be for trial.

In the spring of 2006, McElroy will die from an apparent heart attack, not long before the March case comes to trial.

For weeks after his death, McElroy's office will remain just as it was, with papers all over the place and with the March case files in a state of documentary limbo because other detectives are hesitant to go in and reassemble the evidence books.

Finally, Pridemore comes across the photocopy of the bounced check to the University School of Nashville. It was written on the account of Janet March at Union Planters Bank on July 22, 1996, in the amount of $3,446.86 and noted "Samson" in the lower left corner. Even though Janet's checking account was not a joint account, the check was signed by Perry in his unique but illegible scrawl. All the checks that make it into the evidence book are from Janet's account. It seems when it came to family funds, Perry had no account of his own. Everything ran through Janet's account. That this could be a point of contention would not be hard to fathom.

Either the check was not mailed to the school for several weeks after it was written, or the school held the check for an extended time before depositing it. The bank had refused to honor the check to University School once before Janet disappeared, and then again after her disappearance. The processing dates on the back of the bounced check jump off the page like bookends enclosing Janet's final days.

And then there is Perry's typed letter to Leigh Reames and her husband dated August 13 asking for more time in which to pay the amounts due from the sexual harassment claim at Bass, Berry, and Sims.

Cash flow within the March household was clearly a problem.

There is also no dispute that when the police searched 3 Blackberry Road pursuant to the search warrant issued on September 17, the hard drive of the couple's home computer had been ripped out.

But does this mean there had been a murder?

Or was it a husband trying to be sure others did not find out about the Reames sexual harassment settlement and his letter of August 13 asking for more time?

Any introduction of testimony about the missing hard drive will open up its own can of worms for the prosecution. The evidence would most logically be presented to the jury through the lead detective at the time, Detective David Miller. Thurman knows it will invariably come out during cross-examination that Miller had called Perry's attorney, Lionel Barrett, and informed him in advance of the search warrant. As a criminal prosecutor, Thurman knows it will be an awkward stumbling block at trial he should not have to deal with.

The delay of two weeks in reporting Janet missing, combined with Miller's call to Lionel Barrett have so far proved such an impediment to a fresh review of any crime-scene evidence that some within the prosecution team say the March case will never make it to the courtroom.

Pridemore changes directions.

"What about the call coming in from Belle Meade about seeing him throw a rug in the Dumpster around the fifteenth? Should we interview that witness again?" he ponders out loud.

On March 15, 2001, Nashville police received a call from Mary Gorham indicating that around the time of August 15, 1996, she witnessed a man pushing a rolled-up Oriental rug into a Dumpster near the Corner Market, a location that would have been within just a few miles of the Blackberry Road address. Gorham went on to state that she spoke to the man (whom she would later identify as Perry March, after being shown his photograph among several other photographs of white males about his same age) who told her that the family dog had died and was inside the rug and to not go near it. The informant went on to recount that she had occasion to return to the Dumpster approximately three hours later and noticed that the rolled-up rug was gone, but that the man was still sitting inside his car just to one side of the Dumpster, as if guarding it.

As much as the two detectives want to tie their suspect to a rolled-up Oriental rug, especially in light of Marissa Moody's statement that she saw Sammy bouncing up and down on a rug on the morning of the sixteenth, and that it was not there when she returned that afternoon, they just don't find the witness's testimony credible. First, with all the media attention that surrounded Janet's disappearance in 1996, why would a witness wait until 2001 to contact police with such potentially critical information? And if Perry was indeed using the city's waste collection to dispose of a body, does it make any sense at all that he would remain by the Dumpster for three hours with his wife's body inside it?

Mary Gorham was not the only Nashvillian to express a belief in the theory that Perry used a nearby Dumpster to dispose of Janet's body. After years in which police were unable to locate her remains, it became frequent cocktail-party talk for armchair detectives to espouse their own theories of what happened to the beautiful young artist. One proposition that seemed to become a kind of grassroots movement across Music City was that Perry did place Janet's body in a Dumpster, knowing that it would end up at the thermal plant in downtown Nashville, located only a few blocks from his law office at Levine, Mattson, Orr, and Geracioti. The thermal plant facility received a portion of the city's garbage, which was then burned to generate energy to provide heat for downtown office buildings.

The theory's implication that Janet's remains were incinerated as part of the energy source that then heated the offices of her murderer, as well as those of the police who were unable to find her, took on its own Hitchcockian mythology.

While the cold case detectives give no credibility to the statement of the alleged Dumpster eyewitness, the most explosive evidence they plan to offer about the events of those late-night hours at the West Nashville apartment complex is the eyewitness testimony of Peter Rodman when he reached his apartment from a late arrival of his United Airlines flight—that he saw a man with an expression "like a squirrel that didn't know which tire to run under," pushing a bicycle at around 1:20 a.m. on the morning of August 16. Rodman stated that he was 90 percent sure the man was

Perry March. The detectives are convinced that this eyewitness was indeed telling the truth, because at the time Rodman approached Detective Mike Smith with his story, it had not come out in the media that Perry was an avid cyclist.

The detectives believe it is quite feasible for Perry to have driven Janet's Volvo 850 sedan to the Brixworth Apartments late in the night of August 15, carrying along his mountain bike in the front passenger seat for a midnight bike ride back to Blackberry Road. On that issue, the detectives feel confident in their ability to provide Tom Thurman with evidence a jury would understand.

And then there is the evidence about Perry purchasing four new tires for his Jeep Cherokee just six days after his wife's disappearance—a task he would later tell the media was accomplished only because it was on the to-do list Janet left for him before she departed on her alleged twelve-day vacation—a position Tom Thurman can easily refute by introducing at trial the actual to-do list, which omitted any reference to new tires.

Pridemore closes one volume and grabs another. "What about the FBI reports?"

"Helpful but not conclusive," says Postiglione.

The Nashville police sent a series of fiber and other microscopic evidence to the FBI lab in Washington for analysis early on in the March case. Depending on whom you asked in the department, the result ranged from good to weak. At the time of the consent search of both of the March vehicles, Janet's Volvo 850 and Perry's Jeep Cherokee, crime-scene investigators removed carpet fibers from the trunk of the Cherokee. The FBI lab test on the fibers demonstrated that they were compatible with fibers found in carpets. Even the colors of the fibers—blue, gray, red, orange, pink, and off-white—would coincide with the dark colors of the Oriental rug seen by Marissa Moody. Yet the strength of the FBI analysis stopped there. The FBI forensic analyst could not testify that the fibers they examined came from "the" Oriental rug because it was never located. In fact, it could not be demonstrated that the fibers came from anywhere within the March home.

The forensic testimony could not be elevated to a degree of certainty that allowed for a very strong building block. The detectives can only hope that the cumulative effect of the evidence will win the day in the end.

What have eight years of police investigation really produced?

First, that a couple was having domestic problems and had a stormy argument. Second, that this same couple was having financial difficulties. Neither scenario was a particularly unique occurrence in Nashville or any other American city. Third, that a husband had written sexually explicit letters anonymously to a coworker. Was that in and of itself even a crime? It had never extended to an extramarital affair, and if it had, that, too, would not have been a crime. Fourth, that a man decided to buy a new set of tires while his wife was allegedly away on vacation. Again, probably not an uncommon occurrence. Fifth, that carpet fibers were found in the trunk of the suspect's vehicle, but fibers that can't be matched to any other possession of the suspect or victim. A circumstantial evidentiary component at best. Sixth, that a man who resembled Perry March was seen riding a bicycle in the middle of the night near the same location where his wife's car was found two weeks after she was reported missing, and that a mountain bike could fit inside a Volvo 850 if its front wheel was removed. Possibly very pivotal evidence—if a jury finds Peter Rodman believable.

But what did the police not have in this case?

No evidence that a crime was even committed inside 3 Blackberry Road. No blood or other DNA evidence. And most important, no body.

As for right person, wrong theory—without a body, the presentation of any theory would be almost entirely circumstantial. Thurman is still convinced that the answers to the Janet March mystery lie with Perry's connection to his former client, Paul Eichel, even though the investigative pressure applied over the last two years to the family members of Eichel and those peripherally connected to him has produced nothing definitively connected to the case. Yet, as the end of 2004 is fast approaching, the prosecutor has no solid evidentiary building blocks that establish his theory.

When asked about whether they agree with Thurman's assessment of what happened to the body of Janet March, the cold case detectives are quick to say they have the greatest respect for the man they have worked with on many of Nashville's most high-profile cases. They say, "Deputy District Attorney Thurman and his office try the cases, and we investigate them. If we don't agree on something, we discuss it and end up resolving the issue."

So they keep working, keep hammering out the issues.

After eight years with the Janet March investigation as an open case, all the principal evidence the DA's office has to work with is evidence that they knew about in 1996, or at least by early 1997. The other seven and a half years have not produced anything that is going to be the smoking gun, or even close to it.

Although they will not admit it publicly, Postiglione and Pridemore know they have a marginal case at best. They need a miracle.

In 2005 they will receive one, and from the most unlikely source.

CHAPTER 23

A Midnight Bike Ride

After weeks of reassessing the voluminous files and going over countless reports and statements, Postiglione and Pridemore both realize that the best they can hope for at this juncture, eight years after Janet March's disappearance, is a circumstantial case. It's time to get realistic about finding the body. Contrary to their assessment, Deputy District Attorney Tom Thurman, the prosecutor in the DA's office spearheading the case, still believes that if the cold case detectives will press hard and reanalyze every one of the hundreds of leads and witness statements, something will break in their favor, and they will be able to locate Janet's body.

Or what is left of it.

Publicly the authorities follow the party line with all unsolved criminal cases, the same position that their captain, Mickey Miller, adopted when interviewed by the *Tennessean* for its article of February 25, 2001, on the twenty-sixth anniversary of the disappearance of nine-year-old Marcia Trimble: "Somebody, somewhere out there, knows something that could help us. It could seem to be such simple information that they haven't thought it was worth mentioning. But it could be. Call us."

With the March case, cold case detectives Postiglione and Pridemore aren't so confident.

Before they took over the investigation, their predecessors had completely written off the March estate in Forest Hills. Postiglione and Pridemore concurred. With the search in September of 1996, the department had pulled out all the stops—cadaver dogs, helicopters with heat-seeking radar, and scores of police recruits combing every square foot outside, while a team of their best forensic investigators, led by Sergeant Johnnie Hunter, analyzed every inch inside.

The bottom line—and they knew it when they were assigned this case—is that too much time had elapsed between August 15 and the date Janet was reported missing, August 29. Two full weeks to dispose of a body, alter the crime scene, and clean up evidence.

If only Janet's family had not waited fourteen days to report her missing.

The delay may prove to be an insurmountable obstacle in their investigation.

Postiglione, whenever asked by the media about the status of the March case, always has the same response: "You go where the evidence leads you." And for the two veteran detectives the evidence leads to Perry—at least by the process of elimination. In over eight years of police investigation, admittedly eight disjointed years with three different lead detectives (David Miller, Tim Mason, and Brad Corcoran), no one else has entered into the *orbit of opportunity* as a possible suspect. Perry admitted that he and his wife argued on the night of August 15 and that they had been having marital problems for quite some time. In his lengthy handwritten statement tendered to police on September 10, he did not offer up any other name. He did not allege that his wife was having an affair or that she had planned a trip with one of her many girlfriends. He said, simply, that she left.

Experienced investigators know that in the disappearance of a wife, the husband is always the first suspect. He is the

one person with whom the victim has the most daily interaction—the greatest opportunity for conflict. Experienced
homicide investigators also know that murders happen for
one of two reasons—sex or money.

In this case, Postiglione and Pridemore speculate that it
may have been both.

The detectives believe that Janet may have come upon a
copy of Perry's typewritten letter to Leigh Reames dated just
two days earlier, asking for more time to pay the balance of
the monies he owed in settlement of a sexual harassment
claim. Janet may have pressed Perry for the details and an
argument may have quickly ensued. And this would have
occurred just a day after Sammy's tuition check to
University School of Nashville, Janet's alma mater, in the
amount of $3,446.86, bounced, just after the confrontation
the couple had about that embarrassing development.

With no one else inside the *orbit of opportunity,* they concentrate all their efforts on making a case that will stick
against Perry.

One thing they feel unwavering about is that if Perry
murdered his wife on the night of August 15, he had to have
moved her Volvo sedan before their two young children
awoke on the morning of the sixteenth.

They set out to be sure they could prove in court just how
he could have accomplished such a gutsy maneuver. They
personally drive and also have a patrolman bike several alternative routes from 3 Blackberry Road to the Brixworth
Apartments and conclude that 4.8 miles is a fair estimate of
the distance Perry would have to travel in each direction on
that night. Postiglione and Pridemore reject any route via
Belle Meade Boulevard, as it is a large divided four-lane
roadway, constantly patrolled by the Belle Meade police.
Being a police officer in the exclusive city of Belle Meade
usually did not provide much in the way of criminal activity,
so catching speeders along "the Boulevard," as it is referred
to in Nashville, is a major part of the patrolmen's daily activities in the tiny city, which Perry would have known.

The detectives believe instead that he continued along

Lynwood, then made a turn to the right and went down the hill through a portion of the residential sections of the Green Hills community. On this route, Perry would have come within a block or two of where the body of Marcia Trimble had been found, just down the street from her own Green Hills home on Copeland Avenue.

The footprints of Nashville's two most notorious criminal cases had crisscrossed on this August night.

After continuing on several more blocks toward Ensworth School, he would have ended up at the back, and much more private, entrance of Brixworth.

But why the Brixworth Apartments? The detectives speculate that it was one of the few places within a five-mile radius where he could park a car along with scores of other ones and its sudden appearance would not seem out of place. It was a location used by dozens of other people, but unlike a commercial shopping center such as Belle Meade Plaza or a grocery store like the Belle Meade Kroger, at Brixworth it would not seem strange for someone to drive into the parking lot as late as midnight or after.

The detectives wonder: Did Perry have some prior connection to Brixworth? What may have planted the seed in his head in the predawn hours of August 16?

It would have been a safe bet that by midnight on August 15, the Nashvillians who resided in the refined neighborhoods of Forest Hills, Belle Meade, and Green Hills were fast asleep in their comfortable beds, dreaming of their Saturday plans at the country club, the golf course, or the spa.

Yet at the Brixworth Apartments, which was positioned on the edge of one of the nicer sections of Nashville, its residents were more middle-class folks, like Peter Rodman.

Rodman was just arriving home after working a flight to Nashville as a flight steward from United Airlines. It was 1:20 on the morning of the sixteenth before he finally made it home. It had been a very long day and he just wanted to get some sleep. He didn't expect to encounter anyone out at this time of night, especially a guy pushing a bicycle.

Detective Mike Smith's report, filed in early February 1997, just one of hundreds of reports buried inside the thousands of pages that made up the multivolume March case file that Postiglione and Pridemore inherited in 2000, sets out the facts.

The previous evening, Smith had crossed paths with Rodman at the bar at the Sunset Grill. One of Nashville's most popular eateries, Sunset Grill is just down the street from the Bound'ry, where Janet spent her last girls' night out on August 13, and only a block or two from Fannie Mae Dees Park, where Sammy's sixth birthday party was held on August 27.

On this crisp February night in 1997, Mike Smith just wanted to enjoy a few drinks or a late dinner among some of the city's beautiful people. Peter Rodman was probably there for the exact same reason. Before becoming an airline steward, Rodman had had a career within the broadly woven tapestry that is the entertainment scene in Music City. He had a radio show in Nashville on Lightning 100, a combination entertainment/political talk show. During that time, Smith and Rodman had crossed paths, so when Rodman saw Smith across the bar, he made his way through the maze of patrons in his direction.

"Listen, Mike, I need to talk you. I read that article in the *Scene* about the Janet March case," Rodman said, his eyes wide behind his glasses.

In an investigative piece with just the right mix of meticulous details and gossipy rumors, Willy Stern's two-part story, "A Good Thing Gone Bad," which ran on January sixteenth and twenty-third, and later went on to win first place feature story in the Alternative Newsweekly Awards, took the entire city deep inside the March case.

Stern had obviously had some sources close to the investigation. One prominent source was David Miller, who had headed the March investigation from its inception. But the second installment of Stern's series in the *Scene* was prefaced with a lengthy editor's note: "On the morning after the [first] *Scene* article appeared, Metro homicide detective

David Miller was relieved of his responsibilities as chief investigator on the March case." The note continued: "Even while he was heading the March investigation . . . Miller was responsible for a heavy case load. During the month of December, with the March investigation still under way, Miller was assigned to the eleven thirty p.m. to eight a.m. 'graveyard shift,' a schedule that made it even more difficult to investigate an already difficult case." Miller was credited with overseeing 1,244 missing persons cases in Davidson County in 1996, with only one unsolved case—Janet March. Finally, the editor's note said, "Numerous sources close to the Police Department say the department is particularly sensitive about the intense publicity surrounding the March case. The same sources say that Miller has been used as a scapegoat by department officials, who have little hope of solving a virtually insolvable case."

It would be the fallout from his cooperation with Stern, along with his earlier unexplained call to Perry's attorney, Lionel Barrett, before the issuance of the September 17 search warrant for Blackberry Road, that would precipitate the removal of David Miller as lead detective from the March case.

The picture of Perry that had appeared as part of the piece had jumped out at Rodman. He had seen that face before. He told Smith that he'd seen Perry at his apartment complex the night Janet disappeared.

Smith took a minute to let this sink in, wanting to get it right. "I was called to the Brixworth the day the car was discovered," he said. "I canvassed a lot of the residents, but I don't remember you."

"I'm gone a lot. I fly with United Airlines, and I'm gone for days at a time. I was coming home from a flight and got to my apartment—the parking lot—around one twenty in the morning. I had stopped at a market and I was getting some beer and milk out of my car when I saw Perry March in the parking lot and he was pushing a bicycle."

The detective's puzzlement was evident. Rodman went on: "I think maybe a mountain-bike type."

"But wasn't it dark?"

"Not really. The complex has streetlights everywhere, especially between the buildings and the parking lots."

"And did he see you?"

"Oh yeah, our eyes met. It was weird." Rodman hunched forward. "Here's this small guy, slender, fairly fit, with curly hair, and he's wearing a jogging suit of some kind. Something about him—I don't know. I felt—cautious. He just froze. It was like watching a squirrel that didn't know which tire to run under."

"Did he say anything? Or did you?" Smith asked. His leisurely evening had now become a work night.

"It all happened so quickly. I grabbed my milk and beer and headed for my apartment. He just walked out of my view. Pushing that bicycle."

"So why tonight?" the detective asked. "Why didn't you go to the police before now?"

"I just read the article a few days ago, and I didn't know exactly what I should do or who to contact. I saw you tonight—and it clicked. I knew you'd tell me what I should do."

Smith's mind was whirling. He was thinking, this could be the break in the case they'd been hoping for. "And you're *sure* it was Perry March?" he asked, looking Rodman in the eye.

"I am ninety percent positive."

"And you know it was on August fifteenth of last year?"

"Actually, it was in the early morning hours of August sixteenth," Rodman clarified. "Like I said, I arrived home around one twenty in the morning. After I read the *Scene* article, I went back and reconstructed my travel dates for August—you know, when I was in Nashville and when I wasn't. I checked with United World Headquarters to see when I got home, and it was definitely in the very early morning hours of August sixteenth."

"Right, right. I'm glad you came over. Listen, you'll need to come down to the station and give a formal statement."

"Sure, Mike . . . anything I can do," Rodman replied, an eager grin surfacing on his face.

•   •   •

Postiglione and Pridemore go over Smith's report yet again. They have already noted to themselves from their initial review of the massive case file that Perry was an avid bike rider and owned a mountain bike. In fact, it is one of the items listed as being at the house during the search of Blackberry Road on September 17. The case file also establishes that the local Volvo dealer confirmed that its Swedish designers had specifically made sure an owner could carry a bike inside the trunk of this particular 850 sedan.

But the cold case detectives do not think that's where Perry stored his mountain bike, his means of getting back to Blackberry Road by backtracking along the quiet residential streets of Green Hills, Belle Meade, and Forest Hills. They are convinced he stored it in the front passenger seat. They base their conclusion upon the fact that a stroller was found inside the Volvo's trunk when it was discovered on September 7 at the Brixworth.

Nashville's gentle rolling hills and abundance of public-park bike trails make it a biker-friendly destination for mountain bikers. The principal spot where most of the Nashville yuppies buy their high-priced mountain bikes is Cumberland Transit, located just down the street from the Vanderbilt campus. Postiglione and Pridemore meet with the owner of Cumberland Transit and he explains to them that indeed with a simple mechanical maneuver, a bike rider could disengage and remove the front wheel from his bicycle, and in this altered condition, the bike could easily be stored in the front seat of most sedans. The shop owner, in fact, indicates to the detectives that he routinely transports his mountain bike in the front passenger seat of his Honda Civic, which is measurably smaller then a Volvo 850 sedan.

It will be years later before the theory of Perry's midnight bike ride will play out before a jury in the murder trial. Both Travis West, manager of Cumberland Transit, and Peter Rodman will be called as prosecution witnesses to offer their testimony.

For Peter Rodman, the chance encounter with Mike
Smith at the Sunset Grill will have larger repercussions.
When the March trial is aired before a national audience on
Court TV, Rodman will later view his role as a witness in the
March trial as a rekindling of sorts of his career as a per-
former. In fact, after the trial is over, he will be seen around
Nashville handing out video CDs labeled "Peter's Rodman's
trial testimony in the Perry March case."

Janet March in 1989, at her first show in Nashville,
as her artistic career was blossoming

(The Tennessean; *Ricky Rogers, photographer*)

Perry's Turn For Janet's 12 Day Vacation

1. Feed the Children nutritious food - 3 meals per day
2. Coordinate Deneane and Ella
3. Pay Deneane and Ella
4. Buy Raffi's Birthday present
5. Get Sam to and from Raffi's party on Sunday
6. Do Children's laundry
7. Be with Children all day - don't pawn off on Mom and Dad
8. Keep list of Sammy's Birthday party RSVP
9. Go through Bill Drawer and pay bills
10. Call Shaun Orange $$$$ and dead trees
11. Bell South Mobility
12. Video Place
13. Make sure Children have bath everyday
14. Read to Tzipi
15. Do educational activities with Sam
16. Spend quantity and quality time with your Children not
    your guitar or computer or clients
17. Pay Dr. Campbell
18. Get OPEs back
19. Cancel credit card charges for computer crap
20. Change burned out light bulbs
21. Clean-up garbage area - children will get sick
22. Clean-up your closet
23. Call Steve Ward about driveway

I agree to do all of the above before Janet's Vacation (in
response to Perry's cowardly, rash and confused vacation) is
over.

August 15, 1996

12-Day Vacation List:
Perry alleged that Janet wrote the "to do" list
for him on August 15, 1996, and then left for 12 days.

(From official police records, Nashville Police Department;
official court document entered into evidence at murder trial)

MISSING PERSON

METROPOLITAN NASHVILLE POLICE DEPARTMENT

Janet Gail Levine March is a female, white, 33 years old, DOB 02-20-63, 5'4", 104 lbs, brown hair, brown eyes, SS# 409-86-5820, TDL# 53097502, NCIC # M956251899. She has been missing since 08-15-96. There has been not family contact since that date. Victim's welfare and mental health are in question. Victim was last known driving a 1996 Gray Volvo 850, 4 door, TN Tag 844CBD

If located, contact Detective Brad Corcoran, Metropolitan Police Department, Homicide / Violent Crimes Unit (615) 862-7546 / 862-7781.

Janet March was reported missing August 29, 1996.

(From official police records, Nashville Police Department)

The March house at 3 Blackberry Road

(From official police records, Nashville Police Department)

Janet March's Volvo, as found at the
Brixworth Apartments on September 5, 1996

(From official police records, Nashville Police Department)

Janet's photo identification as provided to police

(From official police records, Nashville Police Department)

Perry March outside Los Angeles jail prior to
being extradited back to Nashville

(Courtesy of Detective Bill Pridemore)

Perry March mug shot, August 12, 2005, upon his arrival at the Nashville Criminal Justice Center

(From official police records, Nashville Police Department)

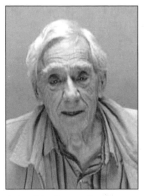

Arthur March mug shot, January 14, 2006, taken in Nashville after being deported from Mexico

(From official police records, Nashville Police Department)

Mug shot of Russell Nathaniel Farris, the inmate who played the part of hit man and testified for the prosecution

(From official police records, Nashville Police Department)

Mug shot of Cornelius King, the inmate who testified that Perry March admitted killing his wife

(From official police records, Nashville Police Department)

Detectives Postiglione and Pridemore point to the site where, according to Arthur March, Janet's body was first buried.

(From authors' collection)

Judge Steve R. Dozier, who presided over Perry March's trials in Criminal Court

(Courtesy of Judge Dozier's office)

Carolyn, Lawrence, and son Mark Levine listen to the closing arguments during the Perry March murder-for-hire trial in Criminal Court Division 1, Judge Steve Dozier's courtroom.

(The Tennessean; George Walker IV, photographer)

Detectives Postiglione and Pridemore at the Tin Angel, with Janet March's painting in the background

(From authors' collection)

CHAPTER 24

An International Tug-of-War

Although the Cook County order did not restrict the Levines' ability to travel with the children, neither did it specifically authorize the Levines to remove their grandchildren from Mexico. After arriving in Mexico, the Levines were able to secure an order from a Mexican court "giving effect to the Illinois order," but the Mexican order explicitly required that the visitation occur in Guadalajara, Mexico. Yet that same night, contrary to the provisions of the Mexican order, they left Mexico with Sammy and Tzipi and flew to Tennessee.

The thirty-nine days of visitation ended, but the Levines did not return their grandchildren to Mexico.

Instead, once they were back in Nashville, Larry Levine turned again to the Nashville court system. On July 3, 2000, the Levines file an Emergency Petition in the Juvenile Court for Custody, Termination of Parental Rights, Guardianship, and Finding that the Children are Dependent and Neglected.

Perry's worst nightmare has come true.

The Levines are attempting to take his children away from him forever. He is not going to let that happen, not without a fight. Perry decides to fight fire with fire. On

August 3, 2000, after the expiration of the thirty-nine-day visitation and the failure to return his children, Perry files in the federal court for the Middle District of Tennessee in Nashville, a Petition for Return of Minor Children Pursuant to International Child Abduction Remedies Act.

The International Child Abduction Remedies Act (ICARA) became part of American federal law in 1995 in order to implement the provisions of the Hague Convention on the Civil Aspects of International Abduction. Both the United States and Mexico are signatories to the multinational Hague Convention treaty, the United States originally signing in 1981 and Mexico in 1991. The Hague Convention was adopted by the signatory nations in order "to protect children internationally from the harmful effects of their wrongful removal or retention and to establish procedures to ensure their prompt return to the State of their habitual residence." Under the Hague Convention, the removal of a child from one country to another is to be considered "wrongful" when it is "in breach of custody rights attributed to a person . . . under the laws of the State in which the child was habitually a resident immediately before the removal."

The principal issue was clearly before the court: What was the state of "habitual residence" of Samson Leo March and Tzipora Josette March? The resolution of this legal question fell upon the shoulders of Federal District Judge Aleta A. Trauger. On October 4, 2000, just two months after the filing of the petition by Perry under ICARA, Judge Trauger releases a lengthy opinion in which she renders her ruling without the necessity of a full trial or even an evidentiary hearing. It is a meticulously framed judicial opinion in which she specifically analyzes and then applies or distinguishes prior decided cases under the Hague Convention and ICARA from around the world. Her incredibly swift decision, when viewed in terms of the months or sometimes years before most court cases are decided, is consistent with the provisions of Article 11 of the Hague Convention: "A court when faced with a petition under the Convention should act expeditiously in proceedings for return of the children."

While clearly acting in an expeditious manner, Judge Trauger leaves no stone unturned.

Perry has the legal burden of showing that the removal of his minor children was "wrongful" as defined by the Convention. If he meets that burden, then the burden shifts to the Levines to establish that one of the exceptions listed within the articles of the Convention applies in their favor.

The record is uncontroverted that the March children had been living with their father in Ajijic, Mexico, since May 1999. The Levines argue that Illinois was the children's "habitual residence" since they had lived there from October 1996 to May 1999. Judge Trauger, quoting from an earlier case on just this issue, writes:

> The concept of habitual residence under the Convention is not to be confused with domicile. Thus to determine the habitual residence of minor children the court must focus on the child, not the parents . . . a child's habitual residence is the place where he or she has been physically present for an amount of time sufficient for acclimatization and which has a degree of settled purpose from the child's perspective.

The court reviewed a lengthy written declaration from Wayne Palfrey, director of the Oak Hill Academy, which established that Samson and Tzipora were quick to learn Spanish after coming to the school, were successful in their course studies, and that both Perry and Carmen were "attentive to the children and engaged in their progress and activities." The declaration went on to say that Palfrey had "enthusiastically recommended Carmen's adoption of both children to the Mexican Family Adoption Agency," after her marriage to Perry in March of 2000.

Judge Trauger wants to accurately assess the "degree of settled purpose" from the children's perspective, so she arranges to have the children brought to her judicial chambers to interview them personally. No lawyers are present and each child is interviewed out of the presence of the other. The judge is assisted by a licensed clinical psychologist, and will later include as part of her written decision her impressions of both children:

> Samson was interviewed first. He seemed happy, relaxed and forthcoming. Samson appears to like all aspects of his life in Mexico (with the possible exception of having to wear a uniform to school). He has learned the Spanish language and likes to speak it, he likes his school, the climate, and being with his grandfather, Arthur March, and he loves Carmen and her children. When asked if he was having nightmares, he stated that he was beginning to have them because he misses his dad and wants to go back to Mexico.
>
> Tzipora, who is six, likewise was relaxed during the interview. She can only be described as playful and delightful in every way. Throughout much of the interview, she was drawing a picture of a little girl thinking about hearts. She likes speaking Spanish, loves her house in Mexico, expressed enthusiastic affection for Carmen and referred to Carmen's children as her siblings. She likes living with her grandparents but missed her father.

Then, with the purity and an innocence that can only come from a child, Tzipi, with the creative heart of a budding artist, expresses to Judge Trauger that what she would most like "is for her father and especially Carmen to come here so that she could hug them and her grandmother and grandfather at the same time."

The Levines argue that Perry should not be allowed to "create a habitual residence for the Children by brazenly refusing to abide by Court orders issued in the United States." In response to their argument, Judge Trauger rules:

> The respondents lose sight of the fact that at the time the petitioner left Illinois, the issue before the Illinois court was a matter of their visitation rights, not the custody of the children . . . At the time of his move to Mexico, there was no custody matter to be decided in Illinois, Tennessee, or any-

where else in the United States. The Levines had not yet sought permanent custody of their grandchildren.

The court determines that Perry March as the petitioner has indeed "carried his burden of establishing that the habitual residence of the two minor children, Samson and Tzipora, is Mexico."

Next, Perry as petitioner has to establish that he was exercising custody rights over his children in Mexico, under Mexican law, at the time of their removal from the country. The court finds that Perry's custodial rights follow logically as a matter of law as the biological father to the children.

The legal burden now shifts to the Levines.

The Levines take the position that pursuant to an exception found within the Hague Convention and ICARA, Sammy and Tzipi should not be returned to Mexico "because there is a grave risk that the return of the minor children to Mexico would subject them to psychological and physical harm."

To support their allegations of "a grave risk," the Levines argue that among other things the children would be expected to reside with "the individual who murdered their mother." The Levines once again present to a court their assertion that Perry murdered Janet. It is the same position that they earlier presented when they amended their probate petition in the Davidson County Probate Court and alleged a wrongful-death action against their former son-in-law.

Judge Trauger does not find their argument persuasive. She concludes that under the Hague Convention, a "grave risk of harm" can exist in only two situations: "putting the child in imminent danger prior to the resolution of the custody dispute—e.g., returning a child to a zone of war, famine, or disease or cases of serious abuse or neglect." She goes on to say:

> Of some importance to this court on this issue is the fact that, throughout three years of grandparent visitation in Illinois, the Levines never claimed March was an unfit parent . . . nor did they seek custody.

At the time of their involvement in this international custody litigation, from the Levines' perspective, what changed everything was that in early 2000 they were awarded a default judgment from Judge Frank Clement's probate court that their son-in-law had killed their daughter, and if he killed their daughter, he can now not be fit to have custody of the children. To help bolster the argument that the Levines knew they would later be making when they flew down to Mexico, Larry Levine addressed the Tennessee House of Representatives Committee on Children and Family Affairs on March 21, 2000, concerning proposed amendments to Tennessee law. When asked why the bill was needed he replied: "Janet March was murdered by her husband and we've got a civil judgment stating that he wrongfully and intentionally murdered my daughter. My grandchildren are living with the murderer right now down in Mexico, and if by some miracle they were ever to come back to the State of Tennessee, I would like the law to be very clear that I have a right to come and ask to take away their custody from the murderer."

Judge Trauger does not find that a default judgment for wrongful death against someone who has not been charged with any criminal charge, a judgment issued as a sanction for not complying with discovery requests, elevates to the narrow standard under the Hague Convention of "imminent danger" or "serious abuse." To the contrary, what she finds from the record before her is that of a loving and involved father whose children are happy, and anxious to return to Mexico.

This exact issue remains the central paradox in the Janet and Perry March story. If you are capable of murder, how can you be a loving parent? Can a man who murders his wife remain a loving father to their children? The easiest approach for Perry would have been to leave his children with the Levines and move to Mexico and start a new life. By following that route, he would have avoided much and possibly all of the legal troubles that followed him for the next decade. The Levines have come to accept that they may never have their daughter back, but they would have had her children—new lives to love. Or was Perry's unwillingness to compromise when it came to his children not the action of a loving parent but actually a selfish act, in the sense that he burdened his children with the constant turmoil of court-rooms, guardian ad litems, judges, and court orders? Or was Perry March simply a man with two different souls?

Judge Trauger rules in favor of Perry and against the Levines stating:

> The risk of delay or frustration in determining the merits of the claim is something the respondents have brought upon themselves. Instead of seeking custody of the March children in the courts of Mexico, as the Hague Convention dictates, they chose to retain them in Nashville and exploit their home court advantage.

The judge directs that the children are to be returned by air to Guadalajara, Mexico, by ten p.m. on October 12, 2000, and that they are to be flown in the company of a family friend or lawyer. The Levines are not permitted to personally deliver their grandchildren. All expenses must be paid by the Levines, including airfare, court costs, and reasonable attorney fees to Perry's attorneys, John E. Herbison of Nashville and Robert S. Catz of Cadiz, Kentucky. Herbison will go on to represent Perry in a series of additional legal battles including acting as codefense counsel in his murder trial.

In a development that is not surprising, the Levines appeal their loss in the international custody case to the Sixth Circuit Court of Appeals in Cincinnati, which issues a stay. The children remain with the Levines pending the appeal. Mark Levine, also an attorney, personally argues the case on behalf of his parents before the three-judge panel. In a written opinion handed down on April 19, 2001, the federal appellate court affirms and adopts what they refer to as Judge Trauger's "well-reasoned opinion." The Levines later file a request for the case to be heard by the United States Supreme Court. Their request is denied.

Two days after the affirmation of Judge Trauger's ruling, the children are placed on a plane to Guadalajara.

It will be four years before the Levines see their grand-children again.

CHAPTER 25

The Brady Bunch

The house that is home to the March family of eight is low and long, sand-colored and very Mexican in its decor, with the mountains as a backdrop. Sammy and Tzipi, home from school, hurry to drop their book bags and change into their bathing suits. Carmen reminds them to use sunscreen. "Wait," she says to Tzipi, and helps her smooth the lotion on her nose, along her cheekbones. Carmen's cinnamon-brown children never have to worry about sunburn.

Sammy and Tzipi jump into the clear blue-green pool, seeing who can make the bigger splash. Their sister and brothers are already playing in the water, shrieking and laughing. Carmen brings out some piedras—raisin-pecan cookies with sugary pink icing—that she brought home from the café.

It's another sun-filled day in Ajijic, and in this land of eternal spring, the mild temperatures make swimming a year-round activity.

Perry has remarked that life in Ajijic is "absolutely ideal." The public was given a window through which to glimpse Perry, Sammy, Tzipi, and their new family when

48 Hours *visited them in Mexico and produced one of the four segments that the CBS show aired from 2002 to 2005. Perry said, "I love it here. I have a wonderful wife. I have a wonderful house. I have a wonderful community around here and this is where I want to live."*

Carmen, who married Perry in March 2000, said, "He's a great husband. He's sweet. He's perfect. He's perfect to me."

When correspondent Bill Lagattuta asked her about her relationship with Sammy and Tzipi, she said, "I do everything for them. They're like mine. They're mine!"

During the months after Larry and Carolyn Levine took the children from Mexico and tried to gain permanent custody—those interminable ten months—Perry was fixated on getting his children back, whatever it might take. Maybe he'd have to send somebody to snatch them. He'd do it. He'd kidnap them back, and it wouldn't be kidnapping at all because they belonged to him in the first place. But the courts came through for him, and now his children are home, safe within their new wonderful family. He reported that the first thing the kids said as they hugged him was "Daddy, why did it take so long to get us home?"

Now that they are back in Mexico, back in the midst of their new blended family, Perry feels whole again. When 48 Hours filmed the Marches, Sammy said into the camera, "He's the best dad in the world." Perry hopes the Levines saw the show. He hopes they saw how happy the kids are in Mexico. They have a grandfather here, too, and sisters and brothers, and a mother. It's a wonderful life.

Perry is home early today. He likes to come home early when he can, have a drink by the pool while he does paperwork, spend time with his kids—all of his kids.

He and Janet used to talk about having a houseful of kids. A random thought like that will zip through his consciousness from time to time, but for the most part that other life back in Nashville is something he has shut out of his mind.

Arthur drops by, joining Perry beside the pool.
"Grandpa! Grandpa!" *the kids shout from the water—and
not just Sammy and Tzipi, but Carmen's kids, too—Daro,
Thomas, and Cinty.*

He waves his thick, rough hand and calls, "Hey, you
little outlaws!" *in his gruff, gravelly voice.*

"Watch me, Grandpa!" *Tzipi calls, promptly dipping
into the water, raising her feet straight up.*

"Want a beer?" *Perry asks.*

"Sure." *Arthur turns back to Tzipi.* "Yeah, that's pretty
good."

*Perry brings him a cold dark bottle that immediately
starts to sweat. Arthur takes a long, thirsty drink and pulls
out a chair from the patio table. He sits down, grunting.*

"Hip bothering you?"

He makes a gesture of dismissal.

*It's a different story if Arthur is in a bar, or surrounded
by a group of attentive listeners. The hip is a very big deal
as he tells all about his exploits as a soldier and the tita-
nium hip that he got after jumping out of an airplane.*

"Did you work today?" *Perry asks.*

"Yep."

*Arthur teaches English at the local hospital. He likes to
tell people he works for the Mexican government.*

*Perry corrals several files that are spread out on the
table and makes a stack.*

"What you got there?" *Arthur asks.*

"Work."

"You work too much. Now take me—I put in maybe four
hours today. That's about right for a day's work."

"I'm not complaining," *Perry says.* "Besides, you're
retired."

*The sun has started its descent. It's a big fiery ball,
growing larger as it dips into the west. Father and son
chat about nothing in particular, and after a few minutes,
Arthur finishes his beer and gets up.*

"Want to stay and eat with us, Dad?" *Perry asks.*

"Nope, I got things to do, people to see."

Arthur has been in Ajijic for a decade now, and he knows just about everybody and just about everything that's going on. He helped Perry get started in real estate. He has all kinds of connections.

"Grandpa, are you coming to my recital next week?" *Tzipi calls out.*

"What recital?"

"Ballet," *Perry says.* "She's a terrific little dancer."

"Friday night. It's next Friday night," *Tzipi says.*

"Sure, I guess I can do that."

"I'll call and remind you," *Perry says.* "Now where is it you're headed?"

"To see a guy, okay?" *He turns to the pool and waves.* "Bye, kids."

"Bye, Grandpa!" *the children shout.*

Arthur glances back at Perry. "I'll call you tomorrow if anything comes of it."

"Come on, kids. Everybody out," *Perry calls.* "Sammy, Tzipi, time for homework."

Sammy and Tzipi complain that they have to get out of the pool, even though they've been swimming for a couple of hours, but they obey. They're good kids. They earn high marks in the local bilingual school and are fluent in Spanish. It is remarkable how they have adapted to the rhythms of this unique culture. Perry told 48 Hours, *"I've never seen them happier," and Arthur has said it, too.*

The children climb out and dry off. "You're shriveled like a prune," *Perry says to no one in particular. The little ones giggle and run off to see their mother.*

Tzipi, of course, does not remember her real mother. Sammy remembers Janet—but he tries not to think about her, about any of that. His dad has told him and Tzipi, "Mommy left home. We don't know what happened to her. It's very sad, but that's the truth." *Sammy likes Carmen. She's nice to him and Tzipi. All of the kids—all six of them—are a real family. He loves his life in Mexico. He tries not to remember anything about Nashville, but some-*

times he thinks about his grandparents, and how his grandmother blinked back tears when he and Tzipi left, and it makes his chest hurt, so he tries not to remember.

To all who witness Perry's interaction with Sammy and Tzipi, he seems truly devoted to them—as he does to Daro, Thomas, and Cinty, and the child they have together, Azul, who at this moment waddles toward him like a duck with her arms outstretched. He sweeps the little girl into the air.

Now that his role as a father has expanded, he says, "We're the Brady Bunch. We have three and three, exactly three boys and three girls."

It is not just Perry's family that is expanding. His business ventures, in partnership with Mexican entrepreneur Samuel Chavez, are prospering. Their diversified interests provide insurance, security, real estate, legal, and financial services for the wealthy expatriates living in the Lake Chapala region. The expats do not know the particulars about the complaints in Tennessee that Perry took money owed to Levine, Mattson, Orr, and Geracioti. Most see Perry as another bright and ambitious businessman who has discovered the perfect life in Ajijic.

Perry's business interests also include a development called Chula Vista Norte, reported by 48 Hours to be "the most exclusive address in Ajijic." In addition, he and Carmen opened Media Luna Bistro & Café in the heart of the lively little town.

He sits Azul on the side of the pool and lets her dangle her toes in the water. The water is tepid, nearly bath temperature. Azul bends over and slaps at the water, laughing her clear, bubbly toddler laugh. Perry holds tight to her little birdlike body.

It's a new life that Perry is living these days, an entirely different life from the Levines' world in Nashville, and Perry—being a person who resides along the fuzzy edges of reality, not quite inside the borders—believes his new life will last forever.

And above all, he is determined that the Levines will never get Sammy and Tzipi. It is his highest priority—to keep his kids out of the clutches of their grandparents. It is an obsession.

CHAPTER 26

Death by Default

In the spring of 2003, another appellate judge, William B. Cain of the Tennessee Court of Appeals, is required to negotiate the legal labyrinth of Levine vs. March.

By July of 1999, the Levines had spent thirty-one months arguing with their son-in-law over every conceivable aspect of their daughter's "absentee" estate. This undying need for litigious conflict was equally attributable to both sides. Judge Cain later characterized the proceedings as "what can only be described as trench warfare."

Judge Cain knew of what he spoke, having served as a trial judge for decades in Maury County, Tennessee, before being tapped to become a member of the Tennessee Court of Appeals. He had spent endless hours in a rural county courthouse in the center of a town square conducting hearings where families in domestic disputes literally disintegrated before his eyes as they spent down their last resources battling over the disposition of inanimate objects. When the case of *Perry March v. Larry Levine et al, No. 99P-1676* was assigned to Judge Cain after an appeal from Orders of Probate Judge Frank Clement, he must have seen the opportunity as a respite from wielding the gavel in the midst of the daily warfare. He was still being paid by the state of Tennessee to work in the realm of human conflict and arrive at a just decision, but the setting was now the Tennessee Supreme Court building in Nashville. Inside the marbled hallways and walnut-paneled courtrooms, Judge Cain and his fellow appellate judges could apply the law in a quiet judicial environment, on their own schedule, away from the intense emotions and personal conflict he had overseen for so many years.

In case No. 99P-1676, it would take Judge Cain twenty-four written pages to find his way out of the convoluted maze that Larry Levine and Perry March had constructed. At the core of what would be a series of endless pleadings and counterpleadings for an unbelievable thirty-one months were: *a cross-stitched baby quilt, a black-beaded evening bag, a* "Mind over Platter" *cookbook, certain missing photos, a wooden footstool, a set of encyclopedias, and the condition of a returned antique secretary belonging to Janet's brother, Mark, and its matching vanity dresser.*

Davidson County probate judge Frank Clement must have thought that the endless shuffle of pleadings by the lawyers was never going to cease in the Janet Levine March "absentee" estate case. In a written order handed down as early as September 17, 1997, Judge Clement had felt compelled to lecture both sides:

The funds available at the time of the hearing, August 15, 1997, after payment of the mortgage but prior to payment of any of the fee requests is approximately $320,000, will be quickly depleted unless substantial changes occur in the litigious protocol established by Mr. March and the Levines.

The Court agrees with all the parties that the fees at issue are more than substantial and is most concerned that the intensely contested proceedings, being the obvious and direct result of the animosity between Mr. March and the Levines and with almost every issue being vigorously contested, will deplete the resources of the Absentee's estate within a few months unless Mr. March and the Levines cease, or at least minimize, the intense litigation that has become the norm in this most tragic case.

Judge Clement's words fell on deaf ears.

For the next two years the Levines and Perry March would continue to argue over the custody and condition of particular estate items including the cross-stitched quilt that Carolyn had made for Janet when she was a baby. The Levines would file a series of petitions seeking to have Judge Clement hold their adversary in "contempt of court" for failure to comply with the judge's own orders.

At the core of the contempt petitions were alleged failures by Perry to deliver "estate property" to the Levines, or that certain property was partially damaged when finally delivered—"a drawer from the antique secretary was shattered and broken in pieces and the matching vanity dresser had a piece of wood broken off." When Perry and the children relocated to Illinois, the Levines established a second residence there so that they could be in the same jurisdiction as their son-in-law. For not only were they arguing over the custody of certain estate property, they were simultaneously battling for visitation of their grandchildren through litigation in both Tennessee and Illinois. Judge Clement would comment on the seemingly incongruous positions of the parties in one of his written rulings:

The acts and omissions of Mr. March, along with other factors, may cause all who participate in these important proceedings to be viewed with disdain by those who wonder who was looking after the children's interest while the money was being spent. There is no doubt whatsoever that Mr. March loves his children. There is no doubt whatsoever that Lawrence and Carolyn Levine love their grandchildren. There is no doubt that the Conservator is admirably performing his duties. Nonetheless, the incessant legal battles between Mr. March and the Levines will exhaust the estate of the Absentee in short order unless a substantial change occurs.

It is as if Judge Clement were begging the parties to consider compromise to be an element within the boundaries of love for one's children or grandchildren. Instead, the parties continued on their path of relentless and protracted litigation. One has to wonder how the human mind and soul do not explode under the weight of such a level of hatred and animosity.

By July 1998, after repeated requests by the Levines, Judge Clement issued an order finding Perry in "civil contempt" for failure to deliver certain personal property in a timely manner. In January 1999 he ordered that Perry "be fined fifty dollars per day until he returns to the Levines the beaded bag and the hand-stitched quilt."

Then on July 16, 1999, after almost three full years of courtroom warfare with Perry, the Levines altered their war plans and unleashed a completely new assault. They amended their original petition in the estate case, and asserted a formal legal claim for the first time that Perry March was responsible for the wrongful death of their daughter, Janet.

It is not a position the Levines first formulated in July 1999. In fact, with the first pleading that they filed in Judge Clement's court in November 1996, the Levines announced to the court the basis on which they felt Perry should not be allowed to inherit any property from the estate: "He has unclean hands, for he refuses to divulge to any appropriate government body or the courts of this state the facts and circumstances regarding the disappearance of his wife, Janet Gail Levine March." The term *unclean hands* is one that lawyers routinely use in contested civil matters when claiming that the judge should rule in their favor because of the prior actions of their adversary involving the matters at issue before the court.

In this case, the reference takes on much more vivid and ghoulish images.

The thirty-one-month delay by the Levines in formally asserting their amended claim against Perry for the "wrongful death" of their daughter will prove to be a very costly procedural error.

Through their amended petition, the Levines were determined to achieve what the Nashville police had been unable to do—to prove that Perry March murdered Janet. In their claim for wrongful death, they allege, "On the night of August 15, 1996, Janet March and Perry March had a heated argument. Perry March inflicted serious bodily injury on Janet March during that argument. As a proximate result of Perry March's violent and wrongful act, Janet March died on August 15, 1996, or very shortly thereafter."

Judge Clement allowed the amendment of the original estate petition to permit the new claim for wrongful death. After objections by the conservator, Jeff Mobley, that it would further deplete the assets of the estate if he had to participate in the wrongful-death claim, Judge Clement ruled that the conservator was not a necessary party.

Eight months later, on February 8, 2000, Judge Cain was at his judicial wit's end with Perry March for his repeated contemptuous behavior, which included walking out of a deposition and refusing to make himself available to continue it. However, as Judge Cain would later point out, this contemptuous behavior occurred before the amendment seeking a claim of wrongful death. In his February order, Clement ruled:

> This court has held on two occasions that Perry March is a willfully disobedient party and has willfully disobeyed unambiguous, specific orders of this Court. The Court finds that Perry March continues to be a willfully disobedient party.

In this same February 2000 order, and as a sanction for Perry's contemptuous behavior, Clement struck the previous answer filed by Perry, and granted a judgment against him for the "wrongful death of Janet Levine March."

Following the order granting the default judgment, on April 4, 2000, Judge Clement denied Perry's application to set aside the judgment, and impaneled a jury to determine monetary damages. The jury returned with a staggering verdict—"$113.5 million in damages against Perry March for the wrongful death of Janet Levine March."

Larry Levine had not found his daughter or her body, but he had accomplished what the Nashville police could not. He had a judicial ruling that formally held that Perry March had killed Janet. The enormous verdict had to be its own bittersweet reward for the years of endless pleadings, motions, and hearings.

The taste of victory, of some level of justice, would last for only three years.

Now, in March of 2003, six and a half years after the initial petition filed by the Levines asking that Perry be denied any inheritance from their daughter's estate, the Tennessee Court of Appeals, through Judge Cain's opinion, rules, "We hold the trial court erred in allowing the amendment. Judgment for default for failure to obey an order to provide discovery is an extreme sanction." In addition to what it deems was "an undue delay" of thirty-one months in filing its amendment for wrongful death, the appellate court also rules that the conservator should have been a required party.

> Without the Conservator being a party to the wrongful death action, he is not bound by the finding of death, wrongful or otherwise . . . we are left with the strange paradox that Janet March is alive (or at least not established by evidence to be otherwise) for the purpose of the absentee estate but deceased for the purpose of the wrongful death action against Perry March.

Judge Cain in his opinion goes on to rule:

> However unfavorably this record reflects upon Perry March, one vital fact remains unchallenged. He has never been convicted of anything. In the eyes of the law, through which eyes alone this Court, and all other courts, must view the unfolding scene, Perry March is innocent of the charges leveled against him by the Levines and will remain so unless

and until he is indicted, tried and convicted of such charges. Being overbearing and obnoxious, as well as in repeated civil contempt of court, does not equate to criminal conviction. The decision of this Court is made after careful consideration of the issues and not because of Perry March but in spite of him.

Considering the conduct of Mr. March subsequent to the filing of the wrongful death action, the imposition of a default judgment is simply too drastic a sanction for his behavior. Throughout the entire proceeding, Perry March has not been the only transgressor. The Levines, in their zeal to sustain their position and to punish Perry March for what they sincerely believe to be the murder of their daughter, have contributed greatly to the problems in this case. The court recognizes the patience and fortitude of the learned trial judge in trying his best to control this litigation, preserve the absentee estate, and maintain the integrity of his court in the face of nearly insurmountable challenges.

The $113.5 million verdict against Perry March and the judicial finding that he was responsible for the death of his wife are set aside. It will be the second time a court has ruled in favor of Perry after years of relentless efforts by the Levines.

One only can wonder what Janet, the "absentee," the mother who was devoted to providing a nurturing, loving environment for her family, would think of all the endless years of acrimony and the dissipation of her estate.

CHAPTER 27

Was the Body Moved Twice?

By 2004 it has been eight years since Janet's disappearance, but Deputy District Attorney Tom Thurman still believes the police can find her body. He has been the point man from the DA's office on this case from the outset, and as an experienced prosecutor with thirty years of trying murder cases, he knows that without a body, securing a conviction for murder will be an uphill battle.

The veteran prosecutor and his cold case detectives are focused solely on Perry. Publicly they will tell the press or anyone else who asks that they continue to follow all leads, but after eight long and unproductive years, Thurman is anxious. He has constructed and deconstructed the events a thousand times, yet he is no closer to knowing the truth. Thurman understands from years in the courtroom that after so much time, memories start to fade and clues simply dry up. He is going to have to get this case before a jury soon or it will be too late.

He doesn't want to go to a jury without a body.

Based upon the timing of Perry's phone calls to his brother, sister, Laurie Rummel, and then the Levines at midnight, Thurman, Postiglione, and Pridemore theorize that Perry had a very short time to dispose of Janet's body on the night of August 15. They are convinced that he did not venture far from 3 Blackberry Road. After the extensive search of the March residence and its surrounding acreage by a small army of officers on September 15 produced nothing, the property was eliminated as a viable option. They are also convinced that after Perry became aware that he was the sole focus of the police investigation, he may have been tempted to relocate Janet's body to a much more remote location.

With the possibility that Janet's body was moved twice, Thurman believes Perry may have had some help. Someone knows something, and he is determined to find out who.

Thurman's anxieties about his case are justified. It has been extremely rare to secure a murder conviction without a body.

However, it happened before, in a case with eerie similarities to the March case. In 1999 Thomas Capano, a powerful and politically well-connected Delaware attorney, was convicted of the first-degree murder of Anne Marie Fahey, the appointments secretary for the governor of Delaware. Capano met Fahey at a political function during one of his frequent trips to the state capital to consult with Governor Tom Carper and other party leaders. Although married and the father of several children, Capano began an affair with the much younger Fahey, which went on for many tumultuous months before Fahey decided she had had enough and rejected Capano's advances.

Just as with Janet March, Anne Marie Fahey simply disappeared one day, never to be seen again. Because she was a member of Governor Carper's office staff, her disappearance instantly became a high-profile media event. The population of Wilmington was consumed with the case as the city was scoured for clues, and the public held rallies and public searches in support of the Fahey family. The national media also descended upon the city and quickly turned the Fahey disappearance into a national news story.

After two years of dead ends, persistent investigation efforts cracked the Fahey case wide open when the police were able to miraculously locate the Styrofoam fishing cooler into which Capano had stuffed the petite body of Fahey after killing her during a violent argument at his fashionable Wilmington residence. He had taken Fahey's body out into the Chesapeake Bay and then miles into the open ocean on his weekend pleasure boat, the *Summer Wind*. He attempted to weigh down the cooler with chains, but it still would not submerge. Finally, Capano stood on the deck of his boat and fired a round from a pistol into the cooler, desperate for the ocean to receive the offering of his dead mistress.

Months later, a Delaware fisherman came upon the cooler, empty, but with a perfectly shaped hole still clearly discernible. Knowledge of the cooler had not yet surfaced, so the angler simply felt he had located a lucky find while out on a fishing excursion. That same cooler would later be brought into a Wilmington courtroom to be viewed by the jury in the Capano murder trial. It was the closest thing the prosecution had to a body, but after Thomas Capano elected to take the stand in his own defense and the jury witnessed his unbridled arrogance, and after a member of Capano's family—who was also on the boat that fateful day—turned state's evidence, it proved enough for a conviction.

Without a body, time of death or cause of death cannot be determined. Worse, it is impossible to prove with direct evidence that there has even been a homicide. For Thurman, finding Janet's body has become the core anxiety in the March investigation. Janet remains an apparition that haunts him. He chases her in his dreams, but she is always just out of reach. She whispers to him, telling him not to give up, that he will find her, and then disappears again into the dark, murky waters of death, her marble-white face evaporating like fog burned off the sea by a hot summer sun.

There is a universal adage in homicide cases: How tells you who, and who tells you why. Without a body, Thurman and his cold case detectives do not know how.

Almost monthly there is a new hypothesis, a new location. Local rivers and lakes in the Nashville area have been searched, along with a limestone rock quarry in Alabama. Numerous construction sites around Nashville, especially those that were pouring concrete in mid-August of 1996, have been examined. Even a garbage disposal business became a potential target when the rumors spread throughout Nashville that Janet's body had been placed in a Dumpster in nearby Belle Meade.

Thurman reasons that the answer to the evidentiary Rubik's Cube he has been unable to solve for eight years somehow lies with Perry's clients. The prosecutor has convinced himself that Perry's client Paul Eichel knows where Janet's body is, and he begins to slowly start turning up the heat.

In 1996 Eichel was making his living, and a very good one, within the underbelly of the city as the king of adult entertainment in Nashville, at one time operating five clubs. Eichel dealt in a world where people sought brief moments of pleasure, escape from their dull and repetitive daily lives. Businessmen, including scores of out-of-towners, would stop in for a drink or two or three and watch shapely young girls gyrate to loud music under pulsating lights, their movements dripping with erotic promise. He moved in a shadowy world where someone who wanted to cross the boundaries of acceptable behavior could meet the right people.

By 2004 Eichel had already served time for income tax evasion. Too much cash and not enough records. He had also been stricken with cancer of the larynx and had to hold a vibrator against the side of his neck to create the necessary resonance whenever conversing with others. The crackling projection of monosyllabic words only added to his unsettling image. One could easily—if erroneously—conjure up that it was a knife or a bullet from a ruthless member of the underworld or a gang member in prison that had left Eichel with this life sentence of parrotlike speech.

Thurman knew that in August of 1996 Perry, as Eichel's attorney, was in frequent contact with the businessman. The prosecutor also knew that in that same month, Perry had contacted Eichel about renting an apartment from him when he had decided to separate from Janet. Thurman secured a search warrant allowing authorities to excavate portions of Eichel's Bellevue farm. Bellevue is another of Nashville's bedroom communities and is located, like Forest Hills, in the western section of Nashville, a short ride down Highway 70 from the March residence. Only ten miles or so from downtown, Bellevue is cluttered with thousands of houses, town houses, apartments, and condominiums, but certain portions of the community have retained their rural roots. Eichel's home is located on a "gentleman's farm," as it is referred to in Nashville. It is one of a series of minifarms still found within Bellevue with enough acreage for horses and for privacy from neighbors and from the road.

A perfect place to bury a body on a dark summer night.

In the voluminous files on the March investigation is the statement from a woman named Karen Dorroll, given in February 2000. Ms. Dorroll said she answered an ad for renting a pool house in the summer of 1998, and the location turned out to be Paul Eichel's Bellevue home. At one point she was left alone with Eichel's daughter, Ashley, who said, "Do you want to see where a dead body was buried?"

Thurman does not stop with a search of the Bellevue property. He and Terry McElroy go to the school Ashley attends, where they pull her out of class and question her in the halls of the school, informing her she better come clean about where Janet's body is buried on her father's farm. The teenager pleads with the police to believe her that she does not know anything, her cries and whimpers echoing up and down the halls.

Terry McElroy and homicide detective Al Gray also pay a visit to Eichel's ex-wife, Susie, asking her just what she knows about her ex-husband's relationship with Perry. Susie has a bad drug habit. Her memory is fuzzy. The detectives report back to Thurman, "Susie Eichel says Janet might be in the cement of the Music City Mix Factory." Thurman takes in the information and muses over it. The Mix Factory is one of the clubs Eichel owned in 1996. The lead may be the ramblings of a junkie, but it seems to Thurman there's more.

Susie has two children by Morris Clinard in addition to Ashley and Josh, her children by Eichel. Morris Clinard, a longtime heroin addict, died in August of 2000, but not before implicating Susie in the Janet March case.

The web grows more tangled. An inmate at Brushy Mountain State Prison, Michael Wayne Johnson, managed to get an interview with police in February of 2002. In his statement, Johnson said that when he was working at Eichel's Bellevue home, back in 1997, he witnessed Morris and Susie putting a body bag in a van. Later, when he was having an affair with Susie, she admitted that the body in the bag was Janet's, and that they had carried it to the Florida Everglades.

A good lead, but by the time Johnson told his story, Morris Clinard was dead. Those who shot dope with Clinard said he was a "pro" and some of the circumstances surrounding his death didn't add up. Did he know too much? Had he talked too much? Morris had told Rose Mary Averett, whose apartment he rented, that Janet's body was moved twice.

Other interviews on file point to Morris and Susie—and to Paul Eichel. Clinard was reported as saying he had done Eichel "a huge favor." His brother said Morris told him that he and Susie had "knowledge of Janet's death." A man who said he worked for Paul Eichel stated that he overheard Eichel and Perry "talking about something [that] had to be done," and later he saw them filling a hole with Quick-Crete. Someone named "Chicago" said Susie told him she helped Morris move the body, for Eichel, and that Susie wore a dress that once belonged to Janet.

Susie apparently told many of her cohorts about moving the body from the Bellevue property. One reported, "Susie said that Paul told her, 'Susie, she wasn't wrapped up in just any rug—it was Perry's living-room rug.' "

Susie denies any part in Janet's death or in moving her

body, but she says, "I heard Paul tell someone that Perry killed Janet."

Thurman brings Eichel in and informs him that if he will come clean about where Janet's body is buried, he will be sure that Eichel's son, Josh, receives consideration for a greatly reduced sentence he is about to start serving for a recent drug possession conviction.

Thurman then secures a warrant to search the Music City Mix Factory. His near obsession with Eichel is further fueled by statements from several witnesses that indicate that in the summer of 1996 Eichel was having a concrete floor poured in the building, and that they had seen Perry at the club around the same time.

All the digging and all the pressure on family members produce nothing helpful for the prosecution.

Yet Thurman is convinced he is still correct. He will not give up his attack on Eichel. By 2005, and still with no body, the prosecutor holds a press conference and in a most unorthodox legal maneuver announces that he has named Eichel a coconspirator in the disappearance of Janet March. Eichel quickly reacts publicly to the prosecutor's procedural assault, his robotic voice delivering his position in a forced mechanical monotone: "I didn't party or dine with Perry March, and I never met his wife. I had three clubs going full blast, I was raising my kids by myself—there's no reason in the world I would risk that. That's why it's so ludicrous."

In addition to Eichel, Thurman also names, as unindicted coconspirators, Morris Clinard and Perry's father, Arthur. No one spoke for the deceased Clinard, but Arthur March was certainly quick to voice his reaction from his home in Ajijic, Mexico: "I wasn't in the fucking country. I didn't get there till she had been gone a week."

Thurman's instincts about a relationship or a connection with Perry's clients was a correct one. He simply had the wrong client.

The high-profile murder case of Thomas Capano might have shed light on how to solve the March case, and exactly whom the prosecutor should have been putting pressure on.

In fact, the events of the Capano investigation might have acted as a road map of what Thurman, Postiglione, and Pridemore could expect to transpire in the months ahead. Thomas Capano and Perry March were both attorneys ostensibly living the "perfect life" and moving in the right circles. Both were also arrogantly convinced that they were always smarter than those around them, and that regardless of their situation, they would always come out on top.

If the police had devoted the manpower in the summer and early fall of 1996 to place a twenty-four-hour tail on their sole suspect, or if the Levines had only hired a private investigator to shadow Perry around the clock during this same time frame, they all would have learned that Arthur did indeed arrive from Mexico a week after Janet's disappearance.

But it would not be his last visit, and Arthur's activities would come to include much more than looking after his grandchildren.

CHAPTER 28

A Family Affair

The Levines' judicial defeat in Nashville's federal courthouse in October 2000, regarding the custody of their grandchildren, is a shock to absorb, but it does not dampen their willingness to return to the courtroom.

On December 6, 2002, both individually and in their capacity as the new conservators of Janet's "absentee" estate, they file a new lawsuit. Over a year earlier, the Levines filed a petition asking that they be the ones to act as conservators of their daughter's estate, replacing the originally named conservator, local attorney Jeff Mobley. The Nashville court granted their petition and on December 19, 2001, Lawrence Levine and Carolyn Levine were formally appointed as co-conservators. Now, in this newest courtroom battle, the Levines elect not only to sue Perry March, but they add the rest of the March family as named defendants: Ron March, Perry's brother; Kathy Breitowich, Perry's sister; Lee Breitowich, Perry's brother-in-law; and Arthur March, Perry's father.

This civil cause of action is based upon allegations that the March family collectively disposed of, in an improper matter, certain assets that had belonged to Janet or to her estate. This time around, the Levines aren't satisfied with seeking compensatory damages of several hundred thousand dollars. They also ask the court to award them punitive damages. They want to punish all the Marches as fully as the law will allow. Furthermore, they ask that a jury be impaneled. They don't want a judge to decide this case. They want ordinary Nashville citizens to hear the evidence.

The Levines feel confident that a jury will recognize the good guys from the bad.

The Janet and Perry March story is really a family story—a story about two different families who were brought into a bubbling cauldron of turmoil and division based upon the intersecting lives of Janet and Perry. From 1996 until 2002, the Levines and Perry March were the ones in the foreground of the intense legal battles. With this latest lawsuit, the remaining members of the March family are formally brought into the seemingly endless river of litigation.

But in reality all the members of the March family have been connected to this story from the very night of August 15, 1996. Telephone records secured by the Nashville police early in their investigation show that at 9:11 p.m., the first person Perry called was his younger brother, Ron, to relate that "Janet has left." That brief conversation was followed by a call to his sister, Kathy, who was staying with her then boyfriend, Lee Breitowich, at 9:14 p.m. The police also learn early on that either that night or possibly the next day, Kathy called her father, Arthur, in Ajijic, Mexico, and informed him that "Janet has left Perry" and he needed to come to Nashville to help with the children.

From this very first night, the Marches were a family doing what a family should do—rallying around a family member in need.

The March familial tapestry was quickly woven more tightly when Perry filed a series a mortgages against the Blackberry Road property in favor of his brother Ron, his sister Kathy, his brother-in-law Lee, and his father Arthur. The basis for these debt obligations was monies Perry said his family loaned him in the early months following Janet's disappearance, after he had left Nashville and his position at the Levine law firm, when he was caring for his children, Sammy and Tzipi, but, according to Perry, had very little income coming in. It was the March family's financial aid from that time that would ultimately land them in the middle of this lawsuit six years later.

The principal attorney representing the Levines is C. J. Gideon with the Nashville firm of Gideon and Wiseman. Gideon is known as a tenacious bulldog who, once he has an opponent in his sights, will proceed methodically until his opponent is either defeated or procedurally exhausted. C. J. Gideon and Larry Levine practiced law the same way: take no enemies alive. Gideon has been at the heart of most all of the civil litigation that the Levines filed against Perry March. It was he who had convinced Probate Judge Frank Clement to issue a default judgment against Perry in the wrongful-death case, a judgment that led to the $113.5 million award against Perry for the wrongful death of Janet. Cold case detectives Postiglione and Pridemore, after taking over the Janet March investigation, had the opportunity to witness C. J. Gideon in the courtroom from time to time. They both agree, "If I ever get in a legal jam, I am calling C.J."

By the twenty-first century Nashville is evolving into a modern metropolis, but in many ways it still resembles the provincial Southern town it used to be. That is especially true in the legal community. Most of the attorneys, particularly the older ones who have been practicing for decades, know one another well. They are friends as well as adversaries.

When the Levines began their legal war against Perry March, many of Nashville's attorneys were directly involved in or affected by the Janet and Perry March story. For instance, C. J. Gideon practiced law with Tom Wiseman. Before becoming a federal judge, Tom Wiseman had been a U.S. attorney and a private practitioner. It was Wiseman whom paralegal Leigh Reames would consult regarding her legal rights after receiving sexually explicit letters from Perry. Wiseman's name would later appear on the list of over fifty prospective witnesses filed by prosecutor Tom Thurman in Perry's murder trial.

The litigation filed on behalf of the Levines against the entire March family is vintage Gideon. The Marches are sued under eight alternate legal theories: fraud, misrepresentation, fraudulent conveyance, champerty, destruction of personal property, conversion, trover, and civil conspiracy. At the center of all these different theories are the same alleged acts by the defendants—that they converted for their own use and gain personal property that they knew belonged to Janet March, Janet's estate, Janet's children, or the Levines themselves. C. J. Gideon, on behalf of his clients, argues that over the years the Levines gave all of the property in question to Janet or her children or loaned them some of their own property. The position of the March family is that they were given the personal property by Perry as repayment for the monies they had respectively loaned him after he left Nashville and was living in Illinois from late 1996 until mid-1999. The Marches will also argue that much if not all the property in question passed to Perry as part of his portion of the marital estate, as her husband, and that it was thus his property to do with as he saw fit.

In 1997, facing a foreclosure action by the Levines against the Blackberry Road house, Perry had filed a *lien lis pendens* against the property based on what he argued was "his undivided marital interest in all property of Absentee Janet Gail Levine March." It was shortly after the filing of this lien in January 1997 that Perry also filed mortgages against the Blackberry Road property in favor of all his relatives. In May of 1997, Perry reached a settlement agreement with the conservator of Janet's absentee estate at the time, Jeff Mobley, just days before the scheduled sale of the estate's principal asset, 3 Blackberry Road, for over $700,000. Pursuant to the settlement agreement, Perry received monies and property (including the 1996 Volvo sedan found at the Brixworth Apartments in September 1996) totaling $73,000 as his share in the equity of the house and as "a credit toward any claim he might have in a subsequent divorce." Based on the settlement, Perry released his lien and the extended March family members released their mortgages.

It seemed in 1997 that a workable compromise had been reached. The Levine mortgages totaling $300,000 were paid off, and this aspect of the Janet March matter was behind everyone. But the Levines later contested Mobley's settlement with Perry, arguing that if he was responsible for Janet's death, he would not be entitled to any portion of her estate. The Tennessee Court of Appeals in a spring 1999 opinion reversed the order approving the Mobley-March settlement and ruled, "There is nothing in the record on which the court could base a determination that it was in the best interests of the absentee (Janet March) to pay a minimum of $73,000 from her estate to settle what appear to be doubtful claims."

The 1999 appellate ruling threw into chaos the prior transactions between Perry and his family, through which he had given them between 1997 and 1999 various personal property to satisfy the debts he felt he owed them for their financial assistance. The Levines wanted all of that property restored to the estate or, alternatively, they wanted the estate to be paid monetary damages. It would be almost three years later before a Nashville jury would be impaneled in Judge Randy Kennedy's courtroom to hear the case of the Levine family vs. the March family. Between the date of filing and the date of trial, the Levines would experience another judicial defeat when the Tennessee Court of Appeals in another probate matter ruling, through Judge William Cain's spring 2003 opinion, would reverse the $113.5 million wrongful-death judgment against Perry.

In a surprise move the day of the jury trial, C. J. Gideon voluntarily dismisses his clients' lawsuit against named defendants Perry March and Arthur March.

By that date, Perry and Arthur have much more to worry about than the Levines and C. J. Gideon.

CHAPTER 29

Clouds on the Mexican Horizon

For Perry, the perpetually blue skies over the Lake Chapala region of Mexico are turning cloudy. The business partnerships that he formed with Samuel Chavez have soured. An additional business venture, Premier Properties, is forced to shut its doors.

And none of this is happening in a vacuum.

The towns of Ajijic, Jocotepec, San Juan Cosala, San Antonio Tlayacapán, and Chapala are laced together by a two-lane road running along the northwest shoreline of Lake Chapala, Mexico's largest natural lake. They support a combined population of approximately sixty thousand people, with North American expatriates representing as many as ten thousand. Most of these transplants who reside in Ajijic are fully retired from their former professions in the United States and Canada and have plenty of time on their hands. Time to take long walks along the cobblestone lanes of Constitución Street, or meet friends for drinks in the sprawling gardens of La Neuva Posada, one of Ajijic's best hotels, decorated with a colorful array of the area's natural plants and flowers.

There is a sense of a small-town community into which
former residents of Toronto, New York City, and scores of
other major cities become quickly acculturated. There is an
active and long-standing art scene, with writing groups,
local theaters, and outdoor concerts. D. H. Lawrence, English
novelist, author of nonfiction works, poet, and painter, lived
and wrote in the lakeside towns and villages of the Chapala
region in the 1920s. His time there most likely acted as an
inspiration for *The Plumed Serpent*, a vivid evocation of
Mexico and its ancient Aztec culture and religion, published
in 1926.

Although nestled away in the Mexican mountains along
the shoreline of Lake Chapala, Ajijic is less than an hour away
from Guadalajara, the capital city of the Mexican state of
Jalisco. Known as both La Perla Tapatia (Pearl of the West)
and Ciudad de las Rosas (City of the Roses), Guadalajara,
with a population approximating five million, represents one
of Mexico's principal centers of culture, finance, industry, and
religion. Across this modern cosmopolitan city, one finds
many striking architectural gems that connect the past and the
present of Mexico—Cathedral of Guadalajara, Degollado
Theater, Plaza de Armas and Cathedral, Octavio Paz Library
at University Square, Rotonda Hombres Jalicienses Ilustres,
Liberation Square, and Chapultepec Tower.

And one also finds the *Guadalajara Colony Reporter*, a
weekly newspaper and the only one in English serving the
city and western Mexico. The paper is staffed primarily by
editors and writers from England, the United States, and
Canada, and its primary readership is the ever-growing expatriate population. In each edition, the news of Ajijic plays
a prominent part. The focus is directed mainly on civic and
community news. The weekly has a small-town presentation, with articles appearing under titles such as "Ajijic
Passion Play Highlights Local Semana Santa Observances,"
"World Tai Chi Day in Ajijic," or "Ajijic Gives Free Bird
Vaccines." But occasionally, the paper's articles will include
news involving a member of the community and with the
hint or promise of mystery: "Well-known Ajijic Resident &

Dog Victims of Hit-and-Run" or "Stolen Art Turns Up in Ajijic."

It was not long after Perry's arrival in the Lake Chapala region that he made the news. In its July 1, 2000, edition, the *Guadalajara Colony Reporter* included an article entitled "Nashville Fixated by Janet March Case." Most expatriates moving to Ajijic had visions of being "freed by distance." A chance to get away from the routine of their former lives, the grind, the repetitiveness. The chance for a fresh start, to clean out the mind's cobwebs. The feeling rock-and-roller Bob Seger described in his song "Roll Me Away"—the feeling of starting over after being lost and double-crossed.

For Perry, Ajijic surely represented being "freed by distance." Distance from the Levines, from the endless court orders, and from the DA's office. But it was never going to mean "freed from the media." Perry had grown accustomed to being the subject of news stories. In fact, some believed that he welcomed this, maybe even relished it. Before he left Nashville for the Chicago area, his televised interview with the Nashville NBC affiliate, WSMV, presents a man not shying away from public scrutiny, but rather one eager to present his "side of the story," drawn to the camera's lens. The camera would again focus on Perry and what had evolved into a national "fixation" on the Janet March case when CBS's *48 Hours* brought their cameras to Ajijic.

The July 2000 article in the *Guadalajara Colony Reporter* could not have surprised Perry. It would be one in over a dozen that would appear in the next several years alerting the expatriate population to the latest developments surrounding the former life of "one of their own." Possibly the paper would have been able to pass on more information to the Ajijic residents and any others among Guadalajara's millions of residents who regularly followed the comings and goings of the "English-speaking population" in 2001 if the plans of the Nashville murder squad had been carried out.

Shortly before the tragic events of 9/11, Detectives Postiglione and Pridemore were scheduled to head to Mexico for some good old-fashioned police investigative work, but the trip was called off. "Nine eleven changed everything," people say, and Postiglione remembers it in reference to the March case. Nine eleven changed everything for the cold case investigation. The year 2001 merged into 2002, and then 2003 arrived, and the detectives never made their trip to the Lake Chapala region.

By 2004 they would have had much more to investigate.

As the business empire built by Perry and Chavez began to implode, disgruntled clients within this haven for American and Canadian expatriates became more vocal. Clients and expatriate residents like Gayle Cansienne began to complain to anyone who would listen, including the *Guadalajara Colony Reporter*, the Mexican government, and local attorneys, that Perry had bilked her out of her life savings of several hundred thousand dollars in a bogus offshore tax-shelter scheme. Other clients of the C&M businesses somehow secured the e-mail addresses of Postiglione and Pridemore and began writing lengthy messages outlining their grievances over excessive fees, services never completed, and files lost in a mysterious office fire.

They were demanding that either the American or Mexican authorities look into the matter.

But according to other expatriate residents of Ajijic, like American Don Leach, Perry was not getting a fair shake in all the local gossip and negative publicity. "I feel bad for Perry because my experience with him has been very very positive," Leach said.

It would not be the first or the last time that Perry March was viewed as both a Dr. Jekyll and Mr. Hyde.

Perry was not the sole target in this crescendo of complaints. Someone wanting to deliver a message to Samuel Chavez targeted him in a drive-by shooting. He escaped injury and was unable or unwilling to provide sufficient information to allow for capture of the shooters, but Chavez apparently understood the message and relocated to Guadalajara.

As the new life Perry had created for himself and his expanded family began to gradually come apart, he would have frequent confrontations with Chavez and others.

During one such heated conversation, a third party was present, Mexican attorney Alberto José Sandoval Pulido. The exchange was in both English and Spanish, as Perry was multilingual, but while Pulido understood most English words, he was by no means fluent.

Yet, during this afternoon, the intent of Perry's threat was unmistakable.

Perry's words would come back to haunt him years later on two separate occasions—once before a judge and once before a judge and jury.

CHAPTER 30

Shuttle Diplomacy

Winter has come to Nashville, and the Thanksgiving dinners of just over a week ago are now being replaced with plans for more family arrivals and Old Saint Nick. The colorful leaves that attract visitors from all over the country to the rolling hills of Tennessee, especially the Great Smoky Mountains, have fallen from the branches. Tree limbs are bare, and the brisk winds of winter have started to arrive. Music City is decked out with the lights and decorations of the holidays, as people scurry around with shopping in mind. Many of the offices in downtown are starting to enjoy their annual Christmas parties, and the pace of business throughout the city has been turned down a notch or two.

But at the district attorney's office and at the offices of the cold case unit in this first week of December 2004, the mood is anything but festive. The decision has finally been made by Tom Thurman and his boss, Torry Johnson, to present the Janet March murder case to a local grand jury. On Pearl Harbor Day, Bill Pridemore enters the chambers of the grand jury, located on the same floor as the DA's office at

222 Second Avenue North, as the sole witness for the state of Tennessee. The Nashville citizen noted as the official prosecutor on the first page of the indictment is Pat Postiglione.

It is the Postiglione and Pridemore show; and eight and a half years of investigative efforts have to be condensed into a logical and well-formulated presentation before a sworn panel of Nashville's citizens. These same citizens have been hearing grand-jury presentments off and on since October, and until a representative from the district attorney's office approaches the podium, the members of the grand jury do not know exactly what criminal case they are about to be presented.

December 7 will prove to be a day they will likely never forget.

Tom Thurman, through his investigators, will lay out in meticulous detail why the state of Tennessee believes that Perry Avrum March, former attorney with the prestigious law firm Bass, Berry, and Sims and former associate with the highly respected firm of Levine, Mattson, Orr, and Geracioti, should be indicted for the murder of his former wife, Janet, on or about August 15, 1996.

The decision by the DA's office to proceed with the grand-jury presentment, without the discovery of Janet's body, is an admission, by all those who have for the last eight and a half years participated in the March investigation, that the case about to be presented will never be any stronger, and it is now or never.

The prosecution team will be entirely wrong in their assessment.

Thurman, Postiglione, and Pridemore know from their decades of experience that even without a body, the chance that a grand jury will not return an indictment is remote. By the nature of the grand-jury system, the defendant does not present his or her "side of the story," so the odds are stacked highly in favor of the state. It is not the grand jury that worries them; it is the actual criminal trial that has always been their primary concern.

The decision to move forward on December 7 only came about after much analysis and debate within the DA's office, as well as months of pre-indictment diplomacy. Tom Thurman, who grew up on a gravel road in a small Tennessee town along the Cumberland Plateau, had to expand his normal role as prosecutor into that of international diplomat and negotiator. With the assistance of the FBI, negotiations with the Mexican government were conducted for months before and after the date of the grand jury appearance. Thurman's worst fear was that the local grand jury would indict Perry March, but the Mexican government would not cooperate in his extradition to the United States.

There were two central points at issue.

The first was the legal disparity between Mexico, the country where Perry March had resided since 1999, and the United States, over the implementation of the death penalty. According to Amnesty International, since 1990, forty nations around the world have abolished the death penalty "for all crimes," bringing the total to eighty-eight worldwide, and another eleven countries have abolished the death penalty for all but "exceptional crimes including wartime crimes." One of those countries was Mexico. Others included Canada, Paraguay, the Philippines, Cyprus, and Turkey. Unlike the United States, these nations apparently concurred with the conclusion of Roger Hood in his 2002 survey of research findings on the relationship between the death penalty and homicide rates; according to Hood: "It is not prudent to accept the hypothesis that capital punishment deters murder to a marginally greater extent than does the threat and application of the supposedly lesser punishment of life imprisonment."

Statistical data seems to support Hood's position. Also according to Amnesty International, in Canada in 1975, the year before the abolition of the death penalty for murder, the homicide rate peaked at 3.09 per 100,000 of population, and by 1980 had fallen to 2.41 before falling to 1.73 in 2003, a reduction of 44 percent. In contrast, according to the Uniform Crime Report released annually by the FBI, in the United

States in 2003 the homicide rate per 100,000 of population was 5.7, or 329 percent greater than Canada's.

As Postiglione and Pridemore knew from firsthand experience, Nashville regularly contributed to the nation's homicide totals. In 1996 there were 91 confirmed homicides in Music City. If the prosecutorial team was successful in their case against Perry March, there would have to be a footnote explaining the belated increase of that total to 92. In 1997 the number of murders in the city rose to 112, including the cold case detectives' two dead kids in a freezer.

The fact that the Perry March case was now embroiled in the international debate over the death penalty should not come as a major shock. Nothing had gone well with this investigation from the start. Now that the prosecutors had finally decided to "roll the dice," why should things prove any different?

The second point brought on by Perry's Mexican residency was the poor track record of Mexico in responding to extradition from other countries. In 1980 President Jimmy Carter signed an extradition treaty with Mexico. It provided for the extradition of a person who has been charged with or found guilty of an offense committed in the United States who had fled to Mexico. The treaty went on to state that an offense is extraditable if it is a crime in both countries and punishable by incarceration for a period of one year or more. In addition, when the offense for which extradition is sought is punishable by death, the treaty said that extradition *may* be refused unless assurances are given that the death penalty will not be imposed, and if imposed, will not be executed.

This possibility of a unilateral decision to refuse extradition was further complicated when the Mexican Supreme Court handed down a decision on October 2, 2001, in which the court ruled that *no extradition would be granted* unless the requesting state gave assurances that a prison sentence of a term of years would be imposed and the suspect eligible for parole. In their ruling, the Mexican Supreme Court stated that the purpose of punishment was rehabilitation, and that life imprisonment is inconsistent with rehabilitation, and therefore a sentence of life imprisonment violates their constitution because it constitutes *cruel and unusual punishment.*

In the fall of 2004, Tom Thurman found himself in the middle of a highly volatile international debate between the government officials of Mexico and the United States. Prosecutors around the country were complaining to Washington about what amounted to the Mexican government dictating how they should pursue their most serious cases if their suspect fled to Mexico after the offense.

One particular case involved the murder of a Los Angeles sheriff's deputy, David March, on April 22, 2002, while on routine uniformed patrol. The gunman who shot him several times at close range, Armando Garcia, fled to Mexico shortly after the shooting. Because Garcia faced life imprisonment without parole for his offense, the Mexican government refused to extradite him. The murdered L.A. sheriff's deputy became a national poster child for the entire extradition debate. Prosecutors around the country became acquainted with the case.

President George W. Bush, always eager to find a law-and-order cause to which to politically attach himself, especially in the post-9/11 atmosphere, elected to speak at the Annual Peace Officers Memorial Service in May 2003, and specifically incorporated references to the David March case in his speech.

Photos are taken of the president consoling David March's widow, Terri. It may have been just another timely photo op for the president, but it was a meeting Terri March would not forget, or allow President Bush to ignore. Years later, her husband's killer still free, she would write a letter to the president stating:

I am living the unthinkable nightmare!!! Sir, I have told you in person, at the National Police Memorial on May 15, 2003, we needed your help. You said, "We're going to get this guy." You looked me in the eye, and I believed you.

Tom Thurman found himself in a catch-22, an illogical and irrational dilemma resulting from dealing with a bureaucracy. He had to convince the Mexican authorities that Perry had committed sufficiently horrific criminal behavior to warrant extradition, yet at the same time assure the same bureaucracy that he would not seek the death penalty and that any potential sentence would incorporate the possibility of parole.

The police theory postulated in this homicide case actually worked to give Thurman more flexibility in his diplomatic negotiations. Nashville authorities from the beginning did not believe that Perry had murdered Janet by carrying out a premeditated act. Rather, all the lead detectives—from David Miller to Tim Mason to Brad Corcoran to Mickey Miller to Postiglione and Pridemore—believed Janet's death was the result of a blow struck during a violent argument.

So first-degree murder was never evidentially "on the table."

What Thurman was dealing with was like a schoolyard game of tug-of-war, but on an international scale. Just when he was convinced he had supplied the right documentation to the Mexican government, through the agreed conduit of the FBI, momentum would swing back in favor of not finalizing the extradition. It became clear that someone was pulling hard on the rope south of the border. Nashville authorities were convinced that Perry was paying bribes to certain Mexican officials to slow down or halt any efforts to remove him from the country.

As 2004 passed and then half of 2005, Perry March was convinced he was invincible inside the borders of Mexico, and that his new life with his new and expanded family in the land of eternal spring would go on forever.

There had been an earlier occasion, in June 2000, when Perry was physically removed from his business offices in Ajijic by Mexican police who without prior warning informed him, "Your papers are not in order." He was hurriedly placed inside a van and rushed out of the small tranquil village. After Perry shouted out the name of a certain Mexican official, the van shrieked to a halt, cell-phone calls were made, and as quickly as it had begun, it ended. "It seems, Señor March, your papers are in order." There was a way to get things done in Mexico and Perry March had become proficient at playing the game. He understood that intimidation got results. It had been his mantra in his personal and business life ever since law school.

Thurman was getting help from inside Mexico as well.

American citizens from the Lake Chapala region who felt they had been treated unfairly or even worse by Perry in a variety of business transactions began writing the offices of the Mexican government, including possibly as high up as the office of President Vicente Fox, voicing their outrage. They would not be the only letters the Mexican president was receiving regarding cases involving someone named March. During this same time, Terri March, the L.A. deputy's widow, wrote him voicing her own outrage over the fact that Armando Garcia, her husband's killer, was still escaping justice and living inside Mexico as a free man.

While the prosecutorial team and the Levines may have viewed Perry as an American citizen hiding out in Mexico to avoid prosecution, a United States Federal Court had in 2001 issued a ruling that the issue of custody for Sammy and Tzipi should be determined by the country where their custodial parent (Perry) resided (Mexico). And as slain officer David March's widow, Terri, was finding out year after year, Mexico was not inclined to extradite its residents, especially those who knew how to "play the game."

On December 8, 2004, the Nashville grand jury conclude that the testimony and supportive documentation presented by Postiglione and Pridemore are sufficient to indict Perry Avrum March on three separate felony charges: murder in the second degree, abuse of a corpse, and tampering with evidence.

However, it will still be eight months, after Tom Thurman and the FBI have endured a bureaucratic nightmare, before the Levines will learn that their son-in-law has been apprehended by Mexican officers while walking on the quiet morning streets of Ajijic.

It will not be until February of 2006 that the victims in the "other March case" will learn that Mexican officials also arrested Armando Garcia.

CHAPTER 31

Trouble in Paradise

Perry's feet bounce along the cobblestone street with a rhythmic precision. The aromas of Ajijic filter out into the bright morning air. The yeasty scent of baking bread mixes with the fragrance of rich coffee and ripe fruits—fresh mangoes, papayas, pineapples, and guavas. Shopkeepers and merchants are just beginning to open up their small establishments. Perry's mouth waters as he anticipates a fresh cup of strong coffee and a delectable pastry he imagines Carmen is just pulling out of the oven at their Media Luna Bistro & Café.

The temperature is ideal, and it promises to be another perfect day in the land of eternal sunshine.

On this Wednesday morning in August, Perry's thoughts are scattered. Images race through his brain like the cars of the freight trains that used to pass through the East Chicago neighborhood of his youth. The doors of many of the railcars would be open as the train rocked down the tracks in its pulsating mechanized dance, and for the briefest of moments Perry would picture himself running alongside, then jumping into an open car, letting the train take him on a magical adventure.

He is so far away from his youth now, so far away from his childhood home. The last ten years have been their own adventure, one filled with extreme highs and lows. But this is home now, as it has been for the last six years. He is surrounded by his children, all six of them, his blended family.

Family remains the center of his world and yet it has been the cause of his deepest pain—first with his mother's death when he was only nine, and then when he was thirty-five he had to endure the other nightmare of Janet's death. But through all the years family has brought him tremendous happiness as well—Sammy, who has matured into a sensitive, handsome young man, and Tzipi, a beautiful, magical little girl, and the newest addition, Azul, whose dark soulful eyes and innocent giggle captivate his heart. And there are Cinty, Daro, and Thomas, who look to him now as their dad. They are all so bright, like little sponges absorbing the knowledge of two varied cultures.

He has loved his perfect life in Ajijic, but now he has to consider the possibility of change. The walls are closing in. Always, he has been one step ahead of his pursuers.

He contemplates how to deal with his family—Carmen, who told 48 Hours *that she couldn't imagine why Perry's first wife left the way she did, and his wonderful children.*

But he knows his dad will be fine. Arthur likes his independence. Perry used to think maybe he would have a new mother someday, but by the time he became a teenager, he knew it would never happen. His dad was different, too set in his own ways, and things have not changed here in Mexico. Arthur will never leave Ajijic. He is a fixture here, a local, as much as any expatriate can become a local. He has a routine that suits him, starting off each day with his friends at the doughnut shop, then off to the hospital to teach English. Arthur knows everyone in town.

From his youth Perry knew he was different, too, different from most others, his mind an unfillable reservoir for information. His view of knowledge as power has always allowed him to land on his feet. Weaker men would have caved under the pressure, the years of battles with adver-

saries as powerful as the Levines, and all the strings they were able to pull with the authorities in Nashville. But he won those battles, and he would be the one to teach Sammy and Tzipi about life, about how their belief in themselves can get them through any tragedy, any battle, any adversity.

With the sun's benevolent rays warm on his shoulders, Perry is alone with all these thoughts as he draws closer to the captivating smells of the Media Luna.

But others are watching his every move.

Special Agent Ken Sena is just one pair of eyes trained on Perry on this morning of August 3, 2005. He has been in and out of Mexico for months keeping tabs on the "target," an on-the-ground observer, hiding in the shadows, blending in with the American expatriates and the many tourists, waiting for instructions. At times it has been frustrating, even exasperating, with all the mixed signals, the go-aheads and then the pullbacks, all depending on the fluctuating position of the Mexican government. He can only imagine what the Nashville authorities must be thinking. But he is used to the ying and the yang of international assignments—the constant stroking of egos, working inside hierarchies, dealing with bureaucracies. Hell, it could be worse. He could be somewhere else in the world, freezing his ass off on this Wednesday morning. It's just the way the game is played, not the way he or most agents want it to be played, but it is what it is.

Besides, in the next few moments, this assignment is going to be over.

All the months of negotiating, of passing along information, pushing for results and then backing off, and then pushing again, are about to come to an end.

"I've never seen anything like it," says Alejandro Ochoa, Perry's gardener, his voice cracking with emotion as he recounts to a translator what he witnessed that day on the streets of Ajijic. "The cars with tinted windows appeared out of nowhere, and men jumped out. They rushed to the curb and grabbed Mr. March. They never showed any ID *or anything. They tried to grab me, too, but I resisted. They let me go, and then sped away with Mr. March in a convoy. The whole thing took less than three minutes."*

Arthur March is just entering the doughnut shop when he learns of his son's fate.

"They have him, they have him, Mr. Arthur!"

"What are you talking about?"

"They have Mr. Perry!"

"Who has Perry?" Arthur demands, his entire demeanor changing, the ever-present smile vanishing in an instant. He forces himself to come to attention, a reflex from so many years in the military. He reaches for his gun—another reflex—and then remembers where he is.

He's sure the Levines are behind this. "First they kidnapped my grandchildren," he says, "and the federal court admitted to it, and we got the kids back. Now they've kidnapped my son."

Arthur rushes out of the doughnut shop. He must get his weapon. "If it's up to me, there's gonna be some bloodshed. I'll get those bastards," he yells, as if he is calling out a promise to his son.

For Carmen it is the second time in five years that Mexican authorities have burst into their lives and bodily removed her husband from their calm environment of Ajijic, from their home. Her heart races like a trapped bird's as she holds little Azul close to her and continues to smile and tries to wait on her customers, as more and more people enter the Media Luna, whispering. The news of the kidnapping has traveled through the tiny village like a tidal wave, shocking everyone it touches. Some of Perry's connections begin at once to distance themselves from him.

But Carmen is not panicked. She knows her smart and courageous husband was able to right this same wrong before. She is confident that Perry can again call the right people at immigration, his inside connections, and he will be home soon, probably before dinner.

But this time, no one is answering.

PART THREE

CHAPTER 32

Old Classmates

When Brent Fossett, a practicing attorney in Los Angeles, receives a call on August 4 from an old Vanderbilt Law School classmate, it is not about a class reunion.

"Mr. March is holding for you. He says he's an old classmate of yours."

"Who?"

"Perry March. He says he went to law school with you."

"Oh—Perry March. Okay, put him on."

"He's calling from jail."

"Jail? Are you sure?"

"The recording said the call was originating from the Van Nuys jail."

Unlike the political wrangling that went on for months in the case of Perry's extradition from Mexico, extradition within the United States is a fast-track process. The process of extradition between states has its roots in the direct language of the United States Constitution. Article 4 addresses, among other things, the responsibilities that the states have to one another. Within Article 4, Section 1 states:

Full Faith and Credit shall be given in each State to the public Acts, Records, and judicial Proceedings of every other State. And the Congress may by general Laws prescribe the Manner in which such Acts, Records and Proceedings shall be proved, and the Effect thereof.

The actions of the Nashville grand jury in early December 2004—handing down three felony indictments—fell within the definition of "judicial Proceedings."

A Person charged in any State with Treason, Felony, or other Crime, who shall flee from Justice, and be found in another State, shall on demand of the executive Authority of the State from which he fled, be delivered up, to be removed to the State having Jurisdiction of the Crime.

Once the governor's office of Tennessee formally requested the extradition of Perry Avrum March, the "fugitive" had only twelve days to decide whether to waive extradition or formally request a hearing and contest his return to Tennessee. Perry March, the bright young Jewish attorney, once tapped to become the next "Harris Gilbert, the next *consigliere* within the Nashville legal community," had never practiced criminal law. He needed counsel—local counsel. And so from the California jail, he called Brent Fossett.

Fossett agrees to stand up before the judge with his old classmate. And in a most odd twist of circumstances, Perry March, an individual who has spent a decade inside and outside the courtroom contesting and vehemently arguing each facet of the events that began on the night of August 15, 1996, and who now faces a criminal arraignment and trial on charges that collectively carry up to thirty-eight years in prison, elects not to contest his extradition back to Tennessee.

The news of Perry's arrest and return from Mexico captures Nashville by surprise. In this Southern city where gossip flows as easily as Jack Daniel's whiskey, the prosecution team has managed to keep the December indictments under wraps for eight months. The grand-jury foreman and his fellow members have apparently heeded the directives of Tom Thurman and have followed the words of the ancient proverb: Speech is silver, silence is golden. The dramatic events crank up the media machine once again. Nashville's principal television stations rush reporters and cameramen onto flights headed for the West Coast, to capture a photograph of the city's most famous fugitive and to sign on: ". . . reporting live from Los Angeles . . ."

Brent Fossett is one of the first to make himself available to the swarm of media, and he presents the best face possible on a horrible situation for his fellow alumnus. "Anyone can see that this is a father who has been ripped away from his family," he says. Fossett adds that Perry was "not given the opportunity to voluntarily appear in Nashville to face these charges. Mr. March wants to get to trial as soon as possible so he can get home and see his family as soon as possible."

Thurman, Postiglione, and Pridemore are more than eager to give Perry March the opportunity to face these charges, but first there is some old business that needs attention.

CHAPTER 33

Let's Make a Deal

It's a warm, breezy afternoon on Long Island. Detective Postiglione is back home, and it feels good. Nashville is fine, but this is home. He's glad to be spending some time with Ronnie in Bayport, something he knows he ought to do more of. Ronnie, his "big little brother," is a beefier version of the detective. Retired NYPD, Ronnie was right in the middle of all the hell during 9/11. All his years on the force, he worked too hard, never took vacation, but he's singing a different tune these days. On Friday Postiglione will watch his niece walk down the aisle. He's never been much for the ceremonial pageantry of weddings, but Debbie's wedding was the excuse he needed to come home for a few days. He thinks a lot about family lately. Working with victims' families has that effect. It has been almost a year since he has seen most of his New York relatives.

He leans back and lets the sun beam down on his face. Perfect. He will never get used to Nashville's humidity. Ronnie is rattling on about how great retirement is when Postiglione's cell phone rings. He looks at the number. "I gotta take this," he says.

The caller is Tom Thurman. It's a call Postiglione has been waiting for.

The call is brief.

Today, Perry March has been deported from Mexico. Postiglione gives his brother a condensed version of the March case. "Looks like I may be going to L.A. to pick him up."

Ronnie takes it in, nodding. "You have to leave before the wedding?"

"Don't know yet. Depends if he waives extradition, or could be somebody else goes, guys from the fugitives section. But it should be my partner and me."

"Sure, it's your investigation."

"Yeah, and if March has something to say, you know—it's a chance we won't get again."

Detective Postiglione spends the rest of the afternoon making and taking calls, trying to get all the facts. Ronnie leaves him in the backyard with his cell phone.

"Don't say anything to the family yet," Postiglione tells him. In the best-case scenario, he'll go to L.A. next week, but he's prepared to leave tomorrow—or today.

Missing family events is nothing new for the veteran detective. Three—or was it four?—summer vacations to Destin, Florida, that his family had to take without him, and there was his son's high school graduation, when he was called out on a double homicide. It's the nature of his work. And this case is important. He's put a lot into it.

Whatever it takes to bring Perry March to justice—he's ready.

Detective Pridemore bends over a stack of paperwork on his desk, wishing he were out on the golf course. The humidity in Nashville during August can be brutal, but he doesn't mind; golf provides him the mental release he needs from the constant chaos of the department. On the links he can escape for a few hours from the harsh realities of work—murder, rape, and brutality. His cell phone rings. Pridemore knows the reason for the call as soon as he hears

Tom Thurman's voice. He knows it has finally happened.
The FBI has grabbed March.

The legally established procedural window to bring Perry
March back to Nashville to face murder charges expires at
midnight on August 13. Once a prisoner waives his legal
right to a formal hearing to contest extradition, the petition-
ing state has only ten days to retrieve the prisoner. After
waiting for almost a decade to place handcuffs on Perry
March, the two cold case detectives are almost denied the
opportunity to catch a plane west and pick him up.

Out-of-town trips are something most of the detectives
vie for—a brief reprieve from the daily grind of police work.
But in this case, once the usual candidates for prisoner pick-
ups are canvassed, the concensus is that Postiglione and
Pridemore should be the ones to bring Perry March home to
face the charges. They have been the two who spearheaded
the investigatory efforts to solve a case most of Nashville
had given up on. They have chased down every single lead
and tip, most of which led nowhere.

They are anxious to make the trip, yet their experience
tells them that the delay in securing the assignment is really
playing to their advantage. Having Perry sit in jail for over
a week before they arrive will make their mission much easier.

On August 12, after spending the night in Los Angeles,
Postiglione and Pridemore get in their rental car and head to
the Van Nuys police facility. The L.A. traffic is a nightmare.
As Pridemore negotiates the car from one crowded freeway
to the next, he promises himself to never curse Nashville
traffic again.

"So how do we want to play this?" he asks his partner.

"You know exactly what we need to do," says Postiglione. "I want his confidence, and I want him to talk."

"Hell, he's an attorney. He'll know to keep his mouth
shut."

"I don't think so. He's narcissistic," Postiglione points
out. "He loves the spotlight. As long as he thinks the media

will be on the story, I think he'll be his normal arrogant self, and we both know arrogant people like to talk."

They arrive at Van Nuys and meet the officer in charge. After the perfunctory introductions and chitchat, there is the review of the paperwork. Always the endless paperwork. It has been thirty years on the force for both Nashville detectives, and retirement is not far off for either. One thing they will surely not miss is the paperwork. It takes up more time than their real investigative efforts. They have promised each other they will solve this one last case before retiring their shields. On this bright sunny California morning of August 12, 2005, they realize that they have a chance in the next twelve hours to fulfill that promise.

"Is the rumor true that O. J. Simpson was in the same cell where they've got March?" Pridemore asks.

"That's what the media's reporting," says Postiglione. "I'm sure he'll view it as a badge of honor, a sign of his deserved celebrity."

After what seems like an eternity, the detectives finally see Perry March approaching down a long shadowy corridor. He is escorted by two burly officers, and his legs are chained together. There is another chain running from his legs up to his hands, which are clasped together inside a restraint that encircles his waist. It is the first time either detective has personally laid eyes on the man who, for years, has been the focus of most of their waking hours. Perry is shorter than Pridemore has imagined from the countless photographs splashed across newspapers and TV. Staring at the bloated and out-of-shape prisoner, he remembers the notation in the file that March became a black belt in karate at age thirteen. Hard to believe.

Postiglione assesses his quarry, the pudgy figure waddling toward him. He readies himself for an opportunity that has taken nine years to surface, the chance to find out what truly happened on August 15, 1996, and where the body of Janet March is. When he arrived in custody from Mexico, Perry employed his old Vanderbilt classmate to represent him, but on this morning he is navigating the legal system on his own.

Postiglione introduces himself and his partner to the prisoner. There is no hostility in Perry's tone; in fact, he is almost cordial. The arrogant, confident, cocky individual that they expected is simply not present. Instead, there is a timid and reticent shadow of the man they expected.

Pridemore exchanges a glance with his partner. He thinks about Janet March and the Levines, about Sammy and Tzipora. He thinks about all the years that they have worked on the case and all the stress it has caused within the department. Unknowingly, he curls his right hand into a fist, and the veins running up his neck begin to protrude. The two Van Nuys jailers sense what Pridemore is thinking, and a grin comes to both their faces at the same time. "Have a nice flight back, Mr. March," one of the jailers says.

The dance between prisoner and cops begins. Perry takes the first steps. He addresses Postiglione. "Am I to walk behind you, sir?" he asks. "May I carry my contact case with me, sir?"

The seasoned detective doesn't show his surprise at the prisoner's subservient demeanor. Instead he calmly joins in on the dance and replies, "That will be fine."

They take photos of Perry to show that he is in good physical condition, retrieve their weapons, and leave the jail. They're running behind schedule but need to stop at a gas station to fill up. While Pridemore is at the pump, Postiglione and Perry talk about L.A., the weather, the traffic—small talk. There is a lapse. Perry stares out the window. He looks as if he's thinking hard. Postiglione seizes the opportunity. "I know as an attorney you know your rights. You aren't required to talk to us at all," he says. "But if you want to engage in any dialogue, we'll listen. Feel free to ask us any questions you may have about anything you don't understand."

March offers a faint smile and nods.

•　　•　　•

The traffic on the trip to the airport is hell. Pridemore wants to pull off the road, get out of the car with his partner, and leave Perry in the car alone. Alone to think about what may be coming next. The streetwise detective senses that Perry is confused. He has been sitting in a six-by-nine cell for over a week. That's not the bright sunny skies of Mexico he has been used to. He has never been arrested before, and he's used to being in control of every aspect of his life and the lives around him; now, for the last nine days, someone else has been calling all the shots. But the prisoner-transfer process has taken much longer than expected, and after returning the rental car and taking the trolley to LAX, they will be lucky to make their return flight at all.

By the time they reach the gate, the time delay has thrown their normal routine totally off. This is not the first time the two veteran detectives have brought a prisoner in from out of state. As experienced cops, they like things to go smoothly, and they know the best way is to be the first ones on the plane. That way they don't disrupt the normal boarding procedures by parading the prisoner in front of the other passengers. In the post-9/11 environment of air travel, knowing they are flying with an individual who requires two police escorts, handcuffs, and legs chains can be damn frightening to passengers.

Entering the Boeing 757 with the prisoner, they are the very last passengers to board. Once inside, they are surprised by a cameraman from a Nashville TV station. The media representative, eager to film the biggest story to rock Nashville in a decade, jumps out of his seat with video camera in hand and ambushes the two cops with their human parcel. Within minutes the whole thing turns into a circus. Postiglione turns to his partner and grunts, "How did they know we would be here today?" Both cops realize there is a leak inside the department.

The head flight attendant rushes over to the cold case detectives and makes no effort to disguise her frustration. "You have taken over my plane!" she says.

Postiglione fires back, "Hey, look, this wasn't staged. We didn't know anything about this idiot with the camera."

Finally they make their way to their assigned seats. To escape the glare of the television camera and the displeasure of the flight crew, the detectives direct March down the aisle and guide him into the window seat. Postiglione slides in next, and Pridemore drops into the aisle seat. Again their standard protocol has been disrupted. The prisoner to be transported is always seated between both escorts.

So far the day has not gone as planned.

By the time the plane reaches a comfortable cruising altitude, Perry dozes off. The flight is almost half over when the in-flight meal is served.

"Can you take these cuffs off so I can eat?" Perry asks.

Postiglione reaches into his pocket for the key. Pridemore gives his partner a look of disapproval. He wants their transport to remain as uncomfortable as possible for the duration of the flight. Postiglione ignores his partner. He senses the dance is about to begin again.

As soon as he completes his meal, Perry begins to talk. "What evidence do you have against me?" he asks.

"I can't go into the evidence. You should know that," says Postiglione.

The dance continues.

"Did you check out the photo we sent to the DA's office?" Perry asks. "The photo of Janet at the Olympics in Athens?"

"We checked it out. We check out every lead."

The veteran cop wants to add that everyone in the department who saw the "supposed" picture of Janet March laughing with others in an outdoor setting at the 2000 Olympics immediately knew it was not her. The detectives knew it was bullshit, probably planted by Perry himself from Mexico or by someone working on his behalf, but they did what their jobs required. They checked it out. They even went to Janet's parents to ask if they thought it could be their daughter. The Levines couldn't believe anyone would mistake the woman in that photo for Janet.

Such a stupid move, Postiglione thinks—whoever did it. One argument that Perry has tried to float with the media is that maybe Janet had a reason to vanish. Maybe she had a secret life she wanted to follow, a life with someone else. The veteran detective knows that if this theory is the seed March is thinking of trying to plant in the minds of potential jurors, the alleged photo at the Olympics makes absolutely no sense. Would a woman who wanted to disappear into another life, a private life where she would never be discovered, place herself at the Olympics, one of the most public events on the planet, and then allow herself to be part of a staged photograph with several others? It makes no sense.

Both detectives have heard over and over that Perry March is very smart and very devious. The episode of the photo at the Olympics proves he isn't so smart. Postiglione knows that in August 1996 March made a mistake, but he had time to cover it up by not reporting Janet missing for two full weeks. Now, under the pressure of confinement, Postiglione knows March will slip up, and this time he and Pridemore will be there waiting.

Pridemore remains silent in his aisle seat. He doesn't want to disrupt a dialogue that he knows his partner is starting to nurture.

"I would like to set up a meeting with Tom," Perry announces. "If we could come to a deal, a deal that would not be more than seven years, I think my wife—I think Carmen would wait for me. I'm going to do the right thing, be a man, and do my time if we can reach an agreement."

A flight attendant approaches to offer beverages. Pridemore waves her off with a frown. She shoots him a look of disgust and returns to the galley mumbling something about Clint Eastwood movies.

"I can't make any deals," Postiglione says. "You know that. You'll have to meet with Tom directly, you or your attorneys. Any deal will require full disclosure of everything, and I do mean everything."

"To be honest, I'm scared shitless about this. But all those representing me might not be out for my best interest.

I know what's best for me. I'll be the best attorney in the room," Perry says. "Just tell Tom we need to talk." The "yes, sir" and "may I do this, sir" have disappeared.

It is evening when they finally arrive at the Nashville Criminal Justice Center, the end of a very long day. The two tired detectives escort their prisoner down the long corridor toward the holding cell. Perry waddles, the heavy chains running from his lassoed feet up to his waist. Postiglione wants to be sure that their discussion on the plane was not just bullshit. He wants to be sure Perry was not just fishing for information.

He says, "I hope you remember the conversation we had on the plane."

Perry comes to a complete stop and turns around to face Postiglione. He does his best to raise his hands up toward his unshaven, haggard face and points at himself. "Look at me. You've got my word."

They walk on. Pridemore drops a little behind to let his partner do his work. He feels his pulse beating hard in his temples. Whatever Perry has to say, he damn well better say it. Time is running out.

"There will have to be full disclosure," Postiglione says.

Perry keeps moving, his chains rattling softly.

They reach the receiving desk. It's over, both detectives are thinking. Then March turns to them and says, "You have certain information about the case and I have certain information about the case. You tell Tom I will tell him everything I know. Everything."

CHAPTER 34

Attending to Some Old Business

Once back in Nashville, things quickly go from bad to worse for Perry. With a bond hearing not yet scheduled, and confined to a jail cell far away from his Mexican paradise and from Carmen and the children, he is slapped with another criminal charge that seems to come from out of nowhere.

In reality, the charge goes back to 1999.

A few months before Perry left Chicago for the land of eternal sunshine, Larry Levine, still in full battle mode against his son-in-law, along with his law partner Michael Geracioti, paid a visit to Deputy District Attorney Tom Thurman. They went to discuss $23,000 in legal fees that Perry received from two clients in the first few months after Janet's disappearance and then, according to Levine and Geracioti, converted to his own use, rather than turning it over to the firm. Tom Thurman was only too happy to help. He presented the matter to a Nashville grand jury, and in June of 1999 Perry was formally indicted for "felony theft in an amount over $10,000 but less than $60,000." At the time of the issuance of the indictment, Perry was already in Mexico, so he was never served with an arrest warrant. Now that Thurman has Perry back in Nashville, he takes the opportunity to serve the murder defendant with the old theft charge.

Perry March does not have many supporters in the Nashville area. However, some in the Nashville legal community comment "off the record" that for anyone else, this matter might have ended up in civil court, with lawyers arguing over who was entitled to certain partnership funds.

The media remains focused on the headline-grabbing murder charges. However, the theft charge may prove just as important. The prosecution announces plans to try Perry on that charge in a separate trial first. If successful, their defendant will face his murder trial not as an ordinary citizen, but as a convicted felon.

The procedural implications of this are enormous from both an evidentiary and trial strategy standpoint.

CHAPTER 35

And in This Corner

It is the age of technology. Instead of the traditional appearance in the courtroom before the magistrate, Perry March is arraigned through videoconferencing. He never even leaves the jail facility. The event takes on a bizarre and surreal air. He speaks into a microphone and looks into a camera. At the same time, a monitor shows him what's happening in the courtroom of Judge Dozier, who has the same equipment. A mass of media with all their cameras is filming the event, which itself is only a video. It is like watching actors shooting a scene in a television movie.

The defendant pleads not guilty.

The charges have been formally presented. Perry March takes on a new title, one he has been avoiding for nine years. From now on until he is proven innocent or guilty, he is now the *criminal defendant*. The bell has been rung and the title match commences. It is the first round of what for now looks to be a twelve-round match. Each side has selected its tag team.

In the prosecution's corner, it is Deputy District Attorney

Thomas Thurman who leads the effort. With nearly thirty years in the DA's office, Thurman, fifty-nine, is a senior trial adviser who has tried the major criminal cases in Nashville for the last decade. He's a homegrown Tennessean who grew up in rural Crossville, Tennessee, earned a master's degree in biology from Tennessee Tech, not far from his Crossville home, and worked for the metro water department while taking night classes at Nashville School of Law.

His mother taught elementary school and his father owned a store that sold men's clothing. Well dressed, with neat, short hair slightly graying, Thurman has a serious and confident manner, but his voice is low-key, matter-of-fact. He is not an orator with a spectacular presentation, but he gets the job done by being tenacious. Among the courthouse crowd, he is known as "The Thurmanator" for his methodical and relentless prosecutorial style. Outside the courtroom, he is still a competitor—a triathlete. Thurman knows how to pace himself for a long stressful contest.

Also at the prosecution's table will be Katy Miller, senior assistant district attorney. Like the deputy DA, Miller graduated from the Nashville School of Law, earning her license in 1981. She began working in the DA's office as an advocate for victims while attending law school. She leads the DA's family protection team, which works on cases involving domestic violence homicides and child deaths.

Tom Thurman and Katy Miller have worked on some of the most serious criminal cases in Davidson County, and they have successfully prosecuted some of the "cold" cases investigated by Detectives Postiglione and Pridemore, including the Paul Reid case. Reid was ultimately given seven death sentences for the murders in fast-food restaurants. Thurman and Miller won the five cases in Davidson County. The cold case detectives also cracked the Richard D'Antonio case—the "Music Row Murder"—and Thurman won the conviction.

In the opposite corner, the defense team is headed by William Massey, with John Herbison and Lorna McClusky at his side. Each brings a special skill to the defense team.

Tennessean reporter Sheila Burke described Massey as the "showman," Herbison as the "streetfighter," and McClusky as the "train conductor."

Bill Massey, age fifty-four, also a homegrown Tennessean, was born in the small town of Fayetteville. A graduate of Memphis State Law School, Massey is a high-profile criminal defense lawyer practicing in Memphis, but with national connections. President of the Tennessee Association of Criminal Defense Lawyers and past chair of the national association, he is a highly sought-after seminar instructor in criminal defense. Massey has a reputation for his ability to connect with juries. He's a smooth talker who loves to do just that—talk. He can sound like a salesman, and the next minute he's sounding like a preacher, making a fervent plea. Massey is as emotional as Thurman is dispassionate.

Like Thurman, he is impeccably dressed and groomed. His thick hair is as white as the cotton fields of West Tennessee, and he wears it parted to the side. A small man, he has a large presence, as he maximizes the use of his voice, expressions, and gestures, while pacing in the courtroom.

Co-counsel John Herbison—the Nashville connection—makes an entirely different impression. A huge man with a protruding belly, Herbison, fifty, could play the office Santa Claus without any padding. His hair touches his collar and covers his ears, and he has a full goatee, with a few gray whiskers peeking out on his chin.

Noted for his appellate work, Herbison has represented Perry at various times during the past six years. It was Herbison who acted as lead counsel in both the successful federal court litigation which returned Perry's children to him, and in the reversal of the $113.5 million wrongful-death judgment handed down by the Tennessee Court of Appeals. He has also made a name for himself defending clients in the adult entertainment industry, clients who may have known Perry in 1996, when Perry bragged that he represented "all the clubs in Nashville." Herbison has a flair for drama. He speaks his mind and is not always careful about whom he ruffles. He publicly lashed out against the police and especially Chief of Police Serpas for "parading my client in front of cameras." The son of a preacher, he is a graduate of the UT Knoxville College of Law.

The third member of the defense team is Lorna McClusky, fifty-two, a partner in the law office of Massey McClusky in Memphis. She graduated from Memphis State Law School in 1994, where she was on the *Law Review*. She is secretary of the Tennessee Association of Criminal Defense Lawyers. Although McClusky does not spend much time in the limelight, she makes her contribution as the "train conductor," keeping the defense team on track as the "showman" and the "streetfighter" do their thing.

The referee will be Judge Steve Dozier.

The judge is the son of a policeman known to many in law enforcement circles as "The Major," the longest-serving officer in the history of Nashville's police force, an officer who retired after fifty years. Like Thurman and Miller, the judge attended the Nashville School of Law and worked during law school for a criminal court judge. Dozier, age forty-eight, practiced criminal law before he became a prosecutor in the Davidson County DA's office. He is a man of quiet demeanor, but a no-nonsense jurist.

As the prosecution and defense teams square off against each other, more than just Nashville is watching—more than just Tennessee. CNN comes calling within the first few weeks.

CHAPTER 36

Collateral Damage

While prosecutors and defense counsel are being interviewed by the national media, Perry is forced to deal with other matters besides his criminal cases. Not the least of his legal woes is the latest in the long line of court actions filed by Larry and Carolyn Levine, this one before he arrived in Nashville.

The Levines wasted no time. Shortly after the announcement of Perry's arrest and subsequent return to the United States, they filed a motion asking for temporary custody of Sammy and Tzipi. The motion said that because Perry had been arrested on a murder charge and was in the United States awaiting trial, the children were no longer in their father's custody. The Levines, as "the children's closest nonincarcerated relatives in the United States," asked the court to let them care for their grandchildren.

Perry has other plans.

The children's lives are in a state of upheaval once again.

Considering the bitter conflicts between Perry and the Levines that have defined the past nine years, it is easy to forget that they operated as a family during that initial anxious and confusing time after Janet's disappearance—Perry, Larry, Carolyn, and Mark, who was in contact with them by phone before he returned from California. Carolyn spent time with Sammy and Tzipi, trying to smooth over what was happening, trying to comfort and reassure them when they wanted their mommy, wanted her to come home. Larry and Perry went together to the airport to search for Janet's car and shared information about calls to hotels and to Janet's friends in Nashville and other cities. At Sammy's birthday party, Perry and the Levines agreed on the story they would tell guests: "Janet is in California. She has an ear infection, so she can't fly."

By the time Perry, along with Larry and Mark, filed the missing persons report, the tension was already evident between him and his in-laws. According to Mark, Perry continued to delay reporting Janet's disappearance to the police until finally, on the fourteenth day, Larry and Mark said, "We're going." They walked out, and after a minute, Perry ran after them, and the three of them went to the Criminal Justice Center. That was August 29. Then Janet's car was found at the Brixworth Apartments on September 5. In Carolyn's words, "The relationship changed."

Carolyn didn't want Perry to take the children to visit Ron in Chicago for Rosh Hashanah, the beginning of the High Holy Holidays. She was trying to provide some constancy in their lives during this bewildering time. Rosh Hashanah, the Jewish New Year, fell on September 13 and 14. Perry let Sammy and Tzipi spend the night with their grandparents on September 11, and the next day he took them to Chicago.

He returned with the children on the fifteenth without telling the Levines, and when Carolyn found out they were back, she also learned that Sammy had broken his arm. She wanted to see him, to know that he was all right—and Tzipi—how was little Tzipi, the baby Janet took everywhere with her? Ella Goldshmid, the nanny, had to tell Carolyn that her instructions were not to let the children see the Levines.

At that point dread came over Carolyn and Larry like a chill; they were sure what Perry was planning. On September 17, the day of the search at 3 Blackberry Road, the Levines obtained an emergency court order to stop Perry from taking Sammy and Tzipi out of Nashville—but they were already gone. This time they would not be back soon.

After Perry moved with the children to Chicago, what had been a strained relationship became a deep, painful rift. The Levines had come to believe what they had refused to accept at first, that something terrible had happened to Janet, and that Perry was responsible. Now he had their grandchildren.

But Larry had worked through the legal system for forty years; now he would use the power of the courts to get his grandchildren—if not his daughter—back to a safe haven. Perry's side of the story was that he had removed the children from Nashville because of the "media circus." He had to get some relief for his family—and make some money to support them.

And so the battle lines were drawn.

Larry and Carolyn fought in the Chicago courts for visitation rights with Sammy and Tzipi, as they fought in Nashville courts to keep Perry from getting Janet's dream house. After two years they entered a Chicago courtroom for a hearing that they believed would result in permanent visitation rights. Another shocking development: Ron, representing Perry, announced to the court that Perry and the children had relocated to Mexico.

It is a cruel dance: the Levines move closer; Perry pulls back.

Perry was ordered by the court to bring the children to the United States for visitation, but more legal action followed, with the Levines filing a wrongful-death claim against him in a Nashville civil court. Again, Perry was a no-show. When he did not appear to fight the charge, the judge ruled against him. Perry's reaction might have been anticipated: he refused to let the Levines have any more contact with his children.

From Perry's viewpoint, the most brutal action on the part of his in-laws occurred in June 2000, when the Levines engaged Mexican authorities to help them execute a visitation order from a judge in an Illinois court. "They are kidnappers!" Perry charged. But the previous month, the grandparents had traveled to Mexico with legal papers from the United States granting them visitation with Sammy and Tzipi, and Perry had turned them away without letting them see the children.

So on that June morning in Mexico, when the Levines arrived at the children's school with their visitation order in hand and whisked Sammy and Tzipi off to the United States, they took steps to get permanent custody of the children. But as Perry told *48 Hours*, "The bottom line is that this treaty says that you can't steal children and try to make custody determinations in the jurisdiction where you stole them to." His lawyers won the case in a U.S. federal court.

The Levines had no contact with their grandchildren for the next four years.

Now the balance of power has once again shifted.

The day after Perry was arrested and deported from Mexico, Carmen March told a reporter from Nashville's NewsChannel 5 that Sammy and Tzipi were with her and she planned to continue taking care of them. "I love the kids. I always take care of them as they were mine," she said.

The Levines quickly filed their motion in federal court asking to take care of their grandchildren. The motion alleged that Perry or "his agents" were hiding the children from Mexican authorities.

On August 10, one week after Perry's arrest, Carmen was contacted again, and this time she said the children were living with a relative in the United States. A Chicago judge had granted temporary custody of the children to Perry's brother, Ron.

On Wednesday morning, August 17, Judge Betty Adams Green presides over a custody hearing in the Davidson County Juvenile Court. As Larry Levine and Perry March face each other across the courtroom, each must be aware of what the years have done to the other—Perry, once the bright, ambitious attorney, now shackled, wearing the required yellow jumpsuit, and Larry, his gaunt face a road map of worry and sorrow. Nine years ago on this day, they drove together to the airport to search for Janet's car.

Judge Green awards temporary custody of the children to the Levines. The next week she rules that the hearing to decide who should get custody of Sammy and Tzipi will take place in Nashville—not in Mexico or Chicago.

Sammy and Tzipi are once again in Nashville.

How have the children fared these nine years?

The public has not seen much of the March children. In spite of the seething hostilities between Perry and the Levines, they seem to be of the same mind when it comes to protecting Sammy and Tzipi from the publicity that has hurtled the Marches and Levines into the harsh spotlight.

But twice Perry allowed TV reporters to visit them in Mexico.

Tzipi, her pigtails bouncing, tells the *48 Hours* reporter, "I was a little bit scared because my grandpa—my other grandpa—was trying to take us back to America." Perry follows up, telling her, "They were trying to grab you, but we're fine now."

But Carolyn Levine said the children "just came running" when she and Larry arrived with Mexican authorities and were finally able to take them back to Nashville. And Mark Levine said Tzipi cried and begged not to go when the Levines had to return their grandchildren to Mexico.

Then there is Sammy, who said in the same *48 Hours* interview that being returned to his father was "the happiest day of my life." But when asked if he ever feels like he's caught in the middle, he blinked his glistening eyes and said, "A lot."

Being "in the middle" is an understatement.

People in Nashville who have never met Sammy and Tzipi March have taken them into their hearts, and they wonder about these children and the loyalties they have forged and the loyalties that have fractured all around them like a house falling down.

In nine years they have lived through the loss of their mother, an uprooting from their home and grandparents and extended family, an uprooting from their father's family, landing in another country. They have adapted to a new step-mother and new siblings in a new culture with their father and grandfather. They have crossed the border when sent back to their mother's parents and crossed again returning to father and grandfather—all this before their father is arrested for their mother's murder.

The shallow roots come up, and they leave the new family behind. A brief stop at their uncle's house before landing back where it all began.

Sammy and Tzipi return to USN, their mother's alma mater and the school they have attended intermittently, return to their old rooms in their grandparents' house in the comfortable West Meade community, among familiar neighbors. They return to the West End Synagogue, to friends who knew them as babies. The children are embraced with joy and tears and all the love fifty extended family members can bestow.

But Sammy tells Judge Green that he and Tzipi want to be returned to Mexico, to stay with Carmen while their father awaits trial.

How will the children sort out this tangle of loyalties?

And their grandfather Arthur will tangle the web even more.

As Perry faces trial for their mother's murder, the DA announces that Sammy March is listed as a possible witness for the prosecution. Within the poisonous relationship and never-ending war between the Levines and Perry March, the children appear to be collateral damage.

CHAPTER 37

The Price Tag for Freedom

When Postiglione and Pridemore escorted Perry March to Nashville from Los Angeles, they expected him to meet with Tom Thurman and make a deal. His last words to them that night were, "You tell Tom I will tell him everything I know. Everything." But it doesn't happen.

The first court appearance in *State of Tennessee v. Perry Avrum March, Case No. 2004-D-3113* is held on September 22, 2005, in the criminal court for Davidson County, Tennessee, Division I, with Judge Steve R. Dozier presiding.

His is a face Perry will be seeing a lot of in the year that follows.

On this warm day, a Southern summer hangs on, unwilling to release its benevolent grip on the Nashville community. The purpose of the hearing is for Judge Dozier to determine the appropriate level of the appearance bond pending the actual trial. Perry faces the three criminal felony charges that were handed down against him by the Davidson County grand jury back in December of 2004: second-degree murder, abuse of a corpse, and tampering with evidence. Bond hearings are usually routine. Witnesses are rare. Rulings are traditionally rendered from the bench immediately after prosecution and defense present their respective positions.

In the March case, nothing is routine.

Perry enters the courtroom through a side door, looking like what Peter Rodman described nine years earlier in his conversation with Detective Mike Smith at the Sunset Grill: "a squirrel that didn't know which tire to run under." Defense counsel, William Massey and John Herbison, greet him with smiles, handshakes, and pats on the back. For a moment Perry's countenance changes and he looks like he could be walking into a backyard cookout with a group of old friends. Once he is seated and the proceedings begin, his demeanor fluctuates between apparent puzzlement in the initial stages of the bond hearing and overly courteous respect for Judge Dozier, like an eager young freshman attempting to impress his first college professor. Periodically Perry will lean toward one of his two attorneys and appear engaged in his own defense; at other times he will seem bored by the entire proceedings, a vacant look in his large, round eyes, as if he is a world away.

The prosecution team led by Deputy District Attorney Tom Thurman calls a series of witnesses in support of what it argues should be an appearance bond in the amount of $2.5 million. There is David Miller, the first lead detective in the investigation and the one who took the initial report of Janet's disappearance on August 29, 1996. Miller relates to Judge Dozier that Perry was initially cooperative, but once declared a suspect, he repeatedly refused to cooperate further with police or allow them to interview his son, Samson.

Cold case detective Postiglione is questioned and presents to the judge—but only after strenuous and heated objections by defense counsel—portions of his conversations with Perry while transporting him from Los Angeles. Postiglione says that during the trip, Perry "offered to make a deal and that he would plead guilty and take between five and seven years to get this behind him." The detective also relates questions Perry asked him while on the plane flight to Nashville: "Has anyone else been indicted?"

The significance of this question will not be fully understood by the prosecution team for at least another month.

This is Tom Thurman's first shot at Perry March inside a courtroom. After many months of contorted conversations and incredibly stressful negotiations with the FBI and the Mexican authorities, Thurman pulls out all the stops to be sure that Judge Dozier understands exactly whom he is dealing with. The ghost of Janet March still haunts the veteran prosecutor, and with all the Levines sitting behind him as he meticulously presents his case to Judge Dozier, he particularly feels the young woman's presence in the packed courtroom on this September day.

Thurman calls as an additional witness, Redina Friedman, an attorney from Chicago, who was one of the guardians ad litem appointed to represent Samson and Tzipora March during the "grandparent visitation case" in Illinois. Ms. Friedman testifies that Perry expressed to her that "he would never comply with an order granting visitation to the Levines and that he could disappear with his kids to Singapore or Mexico." This witness explains that after Perry did indeed leave the United States and fly to Mexico with his children, the judge in Chicago issued a "contempt order" against Perry for his failure to appear as scheduled.

Although Thurman has clearly established through this witness the key element that Perry March has a history of "not complying with court orders," the prosecutor goes further. He uses Ms. Friedman's testimony as a vehicle to present what clearly is evidence related not solely to the central issue of "assuring the defendant's appearance at trial," but rather to his own more important quest to establish what occurred on the night of August 15, 1996. In response to a question by Thurman, and over strenuous objection by defense counsel, Judge Dozier allows Ms. Friedman to introduce double hearsay—statements attributed to Sammy March and related by the young boy back in the late 1990s to another guardian ad litem: "He heard his parents fighting and the next morning he observed a rug rolled up and that afternoon it was gone."

Thurman proceeds with his parade of witnesses.

He calls local Nashville attorney C. J. Gideon, who represented the Levines in various civil cases against Perry March. Gideon's testimony includes the information that Perry had been held in contempt on at least five separate occasions, and that currently there is an outstanding judgment against him in favor of the Levines for $6 million. It turns out that after Judge Cain of the Tennessee Court of Appeals set aside the $113.5 million wrongful-death judgment against Perry in spring of 2003, the Levines hired Gideon to file on their behalf in September 2003 a new and separate wrongful-death case against their son-in-law.

Perry, living in Mexico at that time, once again failed to respond to the litigation filed against him alleging that he was responsible for the death of his wife, Janet, on or about August 15, 1996. In May 2004 Davidson County Circuit Court judge Barbara Haynes entered an Order of Judgment by Default, which included the judicial finding that "there is satisfactory evidence that Janet Levine March is deceased, having died on or about August 15, 1996. In addition, Janet Levine March was exposed to a specific peril of death, namely she was intentionally and wrongfully killed by her husband Perry March."

Four months later, on September 7, 2004, a jury of Nashville citizens heard testimony from Janet's parents, brother, and friends Lori Fishel and Gabi Friedman, from family friend Terry Rosenblum, and from William W. Damon, Ph.D. The jury rendered monetary judgments against Perry March in favor of the Levines, as Janet's parents, and also in favor of the Levines for the use and benefit of their grandchildren, Sammy and Tzipi, totaling $6 million.

Having been successful in introducing testimony through Chicago attorney Redina Friedman as to what Sammy March told others about the events surrounding Janet's disappearance, Thurman calls his most explosive witness, Samuel Chavez, the Mexican attorney, entrepreneur, and former business partner of Perry March. Mr. Chavez describes for Judge Dozier how Perry would leave Mexico for extended periods and travel to Israel and in fact possessed an Israel passport. The witness goes on to relate that when he refused to falsify certain documents, Perry told him, "If you report me I will kill you the way I killed my wife." As if that is not damaging enough, Chavez then testifies that he believes that Perry March is the one who tried to have him shot and killed in May 2000.

Perry can only do his best to remain calm as Chavez stares down at him from the witness stand. Chavez is clearly enjoying this opportunity to get even with his former business partner years later. As Choderlos de Laclos said in *Les Liaisons Dangereuses:* "Revenge is a dish best served cold."

The defense calls Ron March, Perry's brother and former civil attorney, who represents to Judge Dozier that he will financially assist his brother in obtaining a residence in Nashville and that "the only reason Perry left the city for Illinois in 1996 was the effect the media coverage was having on the children." Upon questioning Ron further, however, the judge learns that Perry has bank accounts in Belize, relatives in Israel and Mexico, and that he possibly forged Ron's signature on legal documents filed with the probate court of Davidson County in 1997.

At the conclusion of all the testimony, Deputy District Attorney Tom Thurman argues for a bond of $2.5 million. Defense counsel counters with a suggested bond in the amount of $25,000. Judge Dozier elects to take the matter under consideration and adjourns the proceedings without a ruling.

Five days later he issues a six-page order setting forth his reasoning and rulings. Within the order, Judge Dozier explains that he has weighed all the evidence against the six criteria that the law requires him to consider: "the defendant's length of residence in the community; employment status and financial condition; family ties and relationships; reputation, character, and mental condition; prior criminal record and record of appearance in court proceedings; and the nature of the offense and the apparent probability of conviction."

Judge Dozier sets the appearance bond for Perry March at $3 million—the largest in the history of Nashville.

Perry March will remain in jail pending his murder trial.

On the day that Judge Dozier is conducting the bond hearing for Perry in one Nashville courtroom, in another courtroom of the same building, Judge Randy Kennedy is about to receive the jury's verdict in the civil case of the Levines as administrators of Janet's absentee estate vs. Ron March, Kathy March Breitowich, and Lee Breitowich. The civil jury finds against the defendants and awards a compensatory judgment in favor of Janet's estate in the amount of $134,650 plus prejudgment interest of 10 percent from March 17, 1999, for a total monetary judgment of $222,449.10. Although the jury finds Perry's brother, sister, and brother-in-law to be guilty of fraud, misrepresentation, fraudulent conveyance, and conversion as pertains to their handling of the estate's property including Janet's Volvo, they do not find that there was a civil conspiracy between the parties, and deny the Levines' claim for punitive damages.

CHAPTER 38

Hiring a Hit Man

Perry could not have imagined this for his own book—
@*murder.com*.

The horror of jail.

It's worse here in Nashville, a lot worse than being detained in L.A. Those nine days, he always knew he'd be
leaving shortly. He'll be leaving this place, too, the special
management unit—SMU—of the Davidson County Criminal
Justice Center, but no telling when. Weeks, probably more
like months. The DA and Nashville police were anxious to
get him back here, but he's sure they will love seeing him
rot away in this cell before they bring him to trial and give
him his chance, the chance to show he's smarter than they
are.

In the meantime, he is in protective custody, which is
supposed to be better than what the general population of
the jail gets, but, God, how could anything be worse? It's
like somebody shoved a bed in the restroom of a gas station
and called it living quarters. The 24/7 clamor makes it hard
to sleep, the screeches and clangs and the voices of inmates
yelling for a guard and others yelling, "Fuck you! Stop

hollering!" Every sound echoes in this metal environment. Behind the steel door of the cell, the temperature is always on the chilly side and it's impossible to get warm and toasty under the thin, scratchy blankets that cover the hard bed. And there's a moldy smell, a mix of human body odors and a tinge of disinfectant, a stench that seeps into the skin, and no amount of scrubbing can get it out.

Perry has time to consider a lot of things.

His first night in jail, Perry meets Russell Nathaniel Farris, who is in the cell adjacent to Perry's. The twenty-nine-year-old inmate with a head as slick as a peeled potato has tattoos that ring his arms like vicious snakes and another tattoo at the base of his neck—a question mark. Perry finds the question mark oddly amusing. As scary as Farris looks, he's pleasant enough when Perry asks him for a favor, to call Ron in Chicago. They begin to talk. Farris doesn't spell out his charges, but he says he's in the SMU because he tried to work for the police once, tried to buy some drugs from some badass guys, and those guys are in jail now, so he's got to be protected.

Perry sees an opportunity here. It could be a useful thing to have somebody like Farris on his side.

"I'm an attorney," Perry says.

Farris sees an opportunity, too.

It is the beginning of a strange liaison between an unlikely pair.

As **"house alone, rec alone"** implies, the inmates in SMU spend most of their time alone in their dreary cells. But they get an hour a day outside their cells. They are not prohibited from talking as long as they are not in physical contact with one another. During these mild autumn weeks when Perry and Farris are inmates in the unit, they sometimes go to the roof. Perry often squats outside his new buddy's cell, and they talk through the door. Farris teaches Perry about "fishing," attaching notes to strips of sheets and sliding them outside the cell so another inmate can retrieve them, and they begin to exchange messages.

Farris learns right away about Perry's ongoing war with the Levines, who have gained temporary custody of Sammy and Tzipi now that their father is no longer in Mexico. Perry's intense hatred for his in-laws catapults him into a rage at times, and he makes no secret of the fact that he wishes they were dead, these rich people with their hooks in the police department and the DA's office, these people who are the source of all his problems. He rants about the lawsuits and the Levines' mission to turn Sammy and Tzipi against him. He tells Farris over and over about the time the Levines kidnapped his children and how he was able to get them back, through the courts, and how his dad was ready to send mercenaries after them if that's what it took.

Perry learns right away that Farris has spent a lot of time in jail, starting with juvie. He's been on eight bonds, this street-smart kid who knows the ins and outs of criminal law that Perry never learned in law school or in his corporate law practice.

Farris enlightens Perry about life behind bars, and Perry boasts to Farris about the good life he has enjoyed in Mexico—perfect climate, beautiful women, and "express kidnappings."

"Easy money," Perry says, "kidnapping the children of wealthy parents."

"I could go for some easy money," Farris says.

Over a period of two months, from August 12 when Perry arrives until October 7 when Farris leaves their shared unit, the inmates confide in each other and commiserate with each other, and then they begin to conspire with each other.

"I could use a partner like you in Mexico," Perry says. "You'd love it there. My dad would give you a place to stay." He builds his dad up as a military hero, a Green Beret. "He'd do anything for me. He'd take a bullet for me," Perry says.

Farris knows he's not going anywhere with a $300,000 bond hanging over him. But Perry makes an incredible offer. "I can help you with that. We can help each other."

"How would you come up with that kind of money?" Farris wants to know.

"I may get a book deal with a woman in New York," Perry says. "And I've got property I could sell."

Farris ponders this. He waits to hear what his part of the arrangement would be.

"I'd have no problems if the Levines were out of my life," Perry goes on. "You see what I'm saying? My chances for acquittal would go from forty percent to ninety percent."

The plot starts to take shape.

Now, with each conversation, a critical detail is added until a plan is fleshed out. Perry will help Farris make his bond, and Farris will kill the Levines, and then he'll flee to Mexico, where Arthur March will provide a safe haven for him. Without the Levines' testimonies and influence, Perry will be acquitted and will join Farris in Mexico, and they will make a fortune in the "express kidnappings" racket.

"I've been looking for somebody to help me out," Perry says.

Life has not been easy for Vickie Farris, raising three boys, and Nathan has not made it any easier. In September, she makes a visit to the CJC—a place she knows all too well— and her heart somersaults when her son tells her what he's done this time.

"I never planned to kill anybody, Mama. I just saw a chance to get outta here, so I went along," Farris says into the phone at the glass enclosure where inmates get visits.

"You told him you'd kill those people if he made your bond?"

Farris winces. Nobody gets to him like his mama. "I said I would, but I was just gonna get out and—you know— disappear. What could he do? I mean, he wouldn't be going to the police about it. He wouldn't be telling them he had a deal with me to kill his in-laws and I didn't follow through."

"He could have somebody else do something."

Farris gives a sheepish shrug. "Yeah, that's what I been thinking."

"I'm glad you're finally thinking, Nathan." Vickie shakes her head.

"Mama—don't be that way," Farris says. "I—I'll work something out."

She's silent for a minute, and then she gives him that look *that says she means business. "You've got to tell Justin."*

"Maybe. I'll think about it."

"Listen to me, Nathan. You tell your lawyer about this. Tell him everything." She's over that sinking, hopeless feeling, and now her mind is focusing on the future. "Somehow you've got to make this right, or else—why, if you get out of jail and those people wind up dead, you *could get charged!"*

Farris has thought about this possibility, too. "I been—I been laying awake trying to figure it out."

"Tell Justin Johnson. He'll know what to do," she says, but Vickie Farris already has her own plan.

Larry Levine cannot estimate the number of calls he has received since August 1996, people who at first said they had information about Janet's whereabouts, and later said they knew where her body was buried.

When a woman identifying herself as Vickie Farris calls him at home and asks him to please tell the police to talk to her son who is in the cell next to Perry March, Levine knows better than to get excited, but his blood pressure probably rises just a little as he indulges the faintest hope that *this* caller is legitimate.

The woman is intentionally vague. "My son has information you'll want to hear," she says. "I promise you, you'll want to hear what he has to say about Perry March."

"Why don't you call the police yourself, Mrs. Farris?" Levine asks.

"I don't trust them," she says.

So Larry Levine calls Assistant DA Thurman, who calls Detective Postiglione. "Find out if there's anything to it," Thurman says. He's as skeptical as Levine, and Postiglione is as skeptical as Thurman—but he follows up.

And after hundreds of leads that didn't pan out, this will be the one that does. The miracle that Postiglione and

Pridemore have been praying for in this case for years is about to unfold.

The four of them meet—Nathaniel Farris, Justin Johnson, Postiglione, and Thurman. Farris and his lawyer have talked at length, and Johnson has explained to him that he cannot be charged with conspiracy since he contacted the police. Postiglione has checked out as much of Farris's story as he can. It's true Perry and Farris are in adjacent cells and have opportunities to talk, but he needs more corroboration.

"Would you be willing to record conversations with Perry?" the detective asks.

Farris is hesitant. Like his mother, he doesn't trust the police, but he decides he's got to do this to get out of the mess he's in, and maybe he can get a deal with the DA if he helps them get evidence against Perry. He feels bad for the guy— Perry's pretty stupid for a lawyer—but he's got his own ass to worry about.

Farris agrees to keep talking to Perry about the murder scheme and let the police put a recording device in his cell.

"You'll see I ain't lyin'," he says.

"Here's what you need to do," Postiglione tells him. "You have a court date on October 6. The court records are going to show that your bond has been reduced to a hundred and fifty thousand, and you need to go back and tell Perry. Tell him your girlfriend will be able to make your bond now, so you can be released in a few days. That's what you tell him."

But Farris won't be released. He will be taken to the nearby Williamson County Jail.

"Can you do it?" Postiglione asks, leaning across the table, his dark eyes glinting with intensity. The veteran detective knows that a good defense lawyer could have a field day with this scenario in court if everything doesn't go just as planned.

"I can do it," Farris says.

Postiglione works with the sheriff's department to get the recording devices in and out of Farris's cell. Early in the first taped conversation, Perry says, "I'm one hundred and ten percent on board with everything we've talked about. I can't tell you how excited I am."

On October 6 and 7, Farris turns in a performance worthy of an Oscar, playing the part of the hit man, taking directions from Perry in regard to killing the Levines.

"You have to do it when they're both together," Perry instructs.

He gives Farris the Levines' address and warns him not to endanger his children. He gives him Arthur's phone number in Ajijic and tells him to make contact when he gets out of jail. The two come up with code words: *Buying a BMW* means killing the Levines. Perry gives Farris a list of words to use with Arthur—Oni the dog and Marta the maid—to prove he is who he says he is. Farris makes up the name "Bobby Givings" as his alias.

Everything is settled when Farris leaves the CJC on October 7.

Perry believes his conspirator is a free man, but Farris is a long way from freedom.

"Hello?"

"Hello? Is, uh, this the Colonel?"

"Yes."

"Hey, uh, how you doin'? My name's Bobby Givings. Uh, has, uh, Perry March contacted you?"

"Yep."

The first telephone conversation between Farris and Arthur March takes place on October 12. Five calls are recorded in the next couple of weeks. Perry has indicated that Arthur is the key to the plan. Arthur advises Farris about weapons and tells him, "You've always got a place here."

In their final conversation on October 27, Farris says, "Everything's done." He tells Arthur he'll be in Guadalajara that afternoon.

Arthur sounds perplexed. "There's nothing on the computer," he says.

"I don't have a clue about the computer," Farris says.

When Arthur arrives at the Guadalajara airport to meet

Bobby Givings, he is met instead by FBI special agent Kenneth Sena. "Bobby Givings" is nowhere near Guadalajara; he's in the Williamson County Jail. And Perry is about to get a visit from Detectives Pridemore and Postiglione.

Perry and Arthur are both indicted on October 28. The cold case detectives can scarcely believe this break. They have Perry March's own voice on tape, plotting a murder. On their way to meet him in the booking area of the jail, they contemplate what this means in the whole scheme of things.

Perry eyes them with skepticism. He doesn't know why he's been brought here. Postiglione advises him of the newest indictment against him. He's charged with conspiracy to commit first-degree murder and two counts of solicitation to commit first-degree murder.

Postiglione will remark later, "He did his best to contain his shock that we somehow knew what he was planning to do to the Levines."

Perry doesn't blink. He nods, and after a minute he asks if he can call John Herbison. On the phone with his lawyer, Perry asks, "Was anyone else indicted?" The detectives, privy to the conversation, exchange a glance.

Perry is returned to his cell, his hopes of release plummeting far below 40 percent.

As the detectives leave the jail, Pridemore makes the comment "He might've asked us who the victims were supposed to be, don't you think?"

CHAPTER 39

Like Father, Like Son

The cell phone rings just as Detective Pridemore climbs into his government-issue older-model gray Dodge with tinted windows. It is seven thirty and he is on his way to his office at the Nashville Criminal Justice Center. The January morning sky is a dull gray and the wind is up, sending dry brown leaves scuttling across the pavement.

"Pridemore," he answers without glancing at the number. He's expecting the call.

"Morning, partner."

"Morning, Pat. Any word?"

"They have him."

It is January 5, 2006, and Arthur March is on board an FBI plane on his way from Mexico to Houston. He has just been formally expelled from the land of eternal sunshine, his home since the mid-1990s. On October 28, 2005, Arthur, along with his son Perry, was indicted by the Davidson County grand jury on two counts of solicitation of murder and one additional count for conspiracy to commit murder, in a murder-for-hire plot to kill Lawrence and Carolyn Levine.

With Perry already in custody in Nashville, this time it is
Arthur March who is whisked away from the streets of
Ajijic. The required political dance with the Mexican government and the logistical coordination through the FBI are
much quicker this time around. The evidence that Tom
Thurman and the prosecutorial team have assembled leaves
little to interpretation—hours and hours of recorded conversations between Perry and Nathaniel Farris, between Perry
and Arthur, and between Arthur and Farris in which the three
plot the murder of the Levines.

Arthur, the old military man, says what he wants and
pulls no punches. After learning weeks earlier that Perry was
indicted for a second time, the Colonel knew they would be
coming for him. He had already told the media he was not
like his son. "There will be some bloodshed this time, theirs
or mine!" Yet Arthur still did not truly believe he would be
forced to leave Mexico. He tells anyone who will listen that
he only agreed to put a friend of Perry's up for a while, that
he had never even met "Bobby Givings." And he does not try
to flee Mexico. He is seventy-seven, and this is the only
home he has known for over a decade. Plus Arthur still believes that his political connections in Mexico will protect
him. He is not like Perry. He is not a wheeler-dealer. He has
not pissed off other expatriates in elaborately concocted
business schemes. Arthur has his routine. He goes to see his
friends at the doughnut shop. He teaches English at the local
hospital.

To Arthur, all he has done is try to help his son. It is not
the first time.

Once arrested and in Houston, Arthur March quickly realizes he is in some serious trouble. The bravado vanishes;
his countenance changes. The photographs of him that fly
over the airwaves and into the newspapers show a frail, di-
sheveled man with rounded shoulders, rumpled clothes, and
tousled hair. At times he seems disoriented as he is led into
a Houston courtroom to have his rights regarding extradition
explained to him. The ex-soldier, who likes to tell everyone
he was in the Special Forces, ends up going quietly. Just like

Perry, he waives extradition and agrees to go back to Tennessee without a contested hearing.

It will be January 13 before all the paperwork between Texas and the feds and Tennessee is in order. Detectives Postiglione and Pridemore arrive at the Harris County, Texas, jail at approximately one p.m. By 1:20 Arthur March is formally handed over to the two detectives. They follow the exact routine that they did with Perry six months earlier in Los Angeles. They inform him of his rights and explain that he "is under no obligation to speak with them, but if he wishes to make a statement they will certainly be available." Unlike his son, Arthur does not quiz the detectives about what evidence they have or what kind of deal he can cut. "I'll let the lawyers handle it," he says—his only comment about his legal troubles.

On the ride from the Houston jail to the airport, Arthur chats with Pridemore and Postiglione as if they were the drivers of a shuttle bus. The veteran detectives have arrested and transported suspects for decades. They are excellent at sizing up people. Arthur March reminds them of that distant uncle you only see at Christmas, who likes to tell stories and knows something about everything or thinks he does. He asks both detectives about their families. He is sociable and gregarious. Arthur clearly likes small talk. There is a simplicity and directness about him, unlike his son. What you see is what you get.

In the weeks that follow, Pridemore and Postiglione will learn that Arthur has a lot to talk about.

Part of what they see on this January afternoon is a man in extremely poor health, who has been issued a cane by the Houston police to assist him in walking. The detectives take him to Chili's restaurant inside the airport. "I would like a good steak," their prisoner announces. He looks like he hasn't had a good meal in a month. "I've got an artificial hip and a slipped disc. I am in constant pain," he informs them. While waiting for the flight back to Nashville, the detectives have to assist Arthur with three different heart medications that were prescribed for their "transport." They also have to obtain a motorized carrier for the trip through the airport. Postiglione will later comment, "I thought the old man was going to croak right there in the wheelchair before we ever got him back to Nashville."

By the time the two-hour flight lands in Nashville, Arthur is comfortable in the presence of the two Nashville detectives. The small talk continues. This is the first of many days of conversation the three of them will have over the next several months.

To add to his legal woes, Arthur has been additionally indicted, along with his son, by a Nashville federal grand jury for the crime of "solicitation to commit a crime of violence by use of Interstate Commerce." A series of critical conversations with Arthur take place on February 21. Just before noon, Thurman, Pridemore, and Postiglione meet with him while he is in federal custody. They are accompanied by two FBI agents. The purpose of the meeting is to determine if Arthur can locate the area in Nashville where Perry took him to recover the buried body of Janet March.

Prior to the February meeting, Arthur agreed to make a formal statement to both federal and state authorities regarding his involvement in the recovery and reburial of Janet's body. The now seventy-eight-year-old defendant has been promised that if he will assist in the murder case against his son, Thurman and the entire prosecutorial team will recommend to the federal judge a suggested sentence of eighteen months for all the charges against him. Arthur is assisted in his negotiations with state and federal authorities by Fletcher Long, an attorney from Springfield, Tennessee. Mr. Long becomes one more attorney brought into the Perry and Janet March legal saga. He will end up playing a long-term role.

Through Arthur's statement, the prosecutorial team learns that Perry confided in his dad within a few weeks after August 15, sometime around the Jewish holidays in September. Perry's description to his father of events on that fateful night bore little resemblance to the story he told police two weeks after Janet vanished: "She packed a few things, said, 'See ya!' and drove away." Perry told Arthur that he and Janet had been quarreling, and when he picked up a tool that was handy, a wrench, there was an accident. He did not mean to kill her. Perry asked his father to clean a portion of the driveway where he thought there might be some evidence. Arthur tells authorities that he never saw any blood or other evidence of a death. Either there never was any or Arthur was proficient in his paternal assistance, for the army of police that descended onto the Blackberry property did not find any either.

Arthur goes on to relate that later Perry "told me he needed help with the body." He tries to place the exact time but can only remember that Perry had returned from spending Yom Kippur in Chicago. Arthur isn't sure what happened to make Perry so anxious, but something made it urgent to relocate the body.

After their meeting and "road trip" with Arthur on February 21, 2006, the cold case detectives will be able to piece together this part of the puzzle from ten years ago. They will also learn more about the Jewish holidays, the ten-day period between Rosh Hashanah and Yom Kippur when Jews go to the synagogue and make peace with God.

In a particularly troubling sequence of events, it appears that the activities Arthur describes took place shortly after Yom Kippur, the Day of Atonement.

A Tennessee sun is doing its best to push winter into the past as the caravan of agents, police, and detectives commence their search at the location where it all began—3 Blackberry Road. Pridemore and Postiglione believe they will have the best shot if they can re-create the route for Arthur. They start at the beginning. Following Arthur's directions, they leave Blackberry Road and turn on to Crater Hill Road, and after a short distance on to Lynwood Boulevard and then Foxwood Road. This affluent area of Nashville looks today almost exactly as it did in 1996. Both detectives were a part of the "army of police" in September of that year. The large homes positioned on expansive, manicured lots look like an ideal place to reside in the city—quiet, peaceful, safe.

The caravan continues east onto Tyne and then south onto Hillsboro Road, a main artery running out of the city. Arthur in the lead car gives directions, trying to take himself back to a night almost a decade ago, doing his best to reconstruct how to get to a location he never dreamed he would ever have to revisit. Yet he is not overly anxious or nervous—just an old soldier on a mission. About three miles from Blackberry Road, he directs them to turn left on to Otter Creek, but after a short distance he says, "We turned left, but this doesn't look like it." The cars reverse direction and head farther south on Hillsboro Road and then, at Arthur's direction, left on to Kingsbury Drive. After traveling through an older subdivision with single-level homes dating back to the 1960s, same result. "This is not it, either." Some in the group are beginning to think that their efforts are wasted, but Pridemore and Postiglione appreciate that their "witness" has just turned seventy-eight years old, and according to his recounting, the trip took place late at night, almost ten years ago. The caravan continues on.

A half mile farther south down Hillsboro Road, Arthur shouts out, "Left, left—turn here." The cars file on to Bridleway Trail. It is the main road into a residential development where the homes are only ten years old or less. "I remember a wooded lot and some construction activity and a slight hill," Arthur announces. The caravan turns left again down a short cul-de-sac. Along one side is a wooded lot with cedar trees and scrubby brush. Across the street is a large brick home on a spacious, level lot. Other large homes can be seen in the distance, farther from the main road.

"I think this is it," Arthur declares.

"Let's get out and look around," Pridemore suggests.

"I remember that we turned left from that main road, and then went a short distance, and turned left again," Arthur says. "Perry told me where to go and that it was about fifty yards from the paved road. I got out and Perry drove around. He didn't want anybody to see the car."

"How long did it take you to find the body?" Postiglione asks.

"Just a few minutes. It was where he said it would be. It was in a shallow grave, in a leaf bag, with some dirt thrown over in."

Pridemore looks around at the topography. Any Tennessee country boy knows that where there are cedar trees, there is limestone and very shallow soil.

"I pushed away the dirt and opened the bag for just an instant," Arthur goes on, as if a movie is replaying in his mind now. "I saw it—some bones and some clothing. I slowly dragged the bag up a small hill back toward the road."

Both detectives gaze across the property. It is mostly very flat. But there are a few drainage ditches running through the property that create some rises and valleys.

"Where was Perry?" Pridemore asks.

"He is still driving around, looking back to see if I'm standing back at the road. He meets me at the edge, and helps me put the bag in the trunk."

"Was it heavy?" Postiglione inquires.

"Oh—fifty, sixty, maybe seventy pounds."

The two detectives exchange a brief glance.

"What car were you in?"

"The Volvo."

Within a few days, Postiglione and Pridemore will establish that the property to which Arthur directed them belonged to Sharon Bell. She began developing the large tract in the mid 1990s. Her attorney was Perry March. In late September or early October of 1996, she and Perry had a conversation during which she informed him, as her attorney, that she would need him to look over a contract. She was selling another lot that was scheduled to close on October 8. It was the corner lot.

The lot where Arthur said Janet's body was buried in a shallow grave.

February's excursion is only the first of several more "road trips" that the trio of Arthur, Pat, and Bill will make together. In an odd, almost puzzling kind of way, the three become friendly acquaintances. Arthur is never short on conversation, and the next series of trips will be long drives of several hours from Nashville. The destination this time is Kentucky. As part of his statement, Arthur indicated that after he and Perry picked up the leaf bag late at night, they drove north toward Chicago. Traveling north along I-65, they were "near Bowling Green, Kentucky, I believe" when they pulled off to look for a motel. They rested for a brief time, and then it was time to dispose of the body. Arthur indicated that Perry said, "I can't do it, Dad. Please promise me you will put it in water."

Arthur left the motel and drove through the nearby countryside. He came across a small creek, but it was not deep enough. A short time later he spotted another creekbed, but again one with not enough depth. Daylight was about to break across the Kentucky fields and woods. In the faint angled sunlight of early morning, Arthur saw a yellow school bus coming toward him on a country lane. Once it passed, he knew he had to act quickly. He noticed a large brush pile where fields had been cleared. The pile looked like it had been there awhile, dry, brittle, perfect for a farmer to burn. Removing the leaf bag from the trunk of the Volvo, Arthur dumped the bones under one section of brush, hid the clothes under another section, and then crammed the plastic bag itself into yet a third spot. Returning to the motel, Arthur, the loyal father and the dutiful soldier, reported to his son that the deed was done.

He never mentioned to Perry that the body was not underwater.

CHAPTER 40

The First Trial—Theft

While the media is focused on the upcoming murder case and the more sensational charges surrounding the murder-for-hire plot, the DA's office elects to start the Perry March criminal trilogy with the separate felony charge of "theft over $10,000." There have been reports and rumors floating around the city that behind-the-scenes settlement negotiations were initiated before trial but never went very far. From the state's perspective, this first trial is a test run to see if Perry March testifies and how a Nashville jury responds to the defendant in open court. With all the developments involving Arthur March, Thurman is feeling better about the solicitation and murder cases to be tried in the summer, and, in fact, defers participation in this first trial. Perry, always the optimist and never short on confidence, sees this first trial as a chance for an early victory.

The basis of the indictment is that while an attorney with his father-in-law's legal firm, Levine, Mattson, Orr, and Geracioti, and only weeks after Janet's disappearance, Perry March caused to be transferred to himself certain legal fees—paid by one client who was a personal friend and also from another long-term client—that actually belonged to the firm as a partnership. The state knows that if the jury comes back with a guilty verdict, it will limit March's testimonial options when they prosecute the upcoming conspiracy-to-murder and the murder cases. At the same time, among many attorneys in Nashville, the sentiment is that this first courtroom battle should not even be a criminal case, but rather a civil one between law partners arguing about who earned what fees from which clients. Perry knows that, should the jury fail to convict him in this first trial, the psychological impact for both the prosecution and the defense on his upcoming trials will be enormous.

The entire proceedings are being aired by a local television channel, and after almost ten years, all of Nashville is waiting to see Perry March inside a courtroom.

The courthouse is not really a courthouse.

It is a converted one-story office building in Metro Center, an office park located in sight of the downtown high-rise buildings but an inconvenient drive for the lawyers, judges, and law enforcement officers who work in the shadow of the *real* courthouse. The consistent growth that Nashville has experienced over the last decade has helped precipitate a decision by the city fathers to construct a new courthouse, more modern and more secure, befitting an urban community that is now home to two professional sports teams, but the new structure is still months from completion. Nor will Perry March's trials be played out in the imposing Art Deco structure, whose cavernous halls he used to frequent as a working lawyer. The old Metropolitan Courthouse, with its tall ceilings, wood moldings, wide tile hallways, and marble steps, is under renovation, with a new use for this historic structure once its new replacement is complete.

The building at 601 Mainstream Drive is the temporary home for all the criminal courts and their clerks—if one

can call being in an alternate location for years a temporary
home.

In the lobby, people are backed up at the two lanes of
security screening, waiting to empty their pockets and
place their purses on the conveyor belts. The scene looks
more like an airport than a courthouse. The carpets are a
dull gray, the walls flat white, and all the doors are un-
stained wood. Signs hang from the ceiling: "Quiet—Court
in Session." It's hard to believe a courtroom is anywhere
near the long, narrow hallway with its floor-to-ceiling windows that face the parking lot.

But sure enough, this is the setting for Perry March's
felony theft trial, on April 17, 2006.

Court is supposed to begin at eight thirty. By eight, the
long single hallway is crowded. Prospective jurors are
lined up single file on both sides of the hall. Official tags
designate them as jurors. The pool of about fifty men and
women is an eclectic-looking group. Jeans or shorts and
sandals are the preferred manner of dress—and every ugly
striped shirt ever made has found its way onto someone's
ample torso. No dress clothes in this group, no business
suits. One man wears a tie but the knot is pulled down,
nearly to his diaphragm, and his collar is unbuttoned.

There is no pretense about this ultracasual group, no
effort at formality. This is the pool from which Perry
March will see the "jury of his peers" selected. He has announced on several occasions that he has faith that a Nashville
jury will treat him fairly. On the whole, these men and
women look as if they would rather be anywhere but here,
on this sun-splashed spring day, with temperatures already
in the balmy seventies. If they view their jury service as
grave and solemn duty, their attire does not show it.

Court officers dot the halls, mostly beefy men wearing
sport coats and ties, looking like Secret Service agents
with their microphones and earpieces. An excessive number of court officers, it would appear—but maybe not, considering this is the first Perry March trial, first in the series
of trials that have captured headlines for weeks. The large

men walk the halls communicating to their counterparts in hushed voices. Later, as jurors are dismissed, these officers will escort them back down to the clerk's office. A dismissal from the March jury pool does not guarantee reentry into what is shaping up to be a gorgeous spring day. Anyone who reported for jury duty might become part of a pool in another case, either criminal or civil.

Inside the courtroom, with its low ceiling, spectators and members of the press begin to crowd onto the seven short oak benches with no cushions, every seat uncomfortable. The court officers and court stenographer take their places at the front of the room a few minutes before eight thirty. The prospective jurors are settling in now, voices modulating to whispers.

In this tiny space that is barely able to accommodate the entire jury pool, there has been some attempt to create a judicious ambience. Along the wall behind the jury box are four large oil paintings of previous judges for this court division. Yet when considering the surroundings and the attire of the prospective jurors, the setting is as much a contrast to a traditional courtroom environment as a room at the Bates Motel is to a suite at the Ritz-Carlton.

Judge Steve R. Dozier takes the bench. Middle-aged, wearing glasses, his gray hair shortly cropped, Dozier might be mistaken for a senior partner in a big-ten accounting firm were it not for the black robe that reveals nothing but a white shirt and dark tie. "Good morning, ladies and gentlemen," he says to the prospective jurors, his voice soft and solicitous, his manner controlled.

Perry March enters the courtroom with his attorneys, Ed Fowlkes and Mike Flanagan. Dressed in an olive-green summer suit sent by Carmen from Mexico, a blue shirt, and a conservative dark print tie, Perry could pass for one of the attorneys, with his files and legal books in his arms.

He has no family here, no one to support him except his attorneys.

Fowlkes, lead defense counsel, is a painfully thin man in his sixties, dressed in dark blue with a crisp white shirt and red tie. Co–defense counsel, Flanagan, is flashier, in his trademark dark blue pin-striped suit, with a white shirt and gold print tie. While Fowlkes's thinning hair is combed straight back, Flanagan has thick, wavy, silver hair. But in contrast to his handsome head of hair, he has bags on bags under his eyes, and his face has seen a lot of life.

The prosecutors are a much younger team. With her fair complexion and shoulder-length auburn hair, lead counsel Amy Eisenbeck looks more like a student in law school than an assistant district attorney general. She is pregnant, and dressed in a dark purple suit accessorized with black heels, gold earrings, and red nail polish. Ben Winters is even younger than Eisenbeck. Tall, with thick dark hair cut in the appropriate conservative style, Winters is dressed in a good-looking tan summer suit, white shirt, and yellow tie. The ages of both prosecutors added together probably don't equal Ed Fowlkes's sixty-plus years.

The questioning of jurors begins, and soon the jury for Perry March begins to take shape. The voir dire—"to speak the truth"—gives both the prosecution and the defense an opportunity to "size up" the prospective jurors. Through questions about their backgrounds, what experiences they have had with the legal system before, and what knowledge they have of Perry March, the respective attorneys do their best to select a sitting jury that will be attentive and listen fairly, without prejudices one way or the other. All the attorneys have their own styles—the prosecutors all businesslike and direct, constantly presenting the image that this is serious work for serious people; Fowlkes with his more gregarious approach subtly attempting to ask the jurors to like him, to trust him, even raising a chuckle or two during the questioning.

During the recesses and lunch break, Ed Fowkles makes the rounds. Talkative and animated, he is friendly and folksy, a lawyer who knows all the court personnel and takes the time to speak to them. He's a little like Barney Fife, but with better posture.

Amy Eisenbeck asks Nick Bailey, a former local prosecutor and now a legal analyst with Channel 5, "Do you know if they make copies of the tapes of the trial?"

"I'm not sure, but I don't think they would give those out."

"Oh. My parents wanted a copy," she says.

"Well—I'll ask," he says. "Let me see what I can do."

It's a big day in the young prosecutor's life, and Nick Bailey is going out of his way to appear accommodating to one of the contacts he likes to maintain.

The hallways are so narrow that everyone knows everyone else's business. Attorneys hover in pairs, negotiating their cases. Their clients sit or stand alone, awaiting their fate—settlement or trial. These lawyers could be on their way to the concession stand at a Titans football game, taking a minute to negotiate the division of a client's marital assets. Serious business done in an environment that is anything but somber. For those who administer the justice system, this is clearly just another day at the office. Same routine, just different clients.

The cops and detectives who are waiting to be called in various cases are all gathered in one part of the hall on two benches across from each other, telling jokes, trading war stories. It's like a college fraternity meeting. Before lunch they enter into a loud debate on where they should all go eat.

Prosecutors from other courtrooms periodically exit their hidden room of battle behind the maple door. Many of these prosecutors are women—some in dark blue suits, white blouses, and pearls, others in suits as bright as canaries.

Heels clicking on the hard floor, they approach the rows of cops and detectives and ask, "Which one of you told me—?" or say to one of the group, "Sorry you had to wait, but we won't be needing you."

And wait is what most people do at the Metro Center Courthouse Complex.

One of the lawyers who roams the hallways is John Herbison, Perry March's co–defense counsel in the murder and solicitation cases. The rotund man with shaggy hair wears a blue blazer, blue shirt, nondescript tie, and khaki pants. This is the attorney who said he was too busy to try this particular March case, but here he is, watching, observing, wanting to be seen, waiting for a possible media moment that doesn't happen.

Members of the television media are not allowed to remain in the courtroom during jury selection, so they have been given a tiny room, the one with the sign marked "Drug Court." They crowd around a conference table overflowing with sophisticated listening equipment so they can follow the trial via audio. The TV reporters and technicians resemble CIA agents listening for al-Qaeda chatter. During breaks in the trial, the most notable TV personalities will spend a majority of their time working the crowd, saying hello to defense attorneys, prosecutors, cops, and the print media.

Court resumes after lunch. The afternoon slogs on. One of the court officers comments during the break, "This is like watching paint dry." Jury selection is generally not exciting and never a swift process—but in the scheme of things, the seating of this jury is taking less time than might have been anticipated.

Two attorneys stop at the courtroom, take turns peering in the rectangular windows in the maple door, and then walk on, but not before offering their critique.

"I don't think March will testify," says the first.

"Why is the state even worrying about this case, with the other indictments they have?" the other asks.

"I think it's a test run by the state to see what a live jury does with Perry March."

Selection of the jury takes about five hours. Just before three o'clock, the last of the panel is chosen. The judge directs the jurors to go home and pack; they will be sequestered for the duration of the trial, per a request by the defense team. Judge Dozier also tells them not to talk to anyone about the case or read the newspapers. The reporters dash out of the courtroom to call in their stories:

"Perry March Jury Selected—Five Men and Seven Women, Along with Two Alternates."

Court gets under way Tuesday morning with opening statements.

Eisenbeck tells the jury that Perry needed money to start his own law practice in 1996 and that he couldn't count on financial help from the Levines, because of the problems he and Janet were having. "He had to look somewhere else for the money, and that's where the theft came in," says Eisenbeck.

In his opening statement, defense attorney Flanagan states that March believed he was owed the money in question when he left Levine, Mattson, Orr, and Geracioti in September of the same year. Flanagan contends that this case is "a dispute among lawyers."

Prosecution witness John Wood testifies that Perry tried to talk him and another associate into joining him in his new practice and that Perry told him Janet didn't want him to leave the Levine firm. Peter Rosen testifies that Perry also asked him to join his new firm. The day Rosen intended to turn him down was August 16, 1996, but he says Perry looked "harried" and said he was going home, that he "didn't feel well." On Monday, when Rosen declined his offer, Perry said, "You are getting pussy advice."

State witness Tom Jacobs, a CPA who was the Levine firm's accountant for many years, tells the court that he and Perry had lunch at Kyoto's on August 15, 1996, and Perry asked him what it would take to set up a practice. "When I asked him how he was going to finance it," says Jacobs, "he said he was holding back billings at the firm."

Michael Geracioti testifies that Perry left the firm in a "lurch" when he stopped working that September and moved to Chicago. He says Perry left cases unfinished, and those accounts receivable belonged to the business, not to Perry.

Two of Perry's ex-clients testify for the prosecution. Club owner Paul Eichel says he dealt with Perry, so he wrote a check for $3,000 directly to him. Elliott Greenberg, a former friend who helped pack the rental truck for the move to Chicago, describes himself as one of Perry's closest friends. Greenberg says that when his wife, Diane, became ill and died of cancer, Perry was one of the few who stopped by. "Friendship came first before attorney relationship," he says. He wrote $20,000 in checks to Perry because his friend asked him to do so. He tells the court that only after he was billed and sued by the firm for nonpayment did he realize what Perry had done, that his friend was looking out for himself.

The prosecution's case is more akin to an accounting seminar, with tedious evidentiary details about fee splits and billing records, until Perry's father-in-law takes the stand. When Larry Levine testifies, the proceedings suddenly become laced with all the underlying emotions of the Janet March saga.

Levine says that Perry met with him and Carolyn days before Janet disappeared and told them he wanted to start his own firm. Though he didn't ask for money directly, Perry showed his in-laws a list of expenses he would need for start-up—a total of about $30,000. Levine says he knew Perry and Janet were "fighting pretty good," so he asked Perry, "Where are you going to get the money?"

Carolyn Levine also testifies that she was concerned about the marital problems Perry and Janet were having. She tells the court, "I said, 'Perry, I think you've got the cart before the horse. I think you need to work on your marriage before your career.'"

Eight witnesses testify during the trial that lasts all day Tuesday and a half day Wednesday, but the most powerful witness for the state is Perry March himself. When he elects, after consulting with counsel, not to testify in his own defense, the state plays for the jury portions of the civil video deposition Perry gave in November of 1996, and it allows the jury to witness his unbridled arrogance and uncooperative nature. Jon Jones, representing Janet's estate, asks questions about Janet and Perry's relationship, which are met with rolling eyes or a defiant tilt of the chin. Most disturbing are the painfully long pauses as Perry considers how to answer questions about his treatment of Janet. Did he ever hurt her, or attempt to hurt her, or choke her, or strike her? He never gives a simple "No."

"To the best of my recollection, I have never struck my wife," he says, after thinking about it for a minute.

He testifies that Janet had a "disastrous working relationship" with the contractors building the house, and some of them might have killed her. "I warned her to attempt to modify her behavior," he says, indicating that Janet's dealings with the workmen might have caused her own demise. He shows no hint of sorrow or sadness about his wife's disappearance.

Even Perry's attorney, Ed Fowlkes, will later admit that the most damaging part of the trial was the tape of Perry's deposition.

But when he gives his closing argument, Fowlkes is still hoping against hope. He tells the jury that this is "a civil case." He says, "It's a bunch of sharks feeding on their own young. That's all it is."

The attempt by defense counsel to convince the jury that this is simply a civil dispute between some rich lawyers falls on deaf ears. On Wednesday afternoon, just forty-five minutes after the jury began deliberations, they have a verdict.

The jury foreman announces to a hushed courtroom that Perry March is guilty of theft.

In the hallway, the TV cameras capture the principal participants of the trial. Amy Eisenbeck says, "The jury did the only thing they could do under the facts and the law in this case." Defense attorney Fowlkes declares again that the trial should never have been tried in criminal court. "Surely you don't spend this kind of time and money on a case—a theft case—unless there is some other reason for it." He also says, "The Levines weren't deprived of a dime. They aren't out a dime."

But prosecuting attorney Ben Winters may articulate most clearly the sentiments of the jury, spectators, and Nashvillians at large when he says, "There wasn't a person that Mr. March dealt with that he didn't betray, from clients to friends, to partners, to associates, to in-laws. Everyone he came in contact with, he betrayed."

CHAPTER 41

The Second Trial—Conspiracy

The second act in the Perry March trial trilogy, held in the same "office park courthouse" as the first, begins on June 1, 2006, with the selection of the jury panel out of six hundred potential jurors.

The key players on both sides participate in settlement negotiations up until almost the day of the trial. The state already has its first conviction and is negotiating from a position of strength. Yet Thurman and his team know they are facing weeks of grueling battle in the courtroom and the emotional toll on all concerned, including the Levines, would be enormous. For nearly two weeks, Postiglione and Pridemore are paged repeatedly to escort Perry from his jail cell to the site of settlement negotiations so he can be available to his attorneys for ongoing discussions. The final decision rests with Perry, the client, but there is more involved than his own interests. Although the authorities have agreed to a deal with Arthur in exchange for his testimony against his son, the exact details of where he will serve his sentence are not finalized. With his health deteriorating, his attorney, Fletcher Long, is adamant that Arthur be housed in a facility where expert medical care was available. And in a most bizarre twist, the state even allows Perry and Arthur to meet privately to discuss their respective potential settlements, even though this meeting would allow them an opportunity to coordinate their stories about the relocation of Janet's body. Perry is insistent on serving any sentence in a minimum-security federal facility. Ron March comes from Chicago to meet with his father to encourage him to complete his cooperation with the state. During this same time frame, Ron consults with a prominent Nashville criminal defense attorney, as the state is still looking into whether Ron and his sister, Kathy, have been willing participants or innocent facilitators in the murder-for-hire plot by helping Nathaniel Farris, Arthur, and Perry communicate by routing e-mails. In the end, neither state nor federal prosecutors pursued any actions against Perry's siblings.

On several afternoons both sides think they have reached a deal, only to have Perry back out at the last moment. Arthur will state after the trials that even he had understood that Perry was going to "take the deal." Finally, Thurman has enough, and gives a final deadline. He will not come off his position that Perry serve at least seventeen years in prison. Perry simply will not allow himself to concede defeat.

The tedious process of questioning the jury pool takes place all day Thursday and into Friday. The challenge is to find jurors who have not already formed an opinion about Perry March's guilt or innocence, in light of all the publicity surrounding the case. More than one hundred men and women are excused because they say they can't be impartial. By the end of the day, Thursday, the jury pool is down to seventy. Finally, on Friday morning, the task is finished: twelve jurors and two alternates have been seated.

On Monday, June 5, the evidentiary phase of the trial begins—again in front of Judge Steve Dozier. Dozier is soft-spoken yet deliberate with his words to counsel and the jurors, his whole demeanor one of control and order. This time March faces three felony charges: one count of conspiracy to commit murder, and two counts of solicitation to commit murder.

The facts are again eerily reminiscent of Thomas Capano, the powerful Delaware attorney convicted in 1999 of the first-degree murder of his young mistress. In that case, Mr. Capano, while incarcerated and awaiting trial, conspired with another inmate to try to have a key witness murdered. In this case, the prosecution will argue that Perry March solicited the services of an inmate, Russell Nathaniel Farris, while both were being held in the Nashville jail, to murder Lawrence and Carolyn Levine.

With the indictments in this case, Perry is not scheduled to be the sole defendant. His seventy-eight-year-old father, Arthur, has also been indicted on the same three felony charges, for allegedly agreeing to assist Nathaniel Farris in escaping from the authorities after the murder, and for arranging for a place of residence in Mexico. Months earlier, however, Arthur copped a plea and, in return for an eighteen-month sentence, agreed to testify in the murder case against his son.

As was true in the theft trial, Perry's brother and sister are not in attendance.

For this trial, Deputy District Attorney Tom Thurman, the veteran Nashville prosecutor who has been involved with the March investigation from its outset in 1996, strides into the courtroom. A fastidious man with neatly trimmed hair, "The Thurmanator" is as serious and focused as a school principal preparing to dole out punishment to a wayward youth. Assistant Deputy District Attorney Katy Miller joins him. On the job, Katy Miller is rarely caught smiling—as if the years of dealing with murderers and heartbreaking cases of child abuse have etched a permanent scowl on her face. She is a woman in a man's world—unafraid and effective: Don't cross me, and don't underestimate me.

Both prosecutors have an impressive track record for convictions. These are the "big guns." The theft case was a significant gauge of how Perry March might fare with Nashville jurors, but this case will set the stage for the much more critical drama in August, the second-degree-murder case.

The March team take their places at the defense table. Lead attorney William Massey chews on the end of his glasses that hang around his neck and nods as Lorna McClusky whispers to him. Massey's partner in their Memphis firm, McClusky is described by one of her colleagues as "a gentle woman" but also is reported to be highly organized. As the Memphis attorneys consult about a document in front of them, Nashville attorney John Herbison hangs to the side, brushing his damp hair out of his face. Herbison may be the one out of the trio with whom Perry has the closest bond. Perry called him a "hero" after he helped to get the children returned to Mexico in 2001.

The prosecution and defense teams will face off again in the murder trial—a fact that is never far from the attorneys' minds as they spar with one another these next three days.

In the first minute of his opening statement, Thurman brings the Janet March tragedy into the forefront, taking the three men and nine women on the jury back ten years. "If you had looked at Janet March's life, you would've thought it was perfect. But it wasn't. Her disappearance started a chain of events that led up to today." He previews the witnesses' testimonies: "You'll hear from Carolyn and Larry Levine, how they supported Perry . . ." He prepares the jurors for Russell Nathaniel Farris, the star prosecution witness, who will undeniably come under the defense's hammer for what Thurman characterizes as a "life of crime and drugs." He tells the jury about the twenty-nine-year-old's history of arrests and jail time, leading to the time when Farris and Perry were both incarcerated in protective custody. Briefly, he relates the incredible story of the plot to kill Carolyn and Larry Levine, the plot that, he contends, Perry hatched, the plot in which Farris was a key player, pretending to be a hit man and ultimately taping conversations for the police. Thurman winds up his opening statement by saying, "You'll be shocked when you hear how cold and calculated he is when this man talks about killing the grandparents of his

children. There will be no question, when you hear this
proof, that he's guilty."

Defense attorney Massey sets up a flip chart and a couple
of boards. The visual aids get the jury's attention. Massey
stands before them with hands spread wide and gradually
brings his palms together in front of him as he says, "Come
back to center.

"The story begins with Nathaniel Farris," he says, following up with a long inventory of Farris's criminal activities.
Thurman may have stolen Massey's thunder by alluding to
the inmate's life of crime and drugs, but the prosecutor
barely scratched the surface. The jurors are attentive as
Massey goes down his list. He insists that Farris created the
plan to kill the Levines. "He was extremely savvy," Massey
says. "He used the system to his advantage."

Then he says, "Let me tell you about Perry March." He
paints the picture of a bright lawyer who had a loving relationship with his wife, children, and in-laws before the night
Janet vanished. The Levines unleashed their wrath on him
out of grief, Massey says. Eventually, Perry was arrested and
went to jail. "It was frightening," he says. "Perry had no experience being with people who were accustomed to jail."

Like the prosecutor, the defense attorney relates a brief
chronology of events that occurred when Perry and Farris
were in adjacent cells, but in the defense's version, Farris is
the instigator of the murder plot. This "imaginary plan re-
volved around inflaming Perry," says Massey. He insists that
Farris convinced Perry he couldn't get a fair trial, that he
played on Perry's sympathies, that Perry was "out of his
league." In great detail, Massey presents the plot, the intricate plan for communicating with each other that involved
Arthur in Mexico, the code words.

Thurman sits back, looking content—looking pleased, in
fact. The defense seems to be adding fuel to the prosecution's case.

But Massey makes the point that Perry never intended for
Farris to go through with the plan. He emphasizes, "Perry
said two important things. He told Farris, 'This is impor-

tant.'" The first was to be patient, to wait thirty to sixty days after his release before he carried out the plan, and the second was to implement the complicated system they had set up that involved both Arthur and Perry's sister, Kathy, telephone, e-mail, and "snail mail." Farris would say, "I'm ready to buy the BMW," and ultimately Perry would give the "green light." Massey says, "Perry told him, 'Wait till you hear from me.'"

There is no way the defense can get around the audio- and videotapes that the jury will be presented. The best Massey can do is to put a spin on things that is favorable to the defense: Perry never gave the "green light."

Carolyn Levine, the first prosecution witness, tells the court that Janet and Perry met at the University of Michigan and later moved to Nashville and married. The Levines paid for Perry's law school at Vanderbilt. But not long into the marriage, they began to have problems. Perry had consulted a psychiatrist, and he and Janet had seen the doctor together, but the week Janet disappeared, she had an appointment to see a divorce attorney. Massey follows up with a few sporadic questions about Janet's disappearance, Perry's arrest in 2005, and the fact that the Levines were awarded temporary custody of the March children following his arrest.

Neither the prosecution nor the defense seems to gain much with their questions to Carolyn Levine, but it is important to the prosecution's case that the jurors see the woman Perry is accused of plotting to kill.

Vickie Farris, mother of Nathaniel Farris, is the next witness. She says she visited her son and was concerned by what he told her about Perry March. Not trusting the police, she called Lawrence Levine and told him someone should talk to her son.

The prosecution calls Larry Levine. A talkative witness, he testifies that Vickie Farris did indeed contact him, and he reported what she said to the DA's office. "Every time there was publicity about Janet, I got phone calls," he said, so he didn't know how credible this caller was.

As Katy Miller questions Levine, the story of the murder

plot begins to take shape just as the prosecution has planned—and then Levine surprises the court by saying, "This was not the first time Perry and Arthur March had tried to kill us."

The defense makes a vehement objection to the statement, and the lawyers meet for a sidebar at the judge's bench. Judge Dozier instructs the jury to disregard Levine's statement, and questioning gets under way again.

Massey begins his questioning on a low key, plowing all the same ground covered by the prosecutor: How long have you practiced law? When did Perry work for your firm? The jury, startled by Levine's earlier statement and the vigorous discussion at the bench by lawyers and judge, now settle back into their comfortable seats in the jury box. Massey gives Levine every opportunity to elaborate on the ways he and Carolyn gave support not only to Perry, but to Perry's father as well.

"And you did that because you wanted to," Massey says.

Levine answers, "I did that because Janet loved Perry and we wanted to do everything we could to make her life pleasant and delightful."

Massey's questions come across as repetitious, even boring. The loquacious Southern lawyer seems to ignore the law school caveat "A witness should answer the question but not add additional information." Nothing is yes or no for Larry Levine. He says, "I need to explain . . ." or "Let me answer if I can . . ." following up with expansive details. For the most part, Massey lets him talk. He is even a little folksy with the lawyer on the stand: "Are you the senior partner at the firm?" he asks, to which Levine actually smiles as he says, "I'm the oldest. I guess I'm the most senior." At one point Katy Miller is the one who interrupts, and the lawyers once again convene at the bench. Judge Dozier instructs Levine that if the prosecution wants him to bring out certain facts, they'll ask.

Still, Levine continues to elaborate. Now the air starts to feel charged, as Massey's questions takes on an edge, and Levine's guarded answers seem to indicate that he is alert to a trap and determined not to fall into it. "Did the federal judge send the children back to Mexico?" Massey asks, in reference to the time after the Levines went to Mexico and left the country with Sammy and Tzipi. Levine answers, slowly and deliberately, "The federal court ordered that Mexico should determine where the children's custody should be accomplished, and based on that, the federal judge determined that the children should be sent back to Mexico in 2001."

Massey asks the same question again, and Judge Dozier says, "He's answered the question," but the irritation in his voice is clearly for the witness as well as the defense attorney. His tone indicates that this little power struggle is getting on his nerves.

"Is it fair to say that at this point in time, the relationship between your family and the March family was strained?" Massey asks.

"It was that trip when Mr. March and his father tried to kill us," Levine answers.

"Mr. Levine! Why are you doing this?" Judge Dozier shouts.

"Because that's what happened, sir!" says Levine.

"They didn't ask you that!" the judge scolds, and he follows with a harsh warning that causes Tom Thurman to fidget at the prosecution's table. "The state doesn't want to have to start all over again! Answer the question!" Dozier instructs, remembering his years as a prosecutor and how witnesses can bring up matters outside the scope of the trial at hand and derail months and even years of preparation.

Levine finishes his testimony without any more incidents that threaten a mistrial, but he continues to get in his digs when he can. "Again, Mr. Massey, you've misstated something," he says at one point.

Larry Levine has a reputation for tenacity in the courtroom, and even when sitting in the witness box, he lives up to it.

• • •

Prosecution witness Justin Johnson identifies himself as the attorney who represents Nathaniel Farris. Like all the other lawyers in the courtroom, he is well dressed—dark suit, blue shirt, red tie—but he has long, straight, nearly white hair, with bangs. He adds another piece to the chronology that helps cement the foundation the prosecution is laying for the March-Farris tapes. Johnson says he met with his client on Friday, September 30, 2005, because Farris was concerned about the conversations between him and Perry. Johnson received a call from Tom Thurman on Monday, and after he talked with his client again, they met with Thurman and the police. "We talked about possibilities," Johnson says. Finally, Farris agreed to talk to police, after he was convinced that his coming forward would absolve him of a conspiracy charge. On October 4, arrangements were made to put a recording device in Farris's cell, to tape conversations between him and Perry.

Johnson says the DA's office has not promised Farris help with an earlier sentence.

But Massey pushes the point that the only way Farris could ever "get his freedom" was to "cut a deal." The defense attorney questions Johnson about all of the charges against his client and how many years they all carry. According to Massey's calculations, based upon all his prior convictions and pending charges, Farris's penalties could add up to 180 years, but Johnson points out that it's true only "if he's convicted."

Detective Pridemore, who has watched the proceedings, has a quick lunch with Postiglione, who is waiting to be called as a witness. Pridemore can't discuss the particulars of testimony—later he can tell him how Larry Levine locked horns with Judge Dozier—but he says, "Justin did okay. He held his own." They both wonder how Nathaniel Farris will come across.

After lunch, Farris gets his chance on the stand. He first testifies outside the presence of the jury. He says Perry told him about committing "express kidnappings" in Mexico.

The judge rules that jurors can hear about the alleged plan to conduct "express kidnappings" but cannot be told that Perry claimed to have participated in this type of scheme in the past.

The jury comes in, and the prosecution introduces its star witness.

The twenty-nine-year-old inmate in his state-issued jumpsuit looks the part of the young man whose "life of crime and drugs" has been outlined in excruciating detail by the defense. His head is slick; his arms are covered with tattoos. Of particular interest is the question-mark tattoo on his neck.

He testifies that he quit school in the sixth grade and got his GED in juvenile detention. Thurman asks him about the charges against him, bringing out the reason that Farris was placed in protective custody. At one time he had tried to make some drug buys for the vice squad, and even though he received nothing for his activities, some of his dealings on the street had created a dangerous situation for him among the regular jail population.

In a low, matter-of-fact voice, showing no signs of nervousness, he begins to tell about meeting Perry in August of 2005. The first night Perry was in the SMU, he asked Farris to call Chicago for him. They began to talk. Farris gave Perry the lowdown on prison life. Perry told him about Mexico, the beautiful beaches and beautiful women, and about express kidnappings. After a while, Perry began to talk about killing the Levines.

"Why did you go along with Perry?" Thurman asks.

Farris says, "Because he told me he would make my bond."

After killing the Levines, Farris was supposed to go to Mexico. Arthur March would give him a place to stay, and when Perry was free, the two would carry out express kidnappings in Mexico.

Thurman asks about the means of communication in the SMU. Farris explains "house alone, rec alone" and tells how Perry came to his cell door. Being in adjacent cells, they also were able to exchange notes. Farris explains "fishing": "where you tear your sheet into strips of rope and tie something heavy on the end of it, like an envelope with a lot of paper in it, and you just basically slide it out in the floor so the other inmate can slide their hand out and pull it in."

Farris says their conversations about killing the Levines went on for about a month. He testifies that he went along with the plan, hoping Perry would make his bond, but never intended to go through with it. Then he got worried. "I was concerned about getting charged," he said.

Thurman asks, "Were you worried about what would happen if you got out and you didn't follow through with killing the Levines?"

"Yes, sir," he says. "I thought, what if somebody comes after me?"

That was when he told his mother and his lawyer.

Upon the jurors' first sight of Farris, a few eyebrows shot up involuntarily, but now Pridemore notes from his vantage point that they are paying close attention as the inmate who quit school in sixth grade tells how he played the role of a hit man and had the smart lawyer confiding in him. Maybe the story is simply too incredible for Farris to have invented. His voice is quiet—not boastful but confident. It has the ring of truth.

He testifies that he used the recording device on October 6 and 7, and then, still playing his role, he told Perry his bond had been lowered, and his girlfriend would make his bond. He had created a fictitious girlfriend named Danielle. Farris was taken to the Williamson County Jail, in the contiguous county, but Perry believed he was released. While still in custody, Farris made calls to Arthur March on October 12, 14, 20, 25, and 27, and the jury will hear recordings of each one.

Massey confronts the witness with a long string of convictions he cannot deny. "You've been with the criminal system most of your adult life," Massey says. He calls Perry "your ticket to freedom." He says, "You told Perry that this was your only chance to be free. You pushed Perry toward this imaginary killing." Massey accuses Farris of "petting him" and "cozying up to Perry."

Farris insists he was simply playing a role, a role Postiglione and Thurman asked him to play.

The defense attorney goes into the code words used on the tapes that jurors have not yet heard. " 'Buy BMW'—kill the Levines. Bobby Givings is ready to buy the BMW. Perry had rules. He put down perimeters." Massey often presents his questions as statements, with only a slight inflection of his voice at the end. "You were supposed to do nothing until Perry gave the green light. The bottom line is, Perry had to give the go-ahead." This time there is no inflection, and Judge Dozier instructs him to move on.

Massey calls the plot an "imaginary plan"—one that Perry never sanctioned.

Farris continues to hold up well under intense cross-examination. While Thurman questioned for forty-five minutes, Massey goes on for three hours. When Thurman gets his chance at redirect, he also sees an opportunity to defuse some of the tension in the courtroom. He says, "You've grown hair since I questioned you."

In his crisp style that gets to the point, Thurman returns to a few dramatic statements Perry made, according to the transcripts of the tapes. "I've been searching for a year for someone . . ." and "You have to stick to the plan and get it done."

"Nobody told you to talk to police?" he asks, wrapping up.

"I went to my attorney and we went to the police," Farris says.

The questioning winds down with two further witnesses. Davidson County sheriff Daron Hall testifies that law enforcement did not request that Perry be put in the cell adjacent to Nathaniel Farris in SMU. Next, the testimony of Kevin Carroll of the sheriff's office and the FBI Violent Crimes Task Force focuses on how he got the tape recorders into and out of Farris's cell. Judge Dozier recesses court until eight forty-five Tuesday morning.

It has been an exhausting first day.

• • •

Pat Postiglione is the first witness on Tuesday morning.

Bill Pridemore squeezes into one of the three spectator rows in the small courtroom. He has helped his partner prepare—late nights, early mornings, gallons of coffee. As Postiglione will testify, the cold case detectives not only brought Perry back to Nashville when he was deported from Mexico, but every step of the way, as each astonishing and more astonishing event unfolded, the two were there, at the heart of the drama.

They both know what is at stake in this trial.

Postiglione answers a few preliminary questions. He testifies that he received information about Farris on September 30 and met with him and his attorney on October 4. "He was reluctant initially," Postiglione says; eventually, Farris agreed to record conversations with Perry to confirm that what he was telling police was, in fact, true. Farris's instructions were to return from his court date on October 6 and tell Perry that his bond had been reduced, and that his girlfriend would make his bond the next day. With each answer, the veteran detective turns and speaks to the jurors, making eye contact with them, drawing them into this incredible plan for a double murder. His courtroom experience is clearly evident, as is his New York upbringing. Thirty years in the South have done little to alter his accent.

The lights dim and lines of type are flashed on the screen. Jurors are given earphones. At the same time the first line is highlighted for jurors to follow, the sound of a voice emerges:

"Hey, Perry? Perry? Perry?"

The tapes begin—a total of nearly seven hours of tapes before the day is over.

The jury has heard references to the plot to kill the Levines from both prosecution and defense and from witnesses, but they have not seen the transcript of the conversations between Perry and Farris. Their eyes are fixed on the screen as the audio comes through their earphones.

"It's crunch time," Farris says.

Perry says, "We've got to talk."

A few lines later, Perry says they need to discuss "hard facts." He lowers his voice. "The most important thing is you have to follow . . . follow the rules."

The voices materialize out of the background noises of clanging, shuffling, yelling, flushing toilets. The voice of Farris on tape is raspy, a little manic, hard to reconcile with the quiet, guarded voice jurors heard when he testified. And although the jurors have not heard Perry speak as a live witness, it's hard to fathom that the hard-edged voice on tape belongs to the calm man in the dark suit seated just across the courtroom.

"In 2001, my dad got on the phone," he says. "Four mercenaries, four mercenaries, four mercenaries, fuckin' mercenaries. They were gonna come in, kill the fuckin' Levines, and grab my kids and take 'em back to Mexico."

Postiglione knows the Levines have read the transcripts, but he suppresses the urge to glance at them, to see if they react to hearing these threatening words from Perry's mouth.

"My dad is the totally coolest guy in the world," Perry says. He says Arthur was a Green Beret colonel and has killed three hundred people. "He would give himself up for me in the blink of an eye."

Pridemore thinks about Arthur's deal—eighteen months on the conspiracy charge in return for giving up Perry.

The plan takes shape in conspiratorial tones. Perry gives Farris the Levines' home address and Larry Levine's office address and gives directions to both. "Do it—you have to do it when they're both together." He warns him to make sure the kids aren't there and leave no trace of evidence.

Arthur is the key to the whole thing, Perry says. He gives Farris code words to use with Arthur and has him write the names of Arthur's dog, Oni; Marta the maid; Uncle Mike from East Chicago; and Morrie. He sets up the complicated system of communication: Using the name Bobby Givings, Farris will call Arthur and say he's ready to buy the BMW. Arthur will send an e-mail to Kathy saying, "Bobby Givings is gonna buy the BMW." Kathy will print it out and mail it to Perry.

"Leave me here riding for thirty days or whatever . . . That gives you plenty of time to get what you need to do," Perry says. "You take your time at it, you don't make any mistakes . . . Then thirty days, forty-five days later you do what you need to do."

When Farris says, "If I got caught—" Perry cuts him off: "I don't wanna hear it."

The tapes take place over two days. Toward the end, Perry says, "Okay, let's review."

"I've been searching, and searching, and searching for a year for someone to have as a partner that I could watch my back and win," Perry says.

The sound shuts off and the screen goes blank. The jurors adjust to the light, shifting in their seats.

Pridemore watches Perry at the defense table, hoping to make eye contact, but Perry is busy trying to maintain a stoic expression in the face of the damning words against him— his own.

The next audiotape allows the court to hear several conversations between Arthur March and Nathaniel Farris. Arthur says Perry told him Bobby Givings would call. Farris tells him he will need a little help, and Arthur says, "You just tell me what you want, how you want it done, and it'll get done." Though Arthur is intentionally vague about details, he discusses the particulars of weapons. He says there's a problem with "obtaining an instrument" and tells him "a nine is absolutely illegal." In all their conversations, Arthur assures him that when the operation is finished, "you've got a home."

In their final taped conversation, Farris tells Arthur, "Everything's done. I'm in Houston right now. And I will be in Guadalajara at about two thirty."

In the afternoon, Massey cross-examines Postiglione, trying to do damage control. He continues to press the point that Perry never gave the "green light" for Farris to kill the

Levines and that he was sitting in jail while Farris and Arthur were making plans.

Postiglione points out that the transcripts indicate Perry and Arthur had been talking with each other.

Kevin Carroll takes the stand again, and more tapes are played for the jury. This time, videotapes show Perry kneeling in front of Farris's cell during their conversations.

Reno Martin, an ex–police officer in jail for drug charges, testifies that after Farris left the Criminal Justice Center and they believed he had been released, Perry said he thought Farris would make his first court appearance but not his second.

Michelle Knight, an investigator in the sheriff's department, testifies in regard to a phone call Perry made to his sister, Kathy, on October 15. Yet another tape is played for the court. In an offhand manner, Perry asks, "Have you had any e-mails from Dad?" His sister says she received e-mail from Arthur that said Bobby Givings had called. "He's just someone I knew from up here," Perry says. He carries off the deception with perfect pitch.

On Wednesday morning the trial is delayed, and there is some confusion about Perry's medicine. Apparently he was given his Prozac at five a.m. instead of the night before. After some discussion by the lawyers and judge, Perry finally comes into the courtroom, and the proceedings begin.

The state calls Fletcher Long, Arthur's attorney, who testifies about an incident in which Perry talked to his father. Long was visiting Arthur in the metro jail when Perry walked into the room and said, "Dad, I'm not going to roll on you. You're not going to roll on me. We will wear these jumpsuits with a badge of honor, a badge of honor."

Massey has no questions for the attorney.

A couple of final witnesses round out the state's case. Phillip Taylor conducted the wiretaps on the phone where Perry used to talk to Arthur. Another tape—the court hears Perry tell Arthur, "I was going to arrange for the sale of a car

down there." He mentions Bobby Givings and says, "Never
ever send me e-mails about that."

Special FBI Agent Kenneth Sena, assigned to Guadalajara,
testifies that he placed Arthur under surveillance and ultimately met him at the airport when Arthur had come to meet
Bobby Givings. He says Arthur was pale and shaken. He
was not detained. Sena accompanied Perry to Los Angeles
when he was deported.

At ten thirty the state rests its case.

John Herbison makes the requisite motion for acquittal, saying Perry did not commit an "overt act" and that "free
speech" must create a "clear and present danger." The judge
quickly denies the motion.

Perry March, who stated to the press after his arrest in
August 2005 that he felt confident the citizen jurors of
Nashville would judge him fairly, never takes the stand except, outside the presence of the jury, to say that he does not
wish to testify. He also states that he will not request an en-
trapment defense.

The defense has little to work with. Massey introduces to
the jury excerpts from Arthur March's deposition taken in
February after Arthur's arrest and return to Nashville. The
court enlists a reader to present Arthur's lines, and Massey
and Thurman read their own questions from the deposition.
In the deposition, Arthur says that he never called Bobby
Givings, that Givings called him "all the time." Massey asks
whether Perry ever mentioned harming the Levines, and
Arthur states, "It was my idea."

"Your idea to take them out?" Massey says.

"Yes, long before this ever happened," says Arthur.

"Who suggested that actions be taken against the
Levines?" asks Massey.

Arthur answers, "Bobby Givings." He says that he did
not talk to Perry about any of the matters he and Givings discussed.

During Thurman's questioning, Arthur admits he told

Perry "it was going to happen next week." He says Perry told him to give Bobby Givings as much help as he needed.

The defense's case is less than spectacular.

Closing arguments take place after lunch. Katy Miller methodically reviews the testimony the prosecution has presented, particularly the taped conversations between Perry and Farris.

Massey says of the tapes: "There was a deep anger here. Don't think I'm minimizing it." But he argues that Farris was not a credible witness, and that Perry never intended or agreed to act on his plans for murder. He presents charts, continues to go to his desk to pick up papers. Clearly, the defense attorney is struggling in this last effort to salvage what many are already saying is a slam-dunk case. He talks about the "imaginary plan," saying, "This was a made-up story."

Thurman is given the last word with the jury, pointing out that a conspiracy doesn't require a "green light," and that Perry did not go to the police and say, "This man is out there and we need to stop him." Thurman says, "You can't cover up facts, can't erase the voice of Perry March." He closes by telling the jury, "It's time for justice."

Judge Dozier then carefully instructs the jurors in the applicable law, his voice earnest yet patient, and the jury goes out.

Pridemore and Postiglione hear joking from others in the hall, "We might not have time for a cup of coffee."

The cold case detectives also expect a swift verdict.

But by the end of the day, the jury is still deliberating.

It just takes one holdout.

Local TV station NewsChannel 5 is airing the trial on its cable channel and by streaming video. News analyst Nick Beres and legal analyst Nick Bailey use the downtime to take calls. An overwhelming number of callers are adamant: He did it! It's a no-brainer! The waiting continues into Thursday morning, and the calls keep coming in. Clearly, the March case has Nashville in its grip.

The verdict comes at midafternoon on Thursday. It is a

tense moment for Postiglione and Pridemore, as the jury files in. Postiglione's stress level has been on the rise for the past twenty-four hours; he has not slept much. He can't even look at the jury. With his elbows on his knees, he presses his palms against his temple and waits.

Pridemore tries to make eye contact with Perry again, but the defendant won't give him that satisfaction.

The jury renders it verdict: "Guilty . . . guilty . . . guilty."

Perry remains stone-faced.

Outside the courtroom, the TV cameras catch the Levines as they leave without comment. The reporters ask for observations from the prosecution and defense attorneys. Both agree that the March-Farris tapes were extremely damaging. The camera turns to Postiglione. In his clipped Long Island accent, he says, "Two down, one to go."

CHAPTER 42

The Third Trial—Murder

Following two convictions by Nashville juries, Perry March's defense team requests a change of venue for the third trial—the big one—scheduled for August 7. Judge Dozier responds favorably to the motion, at least in part, announcing that a jury from outside of Nashville will hear the second-degree-murder trial. Massey and his team hold out hope that the entire trial will be moved to another jurisdiction, but on July 13, Judge Dozier announces that the jury will be chosen in Chattanooga and transported to Nashville for the trial.

Reference is often made to "the three states of Tennessee"—East, Middle, and West—each region with its own disposition. Chattanooga, the fourth-largest city in Tennessee, located 110 miles southeast of Nashville, might as well be in another state.

The judge, the prosecution and defense teams, and the defendant, Perry March, travel to Chattanooga, and on Monday morning, August 7, the jury selection begins at the Hamilton County Courthouse. Seven hundred citizens have been called as the jury pool for this occasion. Half of the jurors who show up ask to be dismissed. Judge Dozier cannot tell them how long they will need to be in Nashville; those selected for the jury will basically put their lives on hold until the trial is over.

It will be the first jury in seven years brought to Nashville from another city.

As prosecutors Tom Thurman and Katy Miller question potential jurors, one question is repeated during voir dire: Can you convict someone of murder without the victim's body? The defense focuses on the same idea—no body—but from a different slant: When someone leaves and is never heard from again, does it mean there had to be a murder?

Carolyn and Larry Levine sit in the front row of the courtroom. They scrutinize every man and woman questioned by the lawyers. Who will be sympathetic to Janet? Who will understand what Perry has done to our family? Who will give us justice?

At the end of the day, after seven hours, a panel is seated—six women and six men; nine white and three African-Americans. Judge Dozier is overly cautious; four alternates are selected as well. "Don't go to your computer and google Perry March," the judge warns before he allows them to go home for the night. These men and women from Chattanooga have said they haven't heard much about the March case—incredible to Nashville residents who have lived the saga for a decade, but the lack of exposure of the case in this region of East Tennessee may explain why Judge Dozier chose to go to Chattanooga for the jury. He sends them home to pack. They are allowed to bring books, but none that are murder- or crime-related. Make plans to be in Nashville for a week, maybe longer, they are instructed.

On Tuesday, the sixteen Hamilton County residents board a bus for Nashville and are taken to the Loew's Vanderbilt Plaza, where they will be sequestered. As the jurors transfer clothes from suitcases to drawers and closets, the prosecution and defense teams make last-minute preparations for the trial that is finally about to happen. They're back in Nashville now, where the March case is once again in the headlines of Tuesday's *Tennessean*, with Perry March's face on the front page. The trial *is* the news tonight on the local TV stations. As if they need to whip up excitement among the TV audience, they flash photos of Janet, Perry, and the children from happier days and replay sound bites from ten years of the March story the media has covered. NewsChannel 5, airing the trial live on TV and through streaming video, refers to it as "Nashville's trial of the century." Reporters from Court TV and CBS's *48 Hours* are in town.

For prosecutors and defense counsel alike, this is the biggest case of their careers. Their legal teams work late, taking care of last-minute business, watching the minutes fly by, anxious that there is not enough time before morning.

For Perry March, in his cell at the Davidson County Jail, it is a long night.

Unlike the first two trials, which were held in the unimpressive, one-story courtroom of a converted office building, this one takes place at the new A. A. Birch Criminal Justice Building, named for a former Davidson County Circuit Court judge and the first African-American Tennessee Supreme Court justice. The streets swarm with news vans, their crisscrossing cables and portable satellite dishes littering the sidewalk like a NASA liftoff. Crowds spill from the sidewalks into the high-rise structure located across the street from the stately Metro Courthouse, still under renovation. This is the district in which many of Nashville's law offices are clustered, the pocket of the city that was once Perry March's milieu. Had the night of August 15, 1996, taken a different turn, he might well have been one of the suits with an attaché, heading to the Birch Building to represent a client on this bright, hot morning.

The obligatory security lines are busy. Guards pay close attention as other security personnel examine purses and briefcases and computers. Heels click on the marble floors, and voices echo in the cavernous lobby. Elevators are packed.

"Going to the trial?" the occupants of the elevator cars ask one another.

Some of them work in the building. They wear uniforms with security or maintenance badges or the business attire of office personnel. But many of the riders exit the elevators on the sixth floor. The courtroom is at the end of the hall, which is strewn with even more cables where the camera crews have set up. A reporter steps up to a light and begins to speak into his mike: "We're outside the courtroom where the trial is about to begin . . ."

The courtroom, with its dark paneling and portraits of previous judges lining the walls, is an impressive arena, suggesting the gravity of the drama that is about to unfold, but the mood is more suggestive of a social gathering as cameras set up in the back of the room and spectators find their seats. Bill Massey, wearing red suspenders, and Lorna McClusky scramble to get organized at the defense table, digging in large boxes, then exiting by a side door. Larry Levine goes about the courtroom saying hello, shaking hands, working the crowd. He has been waiting for this day. Many thought it would never come, but he and Carolyn would not give up. A large contingency from Nashville's Jewish community have come to support Larry and Carolyn—the friends and family members who know best the roller-coaster emotions that have defined these ten years.

The courtroom is full at eight thirty.

Judge Dozier is known for running a tight ship, so spectators begin to buzz when the proceedings fail to start on time. Is Perry making a last-minute deal? Is something going on behind the scenes? Then one attorney and another enter the courtroom—Tom Thurman first and then John Herbison. A contrast in styles—Thurman impeccably groomed, almost military in his bearing; Herbison hitching up his pants, looking like a bad-hair day, but it's the norm for him. Bill Massey comes in, McClusky at his side. Massey straightens his jacket, getting it just right. Katy Miller joins Thurman at the prosecution's table. There are also two law students from Vanderbilt sitting with the prosecution, by permission of the judge. They have spent countless hours doing legal research, helping the prosecutors prepare for the broad array of legal issues and technicalities that are associated with a murder case, helping the prosecutors convict one of their own alumni, a former associate editor for their nationally respected *Law Review*.

"All rise," a voice sounds, and Judge Dozier takes the bench. He calls for the court officer to bring in the defendant. Perry enters, wearing a dark suit and a confident smile. The court officer unfastens his handcuffs.

The proceedings begin with an announcement by Bill Massey that threatens further delay. He tells the court that he received an unsigned letter on Tuesday afternoon from someone who claimed he was having a romantic relationship with Janet March in August 1996. According to this source, Janet was upset; she was drinking. She took sleeping pills, and later the author of the letter found her with no pulse. He disposed of the body and kept quiet.

Massey points out that the letter was written on the same letterhead and in a similar type as letters previously received from an inmate at Riverbend Maximum Security Prison, Barry Armistead. He wants to delay opening statements to interview Armistead. Thurman counters, saying he has a file on Armistead, who has tried repeatedly to get consideration from the DA's office. "He has auditioned for us before," Thurman says. "He's not credible." Judge Dozier orders that the prisoner be brought to the Criminal Justice Building so the attorneys can interview him, but he will not delay opening statements.

More discussions and procedural motions follow before the jury finally files in, and Judge Dozier calls on Katy Miller to read the grand-jury indictment. Wearing a windowpane-plaid suit, her dark hair pulled back in a headband, reminiscent of Hillary Clinton when her husband ran for president the first time, Miller stands before the jury. In a dispassionate voice, she begins reading the counts: ". . . Perry Avrum March . . . knowingly did kill Janet Levine March . . ."

And then Defense Attorney Massey has his turn. On behalf of his client, he enters a plea of not guilty on all counts. Perry's deadpan expression seems to indicate that none of these proceedings interest him.

The judge calls on Deputy District Attorney General Tom Thurman to give his opening statement.

It is a solemn moment when Thurman addresses the jury. It is the moment Carolyn and Larry Levine have anticipated for a long time, the moment Perry March has done everything in his power to avoid. The experienced prosecutor acknowledges that the case against Perry March is a circumstantial one, but he promises to present an intricate story of inferred guilt. "Innocent people do not try to have witnesses murdered," he says, referring to testimony the prosecution will produce from inmate Nathaniel Farris. He does not mention March's conviction in the murder-for-hire plot, but he tells the jury that Farris secretly recorded conversations in which Perry plotted to kill Carolyn and Larry Levine, and that the prosecution will play the audiotapes for the jury to hear. Thurman outlines the history of the case, the points that the prosecution will focus on, and the questions that don't make sense if one believes Perry March. He announces what the key prosecution witnesses will contribute. Another inmate, Cornelius King, will testify that Perry admitted killing Janet with a wrench during an argument on August 15, 1996. Videotapes will be produced in which Perry's own father, Arthur March, states that he helped Perry dig up Janet's body from one location near the March home and relocate it in Kentucky.

"This case is about murder," Thurman says. "It's about deceit. It's about abuse of trust."

At the end of twenty-six minutes, Thurman faces the jury and says in a grave voice, "There will be no question in your minds. There's a murderer in the courtroom. He's sitting right there. His name is Perry March."

Perry tries for the bravado, the tilted chin and smug smile that have characterized him during all of his court appearances, but he can't get it quite right. For the first time, as the jurors gaze at him, he looks like the defendant in a murder trial. For the first time, his face shows his confidence shaken a little.

Bill Massey, however, is the kind of defense attorney who can instill confidence in his client simply by the ring of his voice. He speaks with the passion of an evangelist as he tells the jury, "Now, ladies and gentlemen, let's come back to center." He points out that the case is purely circumstantial. "Psychics, cadaver dogs, and inmates—that's what this case is about," he says. At every opportunity, he hammers home the point, "There is no body." Yes, Janet and Perry were having marital problems, he tells the jury. They had been seeing a psychiatrist, who told them they needed a cooling-off period. An animated Massey paints a picture of a woman who was "a little bit spoiled" and a husband who was hounded by the police because they had no other suspect. He criticizes the police work on the case and warns that the jailhouse informants who will testify against Perry March are out to get deals of their own. The defense plans to show a videotape of Sammy March in an interview with a TV reporter. In the interview, young Sammy will say that he saw his mother drive away on the night of August 15, 1996.

After Massey's fifty-seven-minute opening statement, the lines of Perry's face are more relaxed. His attorney has put up a good argument.

Cold case detectives Bill Pridemore and Pat Postiglione have spent the morning in the district attorney's victim/witness area, located on the fourth floor of the courthouse. One section for witnesses has phones and a television. Pridemore and Postiglione wait in the other section of the large area, accessible only by ID cards, used by members of the DA's office and police. They drink coffee, use the phones, and go over and over their testimony. Thurman and Miller come into the secure area during recess, both in good spirits.

The detectives know it's going to be a long wait before either of them testifies.

• • •

Back in court, Katy Miller announces the first prosecution witness, Carolyn Levine.

A small, attractive woman in a classic dark pantsuit with pink accents, Janet March's mother is a reminder of how Janet might have looked if she had lived to be Carolyn's age. The bone structure, thick hair, and expressive eyes—her features were Janet's features, too. Pride resonates in her voice as she speaks of her bright, artistic daughter who not only designed the Blackberry Road house but showed keen business sense when she subdivided the property and sold off the lots for more than she had paid for all of it.

With a sad smile, Carolyn tells how she and her husband treated their son-in-law like a son, how their lives intertwined with the lives of Janet, Perry, and the grandchildren. Miller asks about Janet and Perry's marital problems. Yes, they both confided in her. Perry was often the first to tell her their problems. "He came to me in the spring and said he was afraid Janet was going to divorce him and take the children," she says. Carolyn was planning to go with Janet to her appointment with a divorce attorney on August 16. She knew the couple had been in counseling for several months.

She testifies that her daughter's emotional state changed the week before the night of August 15, the night Perry called her and Larry and said, "Janet is gone."

Perry presented them with a story that they accepted. Janet would be back by Sammy's birthday, in time for his first day of school. "She was going to bring cupcakes to school," Carolyn says.

She admits that Larry wanted to go to the police immediately. "I didn't want Janet to be embarrassed," Carolyn says. Yes, she believed Perry. She believed Janet would be back— but then the police found the Volvo.

"That was a hard day for me," she says, blinking back tears.

After the lengthy testimony of Carolyn Levine, the judge calls for lunch. Everyone is ready. The release of tension in the courtroom is palpable.

Carolyn Levine is a strong woman. She's had to be. She remains composed as defense attorney Lorna McClusky questions her again about the critical two weeks after Janet disappeared. McClusky speaks in a low-key, courteous voice, but she is determined to make an important point. *Who* didn't want to go to the police? The Levines have said Perry delayed for two weeks. Perry has said the Levines were responsible for the delay.

"You didn't want to be embarrassed," McClusky says.

Carolyn says, "I thought, if Perry wants to go to the police, it would be to embarrass Janet."

It's a paradox that has haunted this mother for a decade. Yes, she was suspicious of Perry. Yes, she believed him. Both are true. "My mind was not going to accept what I inevitably came to believe," she says. "I didn't want to believe the worst."

McClusky's cross-examination lasts a little over a half hour. Her probing questions provide Carolyn more opportunity to describe the deterioration of the relationship between Perry and the Levines, the custody battles, the manner in which Perry belittled Janet. Even so, Carolyn never raises her voice, never assumes a hateful tone toward Perry. McClusky cannot break her; she remains the picture of grace and dignity. The soft-spoken woman on the witness stand is a mother whose grief has made her wise, not bitter. She gives well-thought-out answers, supplying precise dates and times, not just because she has been well prepped but because she has lived and relived these scenes, over and over and over for the past ten years.

The prosecution has scored with Carolyn Levine.

It is after three when Carolyn is excused from the witness stand. Massey has determined that there is nowhere to go with the anonymous letter. The inmate, Armistead, who was brought to the Criminal Justice Center earlier that day, has denied any knowledge of it. No miraculous break for the defense seems imminent.

The prosecution has a dozen more witnesses lined up for the remainder of the afternoon.

John Richie testifies that he and John McAllister, workmen from a cabinet shop, were present at the March home installing countertops at about four on August 15, the last day anyone other than Perry and the children saw or heard from Janet. According to Richie, Janet asked them if they would fix a leaky faucet, and Perry, who arrived during the time the workmen were there, provided the tool that McAllister used to tighten the faucet—a pair of pliers.

Later, when Postiglione and Pridemore hear that Richie has said "pliers," they can't believe it. They went over his testimony with him, as they did with other witnesses, and he told them Perry provided a wrench for McAllister to tighten the faucet. "Are you sure it was a wrench?" Postiglione remembers asking, and Richie said, "Yes."

The next witness after Richie is Deneane Beard, the Marches' housecleaner in 1996. She testifies that when she arrived at the March home on August 16, Perry told her Janet had gone to California. The house was already clean that morning. Of special note was the bathroom, where she would usually find strands of Janet's long, dark hair, but not on this day. Janet always left her lists that were handwritten, not typed, she says.

The next witness, Marissa Moody, tells the court that she brought her son, Grant, to the March house to play with Sammy on the morning of August 16. She had talked with Janet the day before to set up the playdate, but when she and Grant arrived, Perry was not expecting her. However, he came out of his office and said Grant could stay. Moody testifies that she saw a rolled-up Oriental rug when she arrived, but when she returned that afternoon, the rug was gone.

Lucinda Smith, divorce attorney, gives brief testimony stating that she had an appointment with Janet for eleven on August 16 and that Larry Levine called that Friday morning to cancel it. When she is dismissed, her expression indicates she might wonder what, of value, she offered in three to four minutes. Her testimony, like Richie's and many of the other witnesses who will take the stand over the next few days, is just one of the building blocks that seems insignificant by itself, but is crucial to the circumstantial case the prosecution is constructing.

Four young women who were Janet's best friends testify during the afternoon. This circle of friends and their husbands, all part of the close-knit Jewish community in Nashville, socialized and raised their children together. The women took trips together. Longtime friends Laurie Rummel and Gabi Friedman had known Janet since school days. Diane Saks says, "I have been friends with Janet all my life." Laura Zinker met Janet in 1988 and the two became close friends. When Zinker and her husband moved to Ohio, Janet visited her and confided that she and Perry were having marital problems. "He was demeaning, degrading, as if she had nothing to contribute," Zinker testifies.

The friends are adamant in their praise for Janet as an exemplary mother—devoted, attentive, one who would never leave her children.

Mitchell Barnett, architect, takes the stand and testifies that he worked with Janet on the Blackberry Road house. "She had the design concept," he says. "I was more or less her technical consultant." Perry rarely came to the job site, he says. "It was Janet's project." On cross-examination, Massey asks, "Would you call her strong-willed?" Barnett says, "I call it focused."

The next witness, Dr. Thomas Campbell, psychiatrist, saw Perry professionally for about thirty sessions from November 1992 to March 1994, and then he saw Janet and Perry together for four or five sessions in the spring and summer of 1996. After Janet's disappearance, Carolyn Levine accompanied Perry to what would be his last session with Dr. Campbell. The psychiatrist describes Perry and Janet as "conflicted" and testifies that he discussed a trial separation with them. "It was a volatile session," he says, referring to August 5, the last time he met with Janet and Perry.

It is almost six o'clock. Perry yawns from time to time.

The spectators have dwindled. Even the lawyers who came into the courtroom starched and animated are beginning to wear down, but Judge Dozier is not ready to call it a day.

Kim Avington Scott was Sammy's kindergarten teacher in August 1996. Due to the nature of her testimony, the judge sends the jury out while she testifies, but she is videotaped. She recalls his first days of school. "He cried because he missed his mother," she says. "He said he didn't get to say good-bye."

The last witness of this long day is Dr. Stacey Goodman, a college friend of both Janet and Perry. She first testifies without the jury; then the jury is brought back in to hear her testimony. She states that after an interview with the *Tennessean* in which she stated that she did not believe Janet would leave her children, Perry called her from Chicago, "swearing, screaming, and threatening." He said, "When I come to Nashville, I'm coming to get you."

It is 6:39 p.m. At last, Judge Dozier recesses for the day.

Pat Postiglione and Bill Pridemore have been secluded in the victim/witness area all day. Now they go to work, meeting with Thurman and Miller. Over sandwiches, they discuss how the case is going—a good first day. It's no surprise to the detectives that Mrs. Levine gets high marks. More coffee is brought in, and they settle down to talk about tomorrow's strategy.

At about eleven p.m., the first day of the trial ends for the prosecutors and the cold case detectives.

The young paralegal who so thoroughly captivated Perry March in 1991 is the first witness to take the stand on day two, but the judge elects to hear her testimony outside the presence of the jury. She is attractive, a slim woman in a flattering suit, with long autumn-red hair. She testifies that she received three sexually explicit letters while working at Bass, Berry, and Sims. After she reported the unsigned letters to her supervisor, the firm investigated and eventually Perry March was identified as having sent them. She reports that she reached a settlement with March for "about twenty-five thousand." She thinks she received $12,000, but she never received the "balloon" payment that was due in 1996. Unemotional, speaking without expression, Leigh Reames gives the impression that she has tried to block out this experience, and what she remembers is a little fuzzy.

Herbison gets his chance to question on behalf of the defense. "You didn't know—*of your own knowledge*—that Perry March wrote the letters," he says.

She says, "No."

Thurman redirects. "Were videos taken of Perry March leaving the letters?"

"Yes."

"Do you have any doubt that Perry March wrote them?"

"No."

The next witness, Cornelius King, also at first testifies without the jury present. An inmate of the Davidson County Jail, King is a young African-American, wearing the required yellow jumpsuit. He testifies to conversations with Perry March in which March stated that he killed his wife. According to King, the couple had an argument because she threatened to leave him and take everything, and Perry said he "wouldn't take that." The altercation turned physical, and Perry hit her with a wrench. He also says Perry told him that her body is "burned in ashes, in water."

Herbison, still acting for the defense, tries to discredit King by bringing out a grievance Perry filed against him. Herbison's manner is noticeably more condescending than Massey's when addressing a witness. He uses ponderous phrasing that confuses King, but King holds his own. He says Perry wanted him to testify against Reno Martin. Martin is another inmate scheduled as a prosecution witness. King says he refused to do what Perry asked, and that was the reason Perry filed the grievance.

The spectators demonstrate keen interest in Reames and King. Both will return to repeat their stories to the jury.

It is almost ten when the jury is permitted to enter the courtroom. All the starts and stops have to be confusing if not irritating to the jurors, already displaced from their homes, sequestered in a hotel. The first witness they hear is Ella Goldshmid, the Russian immigrant who served as the Marches' babysitter for six years. Working through an interpreter, she testifies eloquently about Janet's relationship with the children: "She was the ideal mother, smart, caring, and devoted. She never failed to sacrifice time for the children." Goldshmid says that when she worked on Wednesday, August 14, Janet was not herself. Her face was "gray, stonelike," that day. She says Janet never went out of town without leaving very explicit instructions for her.

During cross-examination, Massey asks, "On August fourteenth, did Janet seem 'down,' 'depressed'?"

"I can't say 'depression' but upset," she answers.

"But when you were interviewed by Detective Hunter, after Janet disappeared, you said, 'Janet was really down and depressed,'" Massey insists.

"I didn't have an interpreter," she says.

Massey presses the point. "But hadn't Janet been 'down' for the last month?"

"During the last month, she did not radiate light," Goldshmid says.

The next witnesses are three detectives who worked the Janet March investigation, Tim Mason, David Miller, and Brad Corcoran. Mason responded to the call on September 7, 1996, when Janet's Volvo was found at the Brixworth Apartments, and continued to work on the case until May 2001. Katy Miller's questions focus on the evidence in the Volvo and the interviews of Brixworth residents that Mason conducted.

David Miller took the initial missing persons report, two weeks after Janet's disappearance, and was lead detective on the homicide case until January 1, 1997, when he was replaced by Mason. Miller has come to Nashville for the trial, returning from Florida, where he has lived since 2001. A balding, soft-spoken man in a gray suit, he gives the appearance of a professor—an absentminded professor—as the questioning proceeds. Though he has been thoroughly prepped to be a witness, he has trouble remembering events.

Miller testifies that he took Perry March's statement and obtained warrants for the searches of the March house and property. Thurman barely touches on the absence of the hard drive from the Ambra computer, choosing not to revisit the fact that Miller had notified attorney Lionel Barrett about the imminent search of Blackberry Road. More testimony about the Volvo and Jeep follows as Katy Miller questions Detective Brad Corcoran, who was a crime-scene investigator and had a turn as lead detective on the case after Mason.

Though Thurman and Katy Miller limit their questions to all three detectives, Massey is prepared with plenty of ammunition to call into question the police work during those days, firing back again and again with questions about particular leads that he insists the police did not follow properly. On his cross of Detective Miller, Massey hands the detective page after page of police reports and witness statements on "sightings" of Janet March, and Miller often looks baffled.

In conjunction with one set of questions, Massey asks Miller about a polygraph test that Nashville investigators conducted of Clyde Sumner, a former worker during the construction of Blackberry Road, who expressed to police his sexual desire for Janet March. Thurman shows a rare burst of emotion, arguing that polygraph examinations are clearly not admissible. "Am I going to get into Perry March's refusal to take a polygraph? In thirty years, this is one of the worst performances I've seen before a jury." Massey quickly defends his line of questioning, and as the two attorneys shout at each other, Judge Dozier's patience wears thin. "Jiminy Christmas," he exclaims, and sends the jury out for lunch. Later Massey asks the court for a mistrial, arguing that the judge's outburst is unfairly prejudicial to the defense. Dozier, exhaling slowly, doing his best to maintain his usual calm judicial demeanor, denies the defense motion.

By the time Kim Garbler takes the stand, tempers are finally in check. A private investigator hired by Larry Levine, she testifies that Perry was angry after she set up a surveillance at Brixworth to look for anything suspicious and that he referred to his wife in the past tense: "She was beautiful, wasn't she?"

Peter Rodman takes the stand late in the afternoon. He testifies that he saw Perry March with a bike at the Brixworth Apartments at about one thirty a.m. on the morning of August 16, 1996.

When asking about Rodman's radio show, Massey says, "Would you characterize your show as 'sensational'?" Rodman states that he never used information about the Marches on his show. As the questioning continues, Rodman grows more adamant that he recognized Perry in the parking lot that early morning, and in February, after seeing Perry's photo in the *Nashville Scene*, he contacted Detective Mike Smith. Massey keeps hammering on the exact date: How could he be sure it was the morning of August 16? Rodman is defensive now, explaining how he checked with his corporate headquarters to figure the exact date that he returned from being out of town.

Detective Smith is called to the stand at six. He confirms that Rodman contacted him after seeing Perry March's photo in the paper.

At six fifteen, after another exhausting day, Judge Dozier finally recesses until Friday morning.

Pridemore and Postiglione, still waiting on the fourth floor, have missed the fireworks in the courtroom, but they meet with Thurman and Miller once again for several hours before calling it a night. The mood, so buoyant the previous night, has altered considerably, like a warm fall afternoon that suddenly turns chilly when the sun goes down.

David Miller, who was the lead detective during the fall of 1996, could have offered so much. Such a disappointment.

So far twenty-two witnesses have testified, and many more are scheduled—plus several hours of videotapes left to present as part of the prosecution's case.

"Let's go home," Thurman says at last, slapping a file folder shut.

Pridemore, finally scheduled to testify the next day, goes over his notes again at home.

The morning of the third day, Friday, the atmosphere in the courtroom is like the aftermath of a storm—the heavy quiet. The first witness, Travis West, manager of a bike shop, testifies that Perry March's bicycle could have fit into the trunk or the front seat of a Volvo. Danny Morris, fingerprint expert with metro police, follows with tedious information about fingerprinting techniques. He testifies that his lab could not match the fingerprints from the Volvo to Perry's.

After the long wait, Detective Pridemore finally takes the stand. In his dark suit and red tie, he looks every bit the part of the professional. He speaks with authority, presenting his credentials of over thirty years on the police force, over two decades as a homicide detective, and four years in the cold case unit. Thurman's questions are brief, focusing primarily on hair and fiber samples Pridemore submitted to the FBI. Pridemore also testifies that he and his partner, Postiglione, brought Perry to Nashville from Los Angeles. Thurman has established narrow limits for Pridemore's testimony; he does not touch on the part the cold case detectives played in breathing new life into the case. That's fine with Pridemore; he doesn't mind a bit if he's on and off the stand in a few minutes.

But that doesn't happen. Massey once again sets out to show poor police work. He refers to the search at the March property on September 17, 1996, and asks Pridemore if he was present for that "spectacle." Pridemore says he was there as a "scribe," not doing the actual searching, and that it was a "typical" search. Massey then hammers the point that police continued to look for Janet or Janet's body even after Perry was indicted. He offers date after date, scenario after scenario where police followed tips, searching for a body. "Did you find the body?" he asks, over and over. Pridemore gets his point in, too, that police followed every lead because "that's our job." But Massey persists. "You were still looking for a body on that date?" and "Did you find a body?" At last Judge Dozier leans toward Pridemore and says, "Let me ask: You've never found her body?" A soft ripple of amusement passes through the courtroom like a wave. Pridemore sees that some of the jurors are smiling. It is a rare light moment in court. Pridemore suppresses a smile, too. "No, we have never found the body," he says.

Carolyn and Larry Levine are not smiling.

Massey's cross of Pridemore doesn't get him very far, and it's clear he doesn't have the steam that he had when cross-examining Miller and Mason. Pridemore is excused. He feels good about his testimony. Now he can watch the trial.

An FBI trace-evidence investigator from Quantico is next to testify. Karen Korsberg examined hairs and carpet fibers that were sent by Pridemore. Her testimony, like Danny Morris's, is extremely tedious, and in the end, some of the jurors are beginning to squirm. One spectator notes during lunch that with the exception of Detective Pridemore, the prosecution's witnesses on Friday morning may have done as much good for the defense as for the prosecution.

But Pridemore has faith that Thurman will tie it all together for the jury, and he knows what's coming next. The video- and audiotapes will make everyone in the courtroom sit up and take notice.

CHAPTER 43

The Camera Never Blinks

In the weeks that followed Janet March's disappearance, Perry had begun to realize that his adversarial relationship with the media was a serious problem. He did not trust the newshounds that publicized his legal and financial woes, the friction between him and Janet's parents, and the police investigation that put him in the role of prime suspect instead of grieving husband. However, criticizing the media's tactics did not win him any points. Finally, in an effort to combat the bad press, Perry decided to take *his* case to the media— to play offense instead of defense. With his attorney Lionel Barrett present, he gave an interview to Annette Nole Hall, a reporter from local television station WSMV, in which he vehemently denied any involvement in his wife's disappearance.

Now, on the third day of the trial, the prosecution plays a series of clips from the interview that Perry gave on October 1, 1996. Hall sits in the witness box as the lights go down in the courtroom, and a younger Perry March is flashed on the screen.

Noticeably, the Perry from that long-ago interview is a

thinner version of the man who sits at the defendant table this morning. In the video clip Perry is adamant that he and Janet did not have a fight. "It was a relatively benign evening," he insists. He is resolute in his statement that he will not let police interview Sammy. "My son doesn't know anything. He was asleep," Perry says, his head cocked at a haughty angle.

Hall confirms that in a subsequent interview, Perry reiterated that his son didn't see anything. She gives the date of the later interview, January 20, 1998.

This is the first in a series of video- and audiotapes that go to the heart of the prosecution's case.

Bill Pridemore, now watching the proceedings from within the courtroom, notes that the jurors are engaged. He smiles to himself when Massey has no questions.

The next witness is Cookeville attorney Jon Jones, one of several attorneys who were involved in the litigation that quickly erupted over the disposition of Janet's assets.

When Perry was questioned by Jones during the period of November 20–22, 1996, he could not have imagined that his own words would come back to bite him on this August day, ten years later.

When Larry Levine insisted that the deposition be videotaped, he could not have imagined how significant the tape would prove, ultimately, in presenting his son-in-law to the public as the manipulator the Levines believed him to be. Or—some would say Janet's father was already preparing for the criminal trial that he believed would take place someday, the trial that he hoped would bring justice for his daughter.

Asked if he and Janet argued on the night of her disappearance, Perry takes a long moment to think about it. "It's a matter of semantics." He says that Janet argued and yelled, but he did not.

Jones asks, "Did you ever strike Janet?"

Perry cocks his head, considering, making furrows in his brow, under the dark curls. "Mr. Jones, to the best of my recollection, I have never struck my wife," he says. "It has always been something that I am proud of. I never struck my wife."

"Did you ever choke her?" Jones asks.

A long pause, and then, "No."

"Did you ever hurt her or attempt to hurt her?"

A longer pause this time—incredibly long—before Perry finally says that he might have grabbed her arm but not with the intent of hurting her.

The Hamilton County residents who have traveled to Nashville to hear this trial are a diverse panel of jurors. One young woman looks like a schoolgirl, with her ponytail, glasses, and white blouse. One juror wears overalls. They are a mix of young, old, black, white, male, female. Some have appeared to be dozing during portions of earlier testimony. But at this moment, as Perry March's videotaped voice sounds in the courtroom, the jurors' faces are frozen in attention. A young black man who has taken notes diligently throughout the trial lays down his pen and leans forward to peer at one of the small monitors that are provided for jurors. The spectators are fixated on the large screen. Heads shake in disbelief when Perry takes a full minute to answer.

Jones asks if Perry knows of anyone with a motive to kill Janet. Perry replies that people who were involved with the construction of their house carried "extreme animosity" toward Janet. He names the contractor, Cooper Cate, and mentions a painter named Ron who "didn't meet her standards." He characterizes Janet's relationship with the contractor and subcontractors as "disastrous," calling it "a constant battle."

Jones and Perry go back and forth about the "bag of marijuana" that Perry alleged Janet took with her when she left. Perry says Janet smoked marijuana on a weekly basis and that she wanted him to use it, too. He only tried it to appease her, he says, with the same evasiveness that characterized Bill Clinton's famous line, "I tried it but I didn't inhale."

When asked if he was involved in a sexual relationship with someone other than Janet, in August of 1996, Perry refuses to answer. He says, "It's none of your business."

At the defense table, the live Perry displays profound

boredom at the answers the younger videotaped Perry gives, that have captured everyone else's attention. His freedom is on the line, but he appears detached from reality, living in his own world.

Pridemore watches the jurors view the video clips. His assessment is that the responses of an arrogant Perry March in 1996 have struck a chord with the jurors. So far, with possibly the exception Carolyn Levine's testimony, showing her strength, courage, and poise, the video is the strongest single item the prosecution has put forth.

Redina Friedman is a certified child legal representative who was appointed as one of the guardians ad litem for the March children in Chicago in March 1999. Her duties were to investigate allegations between the parties—Perry and the Levines—in the dispute over the grandparents' visitation. She testifies that when she visited the March home in Chicago, there were no pictures of the children's mother, a fact Friedman found disturbing. She also stated that Perry responded to her with hostility when she recommended that the Levines get visitation rights. Perry told her he didn't want the grandparents to visit the children because he didn't want them to take Sammy to the police, and that Sammy didn't see or hear anything the night of August 15. According to Friedman's testimony, Perry also told her he could disappear in Singapore.

Mark Levine is the next witness. He testifies that he came to Nashville after Janet's disappearance and went to the March house to look at the "twelve-day note" Janet left. He also found a six-page document, single spaced, written by Janet, a kind of "stream of consciousness" memo of ways Perry had mistreated her. Mark saw the note and asked to print it out, but Perry was embarrassed. Mark says, "Perry kept talking about how this was all affecting *him*." He talked Mark out of printing the document because "Perry said it would always be there." Mark says, "Perry was good at trying to make you want what he wanted."

Mark is clearly his father's son. Like Larry Levine,

whose shouting match with Massey generated a reprimand by Judge Dozier in the conspiracy trial, Mark refuses to let Massey make the point that when the Levines took Sammy and Tzipi from Mexico in 2000, the order allowed visitation only in Guadalajara. Mark insists that the Mexican order enforced the Illinois order, which meant that his parents could visit with their grandchildren anywhere in the world.

It's already five forty-five when Leigh Reames testifies, her first time before the jury. Judge Dozier instructs the jury that the evidence they are about to be presented "may only be considered for the limited purpose of determining whether it provides a motive for the crimes for which Mr. March is now on trial." The paralegal repeats the events relating to the three sexually explicit letters she received while at Bass, Berry, and Sims, the investigation conducted by the firm, and her settlement with Perry. She identifies two of the letters, the two that were found in the garage of the March house on Blackberry Road, and copies are given to the jurors, who linger over them for at least ten full minutes, absorbed in language that they would not normally come across. Pridemore watches for their reaction. One of the jurors shakes her head. Another finishes reading and stares at Perry, who certainly is not looking at the jury.

Though the hour is late and the jurors have an overload of information to digest, one final witness for the day is called to the stand. Katy Miller questions Michael Levine, nephew of Larry Levine. He is a life insurance agent who sold Janet and Perry life insurance policies in 1994. His testimony deals with Janet's $250,000 term life policy, of which Perry was the original beneficiary. After Janet's disappearance, the conservator of her estate, Jeff Mobley, made a request to the insurance company, Union Central, to change the beneficiary to her estate. The request was approved, and Perry wrote the company asking for an agent other than Mike Levine.

The judge has announced that court will be in session all day Saturday and Sunday afternoon. Judge Dozier knows that the flow of the case should not be interrupted, and that these jurors want to get home to Chattanooga. There are still issues to be worked out between the defense and prosecution regarding the testimony of Sammy March, who is now a teenager, about to turn sixteen. The judge says he will consider the defense's request to call Sammy as a witness.

Day three of the trial ends at nearly seven p.m.

Tom Thurman and Katy Miller have called twenty-nine witnesses, and they feel confident that they are building a solid case. It's a tedious process. It's a matter of timing, too. On Saturday morning two other witnesses take the stand to lay further groundwork before the prosecution introduces the most damaging witness they have against Perry March, his own father.

The first witness is Sheree Lee, who was Janet's hairdresser at Salon FX. She testifies that Perry came into the salon where she was cutting Janet's hair, and Janet's demeanor changed. When Perry came to her chair, she leaned away. "Not exactly cowering, but it seemed odd," Lee says. "I made a mental note." A week before she knew Janet had disappeared, she saw Perry in the salon with another woman. "He said she was Janet's best friend," Lee tells the court.

She is followed by Alberto José Sandoval Pulido, a lawyer from Mexico who represented Samuel Chavez, Perry's former business partner. Samuel Chavez also came to Nashville intending to reiterate the explosive testimony he first gave at the bond hearing almost a year earlier, but having received word that his daughter was diagnosed with cancer, he returned to Mexico.

With his striking dark features, slicked-back hair, and light-colored suit, Pulido could have walked off a *Godfather* set. Through an interpreter, he testifies that "Mr. March said if we didn't help him, he would do away with us the way he did with his wife." He says Perry made another statement: "I kill—" followed by a third word that Pulido did not understand.

The jurors have listened to more than thirty hours of testimony. It's the weekend—no break for Saturday, and a short break of only a few hours on Sunday. Yesterday's videotape of Perry's 1996 deposition generated noticeable sparks of interest in the jury box, but this morning the men and women from Hamilton County are tired. Tom Thurman can see it. The jurors need something dramatic to happen. It's time for Arthur March. Thurman is confident that this witness will infuse sufficient drama into the courtroom on this sleepy Saturday morning.

The prosecution has known for a while that Arthur, now incarcerated in a federal prison in Litchfield, Kentucky, would be unable to attend the trial because of his failing health. Thurman introduces the videotaped deposition that the seventy-eight-year-old gave in April, 2006, as part of his plea-bargain deal on the solicitation charges. Arthur March is the closest thing the prosecution has to a body. It's no small thing that a father is implicating his son.

The lights dim. The spectators focus on the large screen in the front of the courtroom; the jurors watch the monitors in the jury box.

The frail man with white hair and a white beard, dressed in a prison jumpsuit, speaks in a raspy voice, without much force behind it. Clearly, Arthur is not the same man who, in a *48 Hours* interview in December of 2005, defied authorities to come after him in Mexico. "I don't go peacefully," he declared. "I don't go like Perry. There's going to be bloodshed somewhere, theirs or mine."

In his deposition, Arthur describes in chilling detail how he destroyed the evidence of his daughter-in-law's remains. About five weeks after Janet disappeared, according to Arthur's testimony, he went with Perry to a site not far from the March home where Perry had buried Janet's body in a shallow grave. The bag, which he calls a "leaf bag," contained bones and clothes and weighed "somewhere between fifty and seventy pounds," Arthur estimated. He and Perry put it in the back of the Volvo and drove north on I-65 to Kentucky, near Bowling Green, where they stopped at a motel. Perry couldn't go through with the rest of the plan,

which was to dispose of the bag in a creek or some other
body of water. Arthur drove around the area, but found no
creeks deep enough. It was getting light; a school bus
passed, running its rural route. Arthur knew he had to dispose of the bag. He spotted a brush pile off the road and decided to dispose of it there, hoping it would be burned. He
dug three holes in the brush, one for clothes, and he says, "In
the next one I put Janet." In the third hole he put the bag.

But he didn't tell Perry the truth; Perry thought he
dumped the body in water.

Arthur relates the story without any indication of remorse. He might as well have been getting rid of a dog's
carcass.

He says that some weeks earlier, Perry told him there had
been an "accident" and Janet was dead. Perry wanted him to
clean up some bloodstains. Arthur washed the driveway and
used bleach on the deck outside the kitchen but never saw
any bloodstains.

He also confesses that he was the one who disposed of
the hard drive from the Ambra computer before the police
could examine it.

It's clear that the deposition is hard on Arthur. His memory is fuzzy when trying to reconstruct the time line for
Massey, who cross-examines him with extreme patience.
Arthur knows it all happened around Yom Kippur, which
was September 23, 1996. At one point he looks at the time
line and says it's all screwed up. "It was after Perry returned
from Chicago that he asked for my help," Arthur says. "He
went to Chicago for Yom Kippur." Arthur stayed in
Nashville at Perry's house sometimes, sometimes at the
apartment. "It was easier for my lady to meet me at the
apartment," he says, referring to Barbara Smith, whose
name had come up in connection with the loading and moving of some items from the home at 3 Blackberry Road to
Illinois.

The frail man is not clear on several facts from a decade
ago, but when asked why he did all these things for Perry, he
is perfectly clear. "He's my son!" Arthur says.

His son leans back in his chair at the defense table, looking away from the videotape of his father.

During the lunch break, Bill Pridemore has a sandwich with his partner in the victims/witness area. He tells Postiglione that Arthur's deposition appeared to have the effect they had hoped. "Technology's a wonderful thing," Pridemore says. "The jurors are loving these videos."

"Wait till they hear the tapes with Perry and Farris," Postiglione says.

Arthur's videotaped testimony continues into the afternoon. Massey's cross-examination of Arthur has consumed much of the three hours, without any revelations that appear helpful to the defense. At last, the screen goes dark and the courtroom lights brighten. The prosecution immediately calls Fletcher Long to the stand. Long, Arthur's attorney, tells the court about the day Perry came into the room at the jail where Long and Arthur were meeting. Perry told his father, "Don't roll on me. I'm not going to roll on you." He tapped his finger against his jumpsuit. "We wear this as a badge of honor—a badge of honor."

The prosecution has its momentum. Thurman's next witness is Dr. William Bass, a forensic anthropologist of the legendary "Body Farm" at the University of Tennessee in Knoxville, made famous by the Patricia Cornwell best-seller of the same name. Massey stipulates to the impressive credentials; essentially, the science of how bodies decompose has come from Bass's research over the last several decades. Dr. Bass explains to the jury that all bodies go through four steps of decomposition, which he calls fresh, bloat, decay, and dry, with the rates of speed varying according to temperature. Other factors that affect decomposition are insects and animals, he says, conjuring up images of blowflies, coyotes, and rats feeding on bodies. Thurman asks what the condition would be of a body weighing about a hundred pounds, after a few weeks in August and September? Dr. Bass is very precise. In the hottest part of summer, only a skeleton would remain by the end of the third week. Bass, the world-renowned expert, turns to face the jury, as if teaching a class, and instructs them that "the skeleton would weigh ten to fifteen pounds."

Bill Pridemore tries to maintain a noncommittal expression as Massey begins his cross. Arthur has testified that the bag of Janet's bones weighed fifty to seventy pounds. Massey first asks about the animals Dr. Bass has mentioned; would they scatter the bones? Dr. Bass says the larger animals like dogs and coyotes would seek a safe place to feed on the bones, maybe a quarter to a half mile away. Pridemore's gut is knotting, burning now, as Massey asks the question and Dr. Bass answers again, "The skeletal remains would be in the ten-to-fifteen-pound range."

Pridemore can't help glancing at the jury. He can't tell if they've made the connection with Arthur's testimony. Arthur's estimate has to be off—a sick, old man might make that mistake after a decade—but Pridemore believes the basics of his story. Still—it's just this kind of thing that can start the dominoes falling in a case.

Michelle Knight, investigator in the Davidson County Sherriff's Office, testifies that she made a DVD of a conversation between Perry and journalist Nick Beres. The tape is played for the court. Perry made the call to Beres after they had met briefly at the jail. Perry wanted to clarify what he had told Beres about his father. He was adamant about the wording—not "I understand why he did what he did" but "I understand his motivation—because he was being threatened with destruction." Perry said, "It's very important."

Pridemore settles back in his seat when Bobby Armstrong takes the stand. Armstrong's testimony that Perry wanted his Jeep's tires changed, shortly after Janet's disappearance, is the kind of testimony that adds another brick to the case. Jurors are sure to follow the logic. Why would Perry want to get rid of tires with 50 percent wear left on them unless he was trying to hide where those tires had been? The explanation he gave was simply that he preferred Michelins. Pridemore looks at the jurors and wonders what they're thinking about the man who spent $458.90 on new tires when his old ones had twenty thousand miles left.

The next witness is Andrew "Bo" Saks, husband of Diane Saks, who had testified on Wednesday. Because Janet and Diane were close, longtime friends, Perry and Bo became friends, too. Bo helped Perry pack the truck when he was moving to Chicago. He testifies that Perry made disturbing comments about the Levines and the police. Massey, on cross-examination, comes down hard on him. "From August 15 to September 18, did you go to his house? You say you were *devastated* by Perry's reaction? Did you reach out?"

Pridemore wonders if Massey is blasting Saks because he's been so helpless to do anything with the other witnesses.

The last witness of the day is Robert Heller, who testifies that early in 1997, Perry wrote and sent him a manuscript entitled *@murder.com*. The final task for the jurors on day four in court is to read from the four-page excerpt of the murder manuscript, in which a beautiful, dark-haired girl is brutally murdered.

Each night, after the proceedings, Perry places a call to Carmen in Ajijic. Each night he is upbeat, his voice animated. Tonight is no different. "Bill is doing a fantastic job with the defense," he says. He knows that his calls are being monitored. When Detective Pridemore reviews the tapes of the calls, he wonders if Perry's enthusiasm is for the benefit of his listeners or if he's trying to keep up an image for his wife.

"How did I look? How do you think I was perceived?" Perry asks. Carmen is able to watch the trial on Court TV.

"You should wear your glasses. You don't smile enough."

"Everything is going our way," Perry says. "We're going to win."

Unbelievable! Pridemore thinks. Surely Perry has some idea of the potential damage from his father's deposition on videotape today. He's a lawyer—or he *was*.

Maybe he's just in denial.

Carmen is more practical. "You have to be prepared for the worst," she says. "You must be strong, Perry, and accept that you're going to lose."

Perry won't entertain the notion of losing.

Nashville is a churchgoing city. Judge Dozier must be aware that many of the city's residents who attend one of the hundreds of churches that represent dozens of denominations will want to follow the trial on TV or streaming video or be present in court, and he surely knows the jurors need a break. He allows a morning—if not a day—of rest. The trial resumes at one Sunday afternoon.

Vickie Farris, mother of Nathaniel Farris, tells the court, as she did in the murder-for-hire trial, about contacting Larry Levine after her son told her that Perry was plotting to kill his former in-laws.

Nathaniel Farris takes the stand next. He repeats the testimony he gave in the murder-for-hire trial, explaining how he secretly recorded conversations with Perry while they were inmates in the metro jail. This jury is not told about Perry's conviction on charges of conspiracy and solicitation to commit murder, but the prosecution plans to play the tapes in court on Monday. Farris holds up under an intense cross-examination, in which Massey hammers the fact of his criminal background and tries to present the murder-for-hire plot as Farris's idea.

Cornelius King, who testified earlier without the jury present, now in the presence of the jury tells about his conversations with Perry while incarcerated. He testifies that Perry admitted killing his wife with a wrench during an argument. "He said that the body wouldn't be found," King says, "because it would be burned to ashes and poured in a lake." The defense makes the point that King did not come forward until March 28, though Perry was supposed to have confided in him months earlier. King says he wrote down what Perry told him and kept the notes in his cell.

The third inmate to testify is Reno Martin, former policeman from Cookeville, Tennessee, who was also housed in the unit with Perry. He testifies that Perry was angry about the custody issue with his children, and referring to the Levines, he said, "It should have been them that I took care of instead of—" Then he stopped suddenly and went pale, Martin says. In cross-examination, Lorna McClusky asks, "So you're the only one that heard these things?" Martin says yes.

All three of the witnesses who were Perry's inmates and are still in jail were attacked by the defense for making "a deal" with the prosecution. McClusky says bluntly to Martin, who was convicted of selling information, "That's what you're doing again today, aren't you?"

All three inmates say they have no promises from the prosecution, but as the day wraps up, Bill Pridemore notes that it's hard to tell what the jurors are thinking, whether they believe the three witnesses or not.

Sunday afternoon is a short session—a good thing, because Monday will be intense. Everyone knows the prosecution's case will be wrapping up early in the week. Thurman and Miller are feeling the pressure to tie up all the loose ends. Postiglione has a case of nerves, thinking about his testimony tomorrow. Pridemore is more relaxed now that he's testified, but his stomach won't stop burning.

Perry places another call to Carmen and tells her how well things are going.

The first item on the agenda for Monday morning is a discussion about Samson March's testimony. The prosecution and defense have agreed not to put Sammy on the stand. The defense will be allowed to play a tape in which Sammy spoke to a reporter while in Mexico, and the prosecution will be allowed to call rebuttal witnesses.

Witness number forty-three is Kevin Carroll, an investigator with the sheriff's department. He explains how he set up the recording devices in jail so that Farris could tape conversations with Perry. He identifies a tape that shows Perry sneaking to Farris's cell during that time period, and the court watches excerpts of the grainy tape that provide a view into the gray cell block. A second tape of the same setting shows Perry going to Cornelius King's cell. Pridemore is thinking this has got to help the prosecution's case. The camera never blinks.

The next witness, Kenneth Sena, is the FBI special agent in Mexico who met Arthur at the Guadalajara airport when Arthur had arranged to meet Farris.

Shortly before ten o'clock Pat Postiglione is called from the victims/witness area, where he has spent five days waiting. He straightens his tie as he enters the courtroom, meticulously groomed, well prepared for this appearance in the witness box.

Postiglione tells about his work on the Janet March investigation, first as a homicide detective and, after February 2002, as a member of the cold case unit. Thurman questions him about the trip he and Bill Pridemore made to Los Angeles to bring Perry back to Nashville, on August 12, 2005. The detective testifies that on the flight back Perry indicated he wanted to close this chapter of his life. "He asked if we could get in touch with the DA over the weekend," Postiglione says. "Several times he mentioned that he would make a deal if he could serve five to seven years actual time."

Postiglione also worked with Nathaniel Farris in regard to the conversations with Perry that Farris recorded on October 6 and 7. Thurman introduces the audiotapes to be played in court. The jurors strain to hear the dialogue between Perry and Farris amid the sounds, clanging and flushing toilets and other voices in the background, reminders that the plot is being hatched in a jailhouse. On a large screen are the lines from the tapes, lots of "uhs" and "Perry, Perry . . . Perry" from Farris, playing the part of a would-be hit man. He does an exceptional job.

Postiglione sits in the witness box as the tapes are presented. He's lost count of the number of times he's heard the tapes, but something in him still reacts when Perry says it won't help just to kill Carolyn, that Farris has to get both of his in-laws. "Do it—you have to do it when they're both together," Perry says, and something in Postiglione's gut says,

Gotcha! Perry gives Farris his in-laws' address. Postiglione thinks about the pleasant, modern-looking house on Vaughn's Gap, with lots of trees, shrubs, and flowers, and a basketball hoop at the end of the driveway. He imagines Perry with Janet and the children driving up to the house, long before the night that changed everything, and now, on tape, Perry is giving out that address to someone he thinks will go to that serene location and pump bullets into Carolyn and Larry.

Judge Dozier calls for a lunch break at noon and resumes promptly at one. The tapes continue. Perry sets up a code for Farris, a.k.a. Bobby Givings, to use when he calls Arthur in Mexico, and tells him to let Arthur know when he's ready to "buy the BMW."

After a grueling three hours, the tapes end. Another break—and Postiglione takes the stand again. His testimony sets the stage for yet another set of tapes, the telephone conversations between Farris, from jail, and Arthur, in Mexico. As with the previous tapes, the lines of dialogue are displayed on a large screen. Arthur doesn't want to know the particulars of the plan, but he skirts the edges of the gun problem, telling Farris, "It better be under a—it can't be a twelve." He says that "when this operation is finished . . . remember you've got a home." Postiglione watches the jurors. They are fixated on the screen.

Postiglione's testimony continues after the tapes. The judge excuses the jury at six, but there is one item of business left before court adjourns.

Scott Parsley, Sammy March's guardian, takes the stand. He establishes that Perry's son, now just two weeks shy of sixteen, is unwilling to testify.

As Postiglione leaves the courtroom, his partner slaps him on the back and tells him, "Good job."

"Thanks—but the hard part's tomorrow," he says.

Tuesday morning, August 15, begins with Massey's cross-examination of Postiglione. The detective is deeply aware that it has been ten years ago, to the day, since Janet March disappeared. The Levines are present in the same front-row seats they have occupied since the first day of the trial. Their supporters are seated all around them, the friends and family members from the close-knit Jewish community. Postiglione glances their way but only briefly. Massey comes out swinging, as he has done with the other detectives, and Postiglione has to be sharp.

Using the tactic that he used with Pridemore—and evidently not deterred by the lack of real results of that tactic—he refers to the many times police looked for a body during the nine years before Perry was indicted. "You didn't find a body," he repeats. When he begins to enumerate the "sightings" of Janet March, Postiglione gets a chance to make a point of his own. He says, "I am not aware of any sightings of Janet March. These were sightings of people resembling Janet March."

Postiglione's testimony, strategically placed near the end of the state's case, has the potential to tie together several pieces of the circumstantial evidence, particularly in regard to the incriminating tapes. From Massey's point of view, this detective's testimony is his last chance to discredit the police. He pushes his points. Massey and Thurman go back and forth over the defense's line of questioning, with the prosecutor saying over and over, "This witness can't know that," and Judge Dozier directing Massey to reword his question. The defense attorney at times is like a long-winded evangelist, alternately beseeching and hammering.

But when Sergeant Pat Postiglione leaves the witness stand, he feels good about his testimony. Finally, he can watch the proceedings from a seat in the courtroom. He finds his partner, who gives him the nod. They have both done all they can do.

Katy Miller questions the prosecution's final witness, Sharon Bell. Bell testifies that in 1996 she owned one hundred acres on Hillsboro Road, one half mile north of Old Hickory Boulevard, and less than five miles from Blackberry Road. She was Perry March's client in 1996, and it was her property where, according to Arthur's testimony, Perry had buried Janet's body. Her testimony is brief.

Tom Thurman says, "That's the state's case in chief."

Herbison asks for a judgment of acquittal, citing instances in which he says the state has failed to make its case. Thurman responds, and the judge denies the motion.

Nobody expected it to end here. Not on this day, August 15, exactly ten years since it all began.

CHAPTER 44

The Defense Steps Up

It's an understatement to say that the defense team has its work cut out for them.

Rumor has it that leading up to the three trials, Massey, Herbison, and McClusky emphatically urged their client to plead guilty and accept the thirty years being offered by the state, but Perry, with characteristic bravado, refused. Now, after nearly seven days of testimony presented by the prosecution, it is clear to all that the "purely circumstantial evidence" has substantial weight.

Pridemore and Postiglione review the case over lunch in the victims/witness area, between bites of sandwiches and chips.

"I still can't figure what happened to Miller," Pridemore says. Neither detective was in the courtroom when David Miller testified on the second day of the trial, but by now they have heard about his poor performance in the witness box. They were also present when Miller returned to the victims/witness area after his testimony, and Katy Miller came in behind him, turning a cold shoulder to him.

"I hated that, for David," Pridemore says. "He didn't seem that nervous before he went on."

"Somebody said he acted like he hadn't even been prepped. I know he was," Postiglione says.

Witness by witness, the detectives go over the testimonies, what each contributed, and speculate about the defense's strategy. It is too risky to put Perry March on the stand, and Sammy March, who might have testified in his father's behalf, is unwilling to do so. All they have left is to attack the state's case. Postiglione and Pridemore agree that the defense could have done a lot more in cross-examination.

"I don't know whether it was laziness or disinterest in their cross, but I couldn't tell where they were going," Postiglione says.

The first witness for the defense is Robert Jackson, an attorney who practiced only divorce law in 1996. He testifies that Perry made an appointment to see him on August 27, and that Perry sent him a packet of information, including the twelve-day vacation list Janet left.

Thurman has no questions.

Next, Kyle Sowell, chief deputy clerk, takes the stand. He testifies about a pleading that was filed on July 30, 1999, allegedly by Arthur March, saying that Larry Levine killed Janet. Thurman makes the point that the pleading was not notarized and not under oath. Sowell says no petitioner ever came forth, and no action was taken.

The next witness, David Roh, worked for the tire store where Perry had the tires on his Jeep changed a few days after Janet's disappearance. Roh's testimony conflicts with Bobby Armstrong's, in that Roh contends there was "nothing unusual about the sale of the tires" Perry bought on August 21, 1996. He does not recall the purchase that Armstrong described in great detail, but he says if Perry had bought four tires he didn't need, Roh would have remembered. Thurman offers the possibility that although Roh made the transaction for the sale, he could have been busy with other customers and Armstrong, the store manager, might have dealt with Perry. Roh says he would have still looked at the tires before finishing the transaction.

The next four witnesses are men and women who work for the sheriff's department. Defense Attorney McClusky questions them about Cornelius King when he was housed in the special management unit. Steve Howard and Sergeant Paul Roberts testify that King asked to be moved because he thought there was a ghost in his cell. Corporal Alicia Baldwin McArthur and Sergeant Sheila Stinson, also of the sheriff's department, testify regarding a claim made by Perry that Cornelius King threatened him with bodily harm. It is obvious that McClusky hopes to discredit the prosecution's witness, but Thurman, in cross-examination, is able to elicit testimony that King had been told about an inmate who was hanged in that particular cell and that the noises stopped when a plumbing problem was corrected. In Thurman's cross of Stinson, she states that the alleged threat by King was basically "the word of one against the other."

The seven defense witnesses have taken up roughly forty-five minutes. Most of the time has been spent by the defense trying to discredit Cornelius King. Now Massey asks for time to prepare for their next witness, the videotaped interview of a younger Sammy March. Judge Dozier calls for a short break.

Bill Pridemore, walking out of the courtroom with his partner Postiglione, says under his breath, "Not much steam so far."

But Postiglione is always nervous during a trial.

It's true, Massey doesn't have much to work with. But you never know about juries. It just takes one—a lone juror who gets hung up on a single point. Postiglione is thinking ahead. Maybe by this time tomorrow, the verdict will be in.

The short break turns into more than an hour. The defense and prosecution have agreed on the parameters for playing the tape of the Sammy March interview. Judge Dozier advises the jury that this tape is not testimony. It is an interview of Sammy in Mexico when Sammy was nine years old.

Though he gave the interview to a NewsChannel 5 reporter in 2000, the TV station decided not to air it until 2005.

It's a poker game at this point. Massey is betting on young Sammy to touch the jury's emotions. Thurman is betting on witnesses he will produce in rebuttal to put the child's statements in the proper perspective.

In an unusual move, Perry March takes the stand without the jury present to say that he does not want his son, Sammy, to testify. He says, "I have no desire to put him into any further spotlight than he has already been put in." It appears that parental love trumps self-preservation. Once again the paradox of a man charged with the murder of his son's mother apparently putting the love of his son first surfaces in the most dramatic of settings. Or is it that he fears Sammy's testimony will hurt, not help, his defense? A few minutes later, he returns to the stand to tell the court that he does not intend to testify. The judge asks, "Do you understand it is your right to make that choice?" Perry says, "I understand."

The jury comes in to hear the tape of Sammy March. It will be the last volley by the defense.

Momentarily, in the darkened room, Sammy's innocent face flashes on the screen. He says he was in his bedroom the last time he saw his mother. She was wearing "her favorite white shirt and brown velvet pants." He says, "She told me she'd be back soon, gave me a good night kiss, and drove away with bags. I went to the window and waved to her, and she waved back."

Do the jurors believe him? Or do they believe that his father has simply told him the story so many times that it has become his own story? Postiglione tries to read the expressions of the men and women from Chattanooga, but all he can ascertain is that they are clearly sympathetic to the child.

He is anxious for the witnesses who he hopes will refute this interview.

The first witness called to refute Sammy's statement is his grandmother.

Carolyn Levine explains the location of Sammy's window in relation to the driveway, using photos that Katy Miller provides. Carolyn says that she has been to the house many times since Janet disappeared. She testifies that from Sammy's window, she could not see the driver of a car—only the top of the car. "How dark would it be outside at eight?" Miller asks.

"It would be dark," Carolyn says. Asked if there were floodlights, she says no.

In further testimony, she says, "I was with Sammy after August fifteenth, and he never said to me what he said on the video."

In cross-examination, the defense asks if she realizes it is still summertime and today is August 15, implying that it is still light at eight.

A cheap shot, Pridemore thinks.

The next witness, Kim Avington-Scott, who was Sammy's kindergarten teacher at USN, testified earlier without the jury present. Now she takes the stand again with the jury present and testifies that in the first days of school, Sammy cried and kept asking people, "Have you seen my mother?" She says, "He told me he was sad because he didn't get to say good-bye to his mother."

Following this poignant testimony, Ralla Klepak, who served as guardian ad litem for the March children in Chicago in 1996, says that Sammy told her his parents were fighting, the last night he saw his mom. The next morning, Sammy said, his mom was gone and there was a rug rolled up at the front door.

The jury is out when the prosecution produces another rebuttal witness, child psychologist Dr. J. D. Woodman, who met with Sammy twenty-eight times between July 13, 2000, and August 20, 2001. He testifies that in his opinion, Perry manipulated Sammy into saying the things he said on the tape. Sammy "wanted to please his father," Dr. Woodman says. He refers to another tape that he discussed with Sammy, in which Perry quizzed the child about who was guarding the house while Sammy and Tzipi were in their grandparents' custody. Perry encouraged Sammy to watch for people who might be coming for him and Tzipi and said they should leave with the strangers if they gave the right "code word." Herbison objects to Dr. Woodman's testimony, and Judge Dozier rules that the psychologist will not testify before the jury.

At five thirty the defense and prosecution rest. Judge Dozier announces that closing statements will begin Wednesday morning, and that the prosecution and the defense will have an hour and a half for both sides to present their respective arguments.

Carolyn and Larry Levine are a somber couple as they exit the courtroom. Still hopeful for justice, they are all too aware that tonight marks exactly ten years since their daughter vanished—since Janet was murdered.

The courtroom is packed on Wednesday. Many of the fifty-plus witnesses who testified are present. Pridemore and Postiglione arrive early to get good seats. The Levines and their supporters take up several rows. Reporters slide into the back rows and cameramen mill about, getting the best angle. The first order of the day is a discussion among defense, prosecution, and judge about how Judge Dozier will instruct the jury. At about nine thirty the judge calls for the prosecution's closing statement.

Wearing a beige suit, holding her notes, Katy Miller approaches the jury.

"You first heard from Carolyn Levine," she recalls for the jury, summarizing Carolyn's testimony as to events from the time Perry and Janet met in college until their marriage deteriorated to the point that they sought counseling and Janet sought advice from a divorce attorney.

Referring to her notes only occasionally, Miller gives a thorough chronology of the events set in motion just prior to August 15, 1996. Using portions of testimony, she weaves the Janet and Perry March story. She reminds the jury of the friends who testified how devoted Janet was to her children; no one could fathom that she would leave her children. Miller paints a picture of Perry as a deceitful husband who concocted an intricate plan to hide the truth of his wife's death, a husband without remorse who desecrated his wife's body, a son-in-law who was treated like a son by his in-laws and repaid that love and generosity by plotting to kill them.

Miller's voice is level, without emotion, but her delivery is clear and her points well organized. She goes through a litany of witnesses—virtually every prosecution witness: Janet's friends, her housekeeper, the children's nanny, Carolyn Levine, Peter Rodman from the Brixworth, the Mexican attorney, the inmates who reported Perry's conversations in jail, the police detectives who laid out the facts from their investigation, and Arthur March. She points out inconsistencies and asks questions: "Would a mother like this miss her son's sixth birthday, the party, the first day of school? Would she leave not knowing who would take care of Sammy and Tzipi?" She refers to the video of Perry's deposition in November of 1996: "Does he look upset? Do the things he says sound like a sad man?" And of Sammy's interview, she says, "Do you believe him? He never told Carolyn. You heard from his teacher: 'My mom left me; I didn't get to say good-bye.'"

Katy Miller ties it all together for the jury.

Miller takes thirty minutes of their allotted time. The judge calls for a ten-minute break, and when court resumes, Bill Massey steps up to face the jury. He has no notes. He folds his hands and says, "A missing persons case is not a homicide."

It's wrong to allow the Levines' use of the police department to chase leads from psychics, he says, wrong to charge Perry March for a crime when police are still looking for Janet.

Sounding like an evangelist, pacing back and forth before the jury box, Massey tells them, "The law may say you don't have to have a body, but you must have proof. The jury can't be placed in the position of guessing. You should be able to look at the puzzle and see it, not make leaps." He pushes his points: reasonable doubt, presumption of innocence, burden of proof.

Like Miller, he recalls for the jury the history of Janet and Perry, but from the point of view of Perry as a victim, a husband in an unhappy marriage, whose wife left him to be hounded by the police. Witness by witness, Massey leads the jury through testimony in which he punches holes. As to the items *not* found in Janet's bag when the Volvo was discovered, he asks the jury, "How many of you have ever forgotten to pack a toothbrush on a trip?" As to Perry's feelings toward the Levines, Massey says, "The Levines took his children!" He points to Peter Rodman's testimony about the man on a bike at the Brixworth Apartments, insisting that Rodman was a radio-show host, looking for a "sensational" story. He explains away Perry's lack of cooperation with police as the natural result of being treated as a suspect.

Massey has hit his stride. He uses his voice well and puts the evidence in the best light for Perry. With the tone of a preacher gearing up for the altar call, Massey then attacks the "inmates' song." The three inmates, King, Farris, and Martin, who testified against Perry were all trying to get a deal. The tapes of conversations between Perry and Nathaniel Farris "don't have anything to do with Janet's disappearance," Massey insists. The man in the tapes is "a man living a nightmare." "If you believe Arthur," he says, "the best you can do is negligent homicide."

Once again he calls the case one of "psychics, cadaver dogs, and ghosts." He says, "You can't buy justice," and closes with an emotional appeal: "They just don't have the evidence. I have to put it in your hands. I have to let go, put Perry March's future in your hands. I don't get to talk to you again."

The jurors are visibly engaged by Massey's style. He sits down. Throughout the trial, Perry has been seen smiling, looking confident to the point of cocky, without good reason most of the time. If he's ever had a time to feel hopeful, it's now. Massey has done a superb job with what he has.

At noon, Tom Thurman steps up to give his portion of the closing statement. He begins by expressing his appreciation to the jury. Massey knows how to play to the jury, to connect

with them. Thurman realizes that his style is not as engaging
as his opponent's. He is more matter-of-fact, nonemotional,
even more so than Katy Miller. But he knows his strengths,
too. Miller has worked from a chronology of the case. Using
a PowerPoint presentation, Thurman outlines the elements
of the case that add up, brick by brick, to solid proof of Perry
March's guilt.

He reminds the jury of Perry's conversation with Sergeant
Postiglione, asking for a plea deal. Then, in an attempt to
discredit Massey's statement that the state's case is full of
circumstantial evidence, he goes through twenty-three
points that he tells the jury are "direct proof" that Janet is
dead.

"The rich, powerful Levines," he says. "Is there any proof
of this? That's an affront to the police department and the
DA's office. If they were so rich and powerful, why would it
take eight years to get an indictment?"

"Is it wrong to look for a body? It's basic human dignity
to look for a body, to give closure to the family," he says.

He tears apart Sammy's statement, listing contradictions
and then listing the people he would have logically told
about waving good-bye to Janet if it had happened. He lists
police, grandparents, Ella Goldshmid, teacher, guardian ad
litem. Sammy did not mention to any of these people the
things he said in the tape. "So that statement was a coached
plan," Thurman says, "a man hiding behind his own child,
no scruples about doing anything to get away with murder."
He follows up with a video clip of Perry saying he would not
let police talk to his son.

"You can infer guilt from a person planning to kill a witness," Thurman says as he moves on to "witness corroboration." He lists Nathaniel Farris, Reno Martin, Peter Rodman,
Cornelius King, and Arthur March. By each name, he has
listed five to ten elements of corroborating evidence.

Finally he presents a list of statements made by Perry:

"Do it when they're both together" . . . "We had an argument" . . . "They will never find the body. It is in ashes and
water."

One of the statements is an excerpt from the manuscript @*murder.com.*

Thurman presents statements made by Arthur March as well, claiming that Perry asked him to clean up an area where blood might be, dispose of the hard drive, dispose of Janet's body.

He presents photos of the Volvo, of Janet's purse, of Perry in a jogging suit, of the March property; a photo of the back of the Jeep. Thurman says, "You can almost see the outline of a body in a bag.

"It is the Janet March case," he says in closing. "It's about the life she didn't get to have. It's been ten years for me to stand here and ask for justice. I ask you to have the courage to return that verdict."

Thurman's strengths have served him well. In fifty-three minutes, he has used all the visual aids at his disposal, and with detailed organization, he has managed to make his points. If his presentation lacks the skill of a polished orator, he has made up for it.

Perry is not smiling.

The court recesses until one thirty, at which time Judge Dozier begins to instruct the jurors. At two fifteen the jury leaves the courtroom to begin their deliberations. Pat Postligione's jitters start in earnest.

Six hours of waiting is not what anybody expected.

At the end of the day, Judge Dozier sends everybody home, but not before the jurors request a list of the exhibits in evidence.

On Thursday morning jurors resume deliberation. Postiglione and Pridemore chat with other detectives, with reporters and lawyers who have business in the courthouse and have stopped in to see what's happening. The longer the jury is out, the more talk they hear about the possibility of a conviction on a lesser included offense—possibly manslaughter.

Pridemore drinks a gallon of coffee and pops antacids. His partner's expression grows more brooding by the hour.

Every now and then they catch a glimpse of Larry or

Carolyn Levine, milling about the courtroom, talking to the substantial crowd that has been there to support them throughout the trial.

"I can't imagine what the waiting's like for them," Postiglione says. They've waited ten years, but those first weeks and these last hours have to be the hardest."

During the lunch hour on Thursday, a buzz goes around the courthouse.

"Did you hear that the jury has asked to see some of the testimonies?"

"*Whose* testimonies?"

"Cornelius King and the Mexican lawyer."

Postiglione and Pridemore hurry to the courtroom to see what's going on.

The jury has, indeed, asked to see the videotaped testimonies from Cornelius King and Alberto José Sandoval Pulido. Massey objects. He wants to present other testimonies to the jury as well. "Play what they request, as well as rebuttal testimonies," he says.

Judge Dozier says he won't send anything the jury hasn't asked for.

"We prefer no testimony," Massey argues. "But if the rule says you have to give these clips, give the others, too."

The jury files in. The tension in the courtroom is thick.

The judge plays only the testimony from King and Pulido. Once again the jury gets to hear Pulido's statement that Perry threatened him and Samuel Chavez, telling them he would do away with them the way he did his wife. "'I kill . . .' and then a third word I didn't understand," says Pulido, through his interpreter.

The next clip is Cornelius King testifying that Perry told him he and Janet got into an argument and "the altercation got physical." King says, "He ended up hitting her across the head with a wrench."

The jury goes back out.

"I can see why Massey wanted to put on something to rebut," Pridemore says as he and Postiglione go back to the fourth floor. "That's pretty strong stuff."

"Yeah, but just the fact that they're looking at it again—I don't know," says Postiglione. "Somebody must be holding out, and they're trying to bring everybody on board."

Pridemore shakes his head. "I sure as hell thought we'd have a guilty verdict by now."

But the afternoon drags on.

CHAPTER 45

The Verdict

Someone brings the word to the victims/witness room: the jury is coming back.

Everybody seems to breathe in for a split second, suck the air out of the room, and then they all get busy—Thurman and Miller, Pridemore and Postiglione. They gather files and briefcases, take a last-minute bathroom break, put on jackets and straighten ties. The Levines, in the family area, are waiting with the stoic expressions that after all these years seem to be etched into their faces.

Postiglione has the worst preverdict jitters he can remember. He can't conceive of a not-guilty verdict. He *knows* Perry March is guilty, but it's always possible that one thing Massey brought out is what sticks in a juror's mind, and that juror is able to sway everybody. Maybe something in the state's case doesn't stack up for the jury, like the weight of the bag that contained Janet's remains, so they say "reasonable doubt." He can't even go there.

"Let's go," say Pridemore. "Showtime."

Pridemore has guzzled coffee all afternoon. His stomach burns like hell. He knows for sure now he has an ulcer. He hopes it's not something worse. When all of this is over, he's got to start thinking about his health. His wife, Denise, fusses at him all the time about not taking care of himself, but like he tells her, getting March convicted is priority one right now. Too much stress, not enough golf. God, he hopes the jury doesn't screw up.

The cold case detectives sit together in the courtroom, second row from the front.

The jury files into the room.

Postiglione's heart is slamming against his ribs like a wild animal in a cage. He clears his throat, sure that everyone around him can hear his furious heartbeat. As the jurors take their places, he tries to read each one's body language. None of them look at Perry—even when Perry and his attorneys rise. What does that mean? Maybe nothing, Postiglione thinks. If he were a juror, he probably wouldn't look at the defendant, either, whatever the verdict.

Judge Dozier asks the jury, "Have you reached a verdict?"

"We have, Your Honor."

It's like a movie in slo-mo, Pridemore thinks.

"On charges of second-degree murder, we find the defendant guilty."

"On charges of abuse of a corpse, we find the defendant guilty."

"On charges of tampering with evidence, we find the defendant guilty."

By the time Pridemore has heard the word *guilty* for the third time, he is already shaking his partner's hand, whispering, "Good job." And then he focuses on Perry, hoping but not really expecting to make eye contact. Perry's expression does not change as he hears the words that will bring another huge change in his life, a life entirely out of his control, the verdict that will send him to prison for decades. He actually raises his chin slightly in that defiant little gesture that may have played poorly with the jury.

The mix of feelings that wash over the cold case detectives is similar, they will discover when they talk about it later, over a few beers. Exhilaration, yes, but a twinge of disappointment that Perry has given them nothing. He has given the Levines nothing, certainly not remorse, not even an emotional outburst of some kind. Just cool control.

He could already be thinking about his appeal.

Massey's disappointment shows in a weak smile. He pats his client on the back and whispers to him. Perry looks down at his hands, but his flat affect does not alter. A moment later a court officer escorts him from the courtroom.

Carolyn and Larry Levine maintain an air of reserve as they leave the courtroom, amid hugs and handshakes.

Pridemore speaks to several people on his way out—he won't remember who. He's thinking about the Levines: they know it's never going to end with Perry.

The journalists and cameramen with DV cams hurry to capture sound bites and quotes.

A dozen mikes extend toward Bill Massey. He is gracious, saying with a reserved smile, "It's been a tough case." The length of time the jury was out gave the defense team encouragement, he says. He rates his closing argument as "positive." A reporter asks, "What was the most damaging testimony?" His answer, not surprising, is Arthur March and the Nathaniel Farris tapes.

Strong testimony in the defense's favor, he says, was Dr. Bass's testimony, which he characterizes as an argument *against* Arthur March's position.

Herbison steps up to the mikes and immediately says, "We do intend to take matters further." Asked what will be the strongest area of appeal, he cites one area as the "discussion on the airplane," referring to Postiglione's testimony about his conversation with Perry on the trip back from Los Angeles.

Postiglione, back in the victims/witness room, will have to wait until the news plays the clip to hear Herbison's statement.

Herbison says the developments since he was brought

back to Nashville hurt the defense's case. The prosecution had a "weak" case before they indicted Perry.

The cameras turn next on Tom Thurman and Katy Miller. From the tone of Thurman's voice, he might have been the loser instead of the winner. Typical Thurman, he shows little emotion as he thanks all who were part of the "tremendous team effort." Not surprisingly, he cites Arthur March's testimony and the Farris tapes as the key elements of the case. "I think anyone listening to those tapes of Perry plotting to kill the children's grandparents could infer guilt," he says.

But he insists that the state had a strong case based on the evidence they had before the conspiracy plot. They knew they needed to move forward because of the potential "loss of witnesses, loss of memory."

Thurman says this case should be an encouragement to the families of victims in which the crime has not been solved for months or even years. These families need to know there are people who care, who are working hard for them, he says.

Katy Miller says she is happy for the Levines, whom she describes as "fine people," not the "evil grandparents."

She and Thurman both mention Dr. Bass's testimony as corroborating Arthur's claims about the "leaf bag."

Postiglione and Pridemore are asked their reaction to the case. Postiglione phrases his comments to the media with a Warholian paraphrase: "Perry March's fifteen minutes of infamy are over. I hope we can all remember Janet now." Pridemore says, "For us this case is still not finished—not until we find Janet's body."

At last, Carolyn and Larry Levine appear, and more than a dozen microphones extend toward them. The Levines have given only one extensive interview during the ten-year investigation, to Bill Lagattuta of *48 Hours*. Someone announces that Mr. Levine has a prepared statement and they will not answer questions. "Where's Tom? And Katy?" Larry asks. Thurman and Miller have finished their interviews and left the crowd, but someone locates them and they return. Carolyn Levine, all smiles, hugs Tom Thurman, and for the first time since the trial began, the prosecutor's granite face softens into a smile. Larry and Carolyn both hug Katy. It is a poignant moment, tears and smiles alike from the spectators. Larry says, "I have a statement to read."

It is a short recitation of all the people who have made this moment possible, from the DA's office and the police force to the members of the jury who gave "careful consideration of the evidence" and to family and friends—"all who supported us during our ten-year pursuit of justice for Janet and for her children."

Ten years and two days.

CHAPTER 46

Aftermath

The weekend unofficially starts on Thursday night in Nashville, and bars and restaurants are hopping. Tonight, in conversations throughout the city, the verdict in the Perry March case is a big item. For a decade Nashvillians have shared their theories about the case. The local newspaper, the *Tennessean*, has run over three hundred articles about the case, with scores more during the ten days that comprised the murder trial. The local CBS affiliate provided "gavel-to-gavel" coverage. It has become the most celebrated case in Nashville history.

The Gerst Haus on Woodland Street, not far from the Criminal Justice Center, is noisy and busy. Cold case detectives Postiglione and Pridemore enter into a haze of smoke—the Gerst Haus has never restricted smoking—and smell the sauerkraut and sausages. The beer-hall decor is a little tacky, the staff has likely never been as far as Memphis, let alone Frankfurt, and the food is expensive for something less than fine German fare, but the Gerst Haus is a Nashville establishment. Pridemore likes the fried pickles. Postiglione goes for the goulash with sweet corn bread. The schnitzel is pretty good, and everybody likes the frosty fishbowls of beer, the large rounded glasses that hold sixteen ounces.

Pridemore and Postiglione, like many of their counterparts in the police department, routinely drop by the East Nashville restaurant for a few beers at the end of a hard week. Some of the guys they know are there every night.

A chorus rises from the bar and the nearby tables. "Hey, Bill! Pat!" A mix of police and people from the DA's office are well into celebrating the conviction.

The detectives greet their friends and join the party.

A couple of beers take the edge off the tension that has pulled at the muscles in Postiglione's neck all day—or, when he thinks about it—those muscles haven't really relaxed in months.

"Come on, do you really believe Arthur March is being truthful?" someone asks, and someone else wants to know, "What about Nathaniel Farris? What kind of deal do you think he'll get?"

All around him the crowd reacts to the verdict. Everyone offers opinions.

"I think Judge Dozier will run the sentences consecutively, and that scumbag will be in prison for the rest of his life," somebody says.

"If he had just let the Levines visit their grandchildren, he'd be a free man today."

"If he'd just kept his mouth shut. Did you hear what they were calling him on Court TV when Farris testified? Perry Canary."

Strangers who have seen the detectives on the news come by to congratulate them—and thank them. "Thank you for getting justice for that family," they say, echoing Larry Levine's words.

Later in the evening, Denise and Margaret, the detectives' wives, join them for the celebration, and Tom Thurman and his wife, Debbie, show up as well. As Thurman and the cold case detectives and their wives head to a table, somebody at the bar says, "Arrogant bastard. That's what convicted him, his own arrogance. He thought he was smarter than everyone else."

"Can't argue with that," Pridemore says.

The verdict is news, and not only in Nashville. On Friday, the *New York Times* runs the story "Ex-Lawyer Guilty in Wife's Murder in TN." Court TV continues its coverage of the case. Tom Thurman is a guest on Ford and Banfield's *Courtside*. The clean-cut, poker-faced "Thurmanator" with his Southern drawl, who looks more like a church elder than the lead prosecutor in a high-profile murder case, is interviewed after his first good night's sleep in a long time.

Ashleigh Banfield wants to know, "What is it about this case that has generated such extraordinary interest by the public?"

Deputy District Attorney General Tom Thurman, who works directly or indirectly on every death-penalty and serious homicide case in Metropolitan Nashville-Davidson County, Tennessee, is well qualified to answer. He has found the March case extraordinary. The fractured loyalties that have defined this case are astonishing, even to the detectives who have worked hundreds of murder cases, even to Tom Thurman, whose job is seeing that murderers pay.

"It has the young attorney with a beautiful wife and a beautiful home, the prominent family, and murder," the prosecutor says. "So many elements of a murder mystery."

And the murder mystery has been solved.

Thurman and the cold case detectives go back to work on other active cases. Carolyn and Larry Levine go home, home to Sammy and Tzipi. The children have to start school the following Wednesday.

Perry March remains in the metro jail until his sentencing on September 6. At the sentencing hearing, Janet's parents and her brother, Mark, present victim impact statements. Larry and Carolyn Levine's statement says, in part: "In taking the life of their mother, Perry March deeply scarred his own young children for the rest of their lives."

Judge Dozier hands down his sentence: fifty-six years.

The next day Perry is moved to the Charles Bass Correctional Facility near Riverbend Prison for thirty days of medical and mental evaluations. On his first day at his new temporary home, he files a grievance.

His cell is too small.

Now he spends his days doing what he knows how to do, writing legal briefs. On October 3, he files a hundred-page handwritten lawsuit to get the children sent back to Carmen in Mexico, arguing under the Hague Convention treaty once again.

Larry Levine responds with a deeply personal statement: "After the trial, Carolyn and I were spent—physically and emotionally exhausted. After the verdict we were looking forward, after ten years of fighting brutality and destruction, to finally going on with our lives; to properly mourning for our daughter, to buying a stone for her at the cemetery even though we do not have her body to bury under it, and to working hard at healing two scarred but amazingly resilient and happy children, freed forever from the demands of an unrepentant sociopath."

By November, Perry has lawsuits in three courts. He has asked for a new trial in the theft conviction. Judge Dozier, who presided over the trial, has denied his motion.

The March case has been solved, the verdict handed down, the sentence pronounced. But there is no end to the number of lawsuits an energetic lawyer can file over a span of fifty-six years.

It is not over.

EPILOGUE

Nashville is not expecting a white Christmas, just dreary, blustery weather with a windchill factor much lower than the actual temperature, typical for Middle Tennessee. On this damp, bone-chilling evening in mid-December, Pat Postiglione and Bill Pridemore raise their collars and hunch against the brisk wind as they leave their cars and head toward the entrance to the Tin Angel. The popular Nashville bistro faces West End Avenue, where cheery lights decorate every establishment along the busy street. The holiday season is in full swing—Christmas, Hanukkah for Nashville's Jewish community of eight thousand, and the celebrations and traditions of the diverse international population that has exploded over the past ten years.

The detectives are keeping a promise they made to themselves, years ago.

"Table for two?" asks the young hostess.

"No thanks. We're just here for a drink."

"Don't I know you gentlemen?"

"We haven't been here before," Pridemore says.

He stops to warm his hands at the freestanding fireplace before following his partner into the bar. Settling on the bar stools, the detectives exchange a glance and a wry smile.

People are always recognizing them now from their appearances on the TV news. They still can't get used to it.

Postiglione nods toward the large painting displayed prominently next to the bar. Thousands of Nashvillians and tourists walk by it every year.

"There it is," he says.

The painting is a bar scene, more dreamlike than realistic. It was painted by Janet March.

"I don't know much about art," Pridemore confesses.

"Me either, but everybody says she had a gift," says Postiglione.

"Yeah, I can see that much. You'd have to have talent to do that—and a good imagination."

"I kind of like it."

Waiting for their beers, the veteran detectives talk about the interview they just had with the *Nashville Scene*. The cold case detectives and Deputy District Attorney Tom Thurman have been named "Nashvillians of the Year" by the *Nashville Scene*, and the story will appear later in the month. The Perry March convictions have elevated the three dedicated government veterans to celebrity status.

And they talk about retirement.

Both plan to retire from the police force in the summer. They will leave with the sweet satisfaction of the Perry March conviction, but there will be many cold cases that their replacements will have to solve. In the offices of the Nashville murder and homicide department, there is a small room down a narrow hallway with no sign on the door. Inside are shelves with row after row of three-ring black binders stacked on their ends. On each is a number and a name. Each one represents an unsolved cold case. Each one represents a human life. The dates go back to the 1970s. One of the names is Marcia Trimble. There are over a hundred others.

The noise level rises as the bar begins to fill up. For a while the detectives nurse their drinks in silence, thinking about all the lives that have been so dramatically affected by the Janet and Perry March story.

Larry and Carolyn Levine remain in Nashville, doing their best to be both parents as well as grandparents to Samson and Tzipora. Sammy is now a handsome teenager of sixteen who attends the University School of Nashville, the school where he was scheduled to start kindergarten in 1996. Tzipi, at twelve, also attends her mother's alma mater. Looking at Tzipi, with her beautiful dark features and high cheekbones, is like looking at her mother, Janet, and at her grandmother, Carolyn, all at once.

Arthur March begins serving a sixty-month federal prison sentence in a federal medical prison in Fort Worth, Texas. When he agreed to testify against his son, the government reciprocated by recommending an eighteen-month sentence. Tom Thurman and the federal prosecutor lived up to their part of the bargain, but federal judge Todd Campbell rejected the settlement, citing he believed the sentence was too light based upon Arthur March's actions. Arthur, who now spends most of his time in bed as the result of multiple health issues, made his feelings known when he granted Nashville's CBS affiliate, WTVF, an interview in November 2006. "I got screwed by the U.S. government," he said. "I'm going to die in prison."

Four days before Christmas, Arthur will, indeed, die in prison. Perry will not be permitted to attend the private graveside service in Portage, Indiana, on Christmas Eve.

In November, *48 Hours* also interviewed Arthur in prison. Pridemore and Postiglione comment that Arthur had the opportunity to retract all of his incriminating statements against Perry, but he did not. He said, "If I'd had any sense, I wouldn't have ever got involved."

Russell Nathaniel Farris, the "hit man" and the state's star witness, did receive leniency of a pending sentence after his testimony in the March murder trial, although Tom Thurman denied that there was any connection. But he was back in jail within just a few days for violating the terms of his release. In an ironic twist, the current charge is for violence against a female.

Carmen March remains in Mexico with her four children, including the daughter, Azul, she has with Perry. There is no record that she has ever been to the United States to visit her husband. Rumor has it that she's had to close the Media Luna Bistro & Café.

Perry March begins serving his fifty-six year sentence in a Tennessee prison in Lake County in the northwest corner of the state. A former inmate, Alex Friedman, was quoted in the *Tennessean* as saying, "It's known for being one of the more serious, hard-core violent facilities. It has a lot of gang members." In his efforts to pursue his appeal, Perry March has no more funds to pay John Herbison and William Massey. Judge Dozier in a hearing in December 2006 declared Perry to be indigent and accordingly available for court-appointed counsel as relates to any future appeal. When asked by the media if he would have done anything differently in preparing for the murder trial of his client, defense attorney John Herbison was quoted as saying, "I would have bought Mr. March a roll of duct tape."

Postiglione and Pridemore have agreed that if Perry had come forward in August 1996, telling the police he accidentally struck his wife during an argument and the blow proved fatal, given the fact that he had no prior criminal record, he could have served as little as four years.

Around Thanksgiving, Nashville's NBC affiliate, WSMV, began airing clips from over six hours of exclusive interviews granted by Janet's brother, Mark Levine—an attempt to tell the family's side of the story after being silent for ten years. In the first segment, Mark relates that his parents have been doing their best to purchase all of Janet's art. On the walls throughout Larry and Carolyn Levine's home, where the children now reside, Janet's works are displayed like a museum collection—almost like a shrine to her memory.

One work of art they have not elected to purchase is the painting at the Tin Angel.

"Another round?" the bartender asks.

"I'm fine," Postiglione says.

Pridemore shakes his head. He says to his partner, "I've got to get home. I promised Denise I'd put the lights on the tree tonight."

"Kind of late this year, aren't you?"

"Yeah, well, I've had a few things to do."

Postiglione looks back at the painting. He raises his glass and says, "To Janet."

Pridemore joins in the toast.

Without a word, they toss some bills on the bar and go out into the cold night.

In his initial interview, Mark Levine went on to explain to the television audience that one painting will never be hung in the Levine home. It is a portrait Janet was painting of her mother. She was never able to complete it.

Like Janet's life, it will forever remain an unfinished canvas.

Michael Glasgow is a native of Nashville. He has a B.A. degree from Vanderbilt University and a J.D. degree from the University of Tennessee. He is currently working on his next book—a true crime story set in both Nicaragua and Nashville.

Phyllis Gobbell, also from Nashville, writes both fiction and nonfiction. She has published stories, articles, and three books. In 2006 she received the Tennessee Arts Commission Literary Fellowship.